PRAISE FOR *HR FOR HYB*

C000001706

The world and the workplace have shifted forever. Companies have been trying to adapt without having a solid resource that could give them direction and a roadmap to thrive in this new environment. Gary Cookson has created the resource that had been missing. Using this book will help you manoeuvre into this new reality so your employees can be hybrid or remote and perform. He's taken a tangible and applicable 'how-to' approach that can fit any organization to engage, anchor and encourage their people.
Steve Browne, SHRM-SCP, Chief People Officer, LaRosa's, Inc, and Author of *HR on Purpose!!* and *HR Rising!!*

Gary Cookson's book provides a much needed and coherent gameplan for the future of work. Fusing research, everyday experiences and practical solutions, it will help you to navigate the uncertainty and redesign your people practices to drive high performance.
Jeremy Snape, Former England Cricketer and Founder, Sporting Edge Digital Learning

Someone needed to cut through the noise of what Hybrid Working means to people (HR) professionals and those with a vested interest in teams and how they work. This book is like Gary Cookson has listened to every conversation, online video call and posted thread. A vivid set of examples through digestible, practical insight and recommendations.
Perry Timms, Founder and Chief Energy Officer, PTHR, Author of *Transformational HR* and *The Energized Workplace*

HR for Hybrid Working brings an accessible, intelligent and well-structured overview to one of the most pressing challenges facing organizations. Gary Cookson's thoughtful work is deeply referenced, full of interesting case studies and, most importantly, hugely practical. If you are looking for resources to help you or your team navigate the world of hybrid working, then this book should be at the top of your list.
David D'Souza, Membership Director, CIPD

The perfect time for the perfect book! *HR for Hybrid Working* is an incredibly thoughtful, practical, and insightful read that takes you through a reflective and forward-looking journey into redesigning organizations and preparing for a newer world of hybrid working. It will encourage you to be more ambitious in your thinking about the possibilities on how and where work gets done, enabling people and businesses to perform at their best whilst enhancing employee experience.

Daphne Doody, Head of CIPD, Northern England

As the demand for Hybrid working increases post-pandemic, many organizations are seeking guidance on how to implement this model. I would recommend Gary Cookson's book *HR for Hybrid Working* as the definitive guide on how you can successfully do so!

Olive Strachan, MBE, entrepreneur and founder of Olive Strachan Resources, Author of *The Power of You*

The world of work is changing, fast. In this essential book, Gary Cookson provides a clear assessment of where people professionals need to change, and provides solid, practical advice on what they need to do. It's a handbook for the future.

Donald H Taylor, Chair, Learning Technologies Conference

We are facing a once in a generation opportunity to reshape the world of work to become more inclusive, more sustainable and more human. The people profession is in a unique position to influence this change, having stepped up during the pandemic in many organizations. Gary Cookson's book provides a timely and comprehensive support to the profession, drawing on his years of experience and creative thinking about the nature of work. *HR for Hybrid Working* is the ideal guide for people professionals in navigating the possibilities of work in the era of Covid-19. Full of practical examples and case studies, it is required reading for HR professionals wanting to change work for the better.

Katie Jacobs, Senior Stakeholder Lead, CIPD

In our changing world, Gary Cookson has managed to encapsulate the thinking on hybrid working through story telling his own experiences, expressing the views of others and using relevant references. This fascinating read is filled with case studies and sketch notes, which not only helps to draw attention to what is happening in businesses but, furthermore, adds a new dimension to summarising the reader's learning. This must-read book is bursting with advice and considerations around hybrid working, the new skills needed, why company policies need to change and why technology has to be an integral part of hybrid working.
Alan Price, CEO, BrightHR

The demand for hybrid working from the workforce has rocketed and organizations are jumping onto the bandwagon to attract and retain talent in this new world of work. It is in this context that Gary Cookson's book is both timely and indispensable. Written from the perspective of a HR practitioner for HR practitioners and people managers, it helps dispel the myths and, more importantly, tackle some of the challenges with hybrid working that lead to lost time and resources if implemented badly. Whether you need to dip into one of the shorter reads or take a deeper dive, this book is for you with practical action plans to enable you to help your people do their best work whilst making sure they feel included, valued and their wellbeing is cared for by their organization.
Shakil Butt (FCIPD, FCCA), HR & Leadership Consultant, Founder of HR Hero for Hire

HR for Hybrid Working

How to Adapt People Practices to Support Employees and the Organization

Gary Cookson

To Rebecca

Thanks for unknowingly featuring in this.

Happy reading.

KoganPage

Publisher's note

Every possible effort has been made to ensure that the information contained in this book is accurate at the time of going to press, and the publishers and author cannot accept responsibility for any errors or omissions, however caused. No responsibility for loss or damage occasioned to any person acting, or refraining from action, as a result of the material in this publication can be accepted by the editor, the publishers or the author.

First published in Great Britain and the United States in 2022 by Kogan Page Limited

2nd Floor, 45 Gee Street	122 W 27th St, 10th Floor	4737/23 Ansari Road
London	New York, NY 10001	Daryaganj
EC1V 3RS	USA	New Delhi 110002
United Kingdom		India
www.koganpage.com		

© Gary Cookson 2022

ISBNs

Hardback	978 1 3986 0575 6
Paperback	978 1 3986 0572 5
Ebook	978 0 3986 0573 2

British Library Cataloguing-in-Publication Data

A CIP record for this book is available from the British Library.

Library of Congress Data

Names: Cookson, Gary (Human resources consultant), author.
Title: HR for hybrid working: how to adapt people practices to support
    employees and the organization / Gary Cookson.
Description: London; New York, NY: Kogan Page, 2022. | Includes
    bibliographical references and index.
Identifiers: LCCN 2022009013 (print) | LCCN 2022009014 (ebook) | ISBN
    9781398605725 (paperback) | ISBN 9781398605756 (hardback) | ISBN
    9781398605732 (ebook)
Subjects: LCSH: Personnel management. | Telecommuting. | Flexible work
    arrangements. | Organizational effectiveness.
Classification: LCC HF5549 .C72453 2022 (print) | LCC HF5549 (ebook) |
    DDC 658.3–dc23/eng/20220303
LC record available at https://lccn.loc.gov/2022009013
LC ebook record available at https://lccn.loc.gov/2022009014

Typeset by Integra Software Services, Pondicherry
Print production managed by Jellyfish
Printed and bound in Great Britain by CPI Group (UK) Ltd, Croydon CR0 4YY

To my wife Katie, and my four children Owen, Faye, Poppy and William. Originally, I was going to write something like 'you wouldn't all be here if it weren't for my successes with remote and hybrid working', but then I realized that was back to front and slightly insulting too.

The opposite is true. My successes with remote and hybrid working (which now includes this book) are there because you have all been there for and with me.

I love you all.

Gary

CONTENTS

FOREWORD

by Siobhan Sheridan CBE, Chartered Companion CIPD

'I discovered that I was drifting without rudder or compass, swept in all directions by influence from custom, tradition, fashion, swayed by standards uncritically accepted from my friends, my family, my countrymen, my ancestors. Were these reliable guides for one's life? I could not assume they were, for all around me I saw old ways of doing things breaking down and proving inadequate.'[1]

Many times over the last few years I have found myself turning to this quotation from Marion Milner. Whether in my work as a chief people officer, a non-executive, a researcher, or a volunteer, it provides a constant reminder to me that there are very few 'right' answers in the world, including in the world of work.

As a practitioner, there have been many occasions over the last 30 years where reflection has helped me to realize the moments that my work has been guided by unspoken beliefs or popular fads that have limited basis in evidence. Reflective practice offers precious opportunities to see the moments where the 'old ways' are breaking down, and to use those to seek to develop better futures, whether that be with individuals in coaching sessions, or organizations in their people strategies. That vital space to notice the challenges and see the opportunities, to notice the stimulus and to choose a response, has often been provided by something discovered within the pages of a book like this one.

To me, the book in your hands provides a space for reflection, an opportunity to pause and think. Whether you are a leader, a manager, a business owner, or a professional in the worlds of Human Resources, Learning and Organizational Development; reflection on this subject, right now, offers the opportunity to craft our future as people who work. Perhaps I am not the only one realizing that something of my own sense of the world of work has been conditioned by 'tradition and custom'. Perhaps you, too, are enjoying the opportunity to allow your own thoughts to emerge about what our future could hold?

Over these recent times, we have begun to pay attention to a range of conversations that were once too quietly spoken in the context of the world of work. Deeply important subjects have found their voice over recent times;

domestic abuse, mental health, burnout, disability, the challenge of being a carer, inequality and so many other questions around inclusion and the role that organizations play in society. Unapologetically, I think it is critical that these unspoken conversations are continued and explored as we seize this opportunity to design our workplaces and workspaces for the future, in ways that are healthier for all of us already in the working world, and for the generations of young people entering it in these unusual times.

Gary has been holding conversations about this subject for a long time, both in his own practice and together with fellow practitioners. He has been inquiring, reflecting, and developing his own perspectives, with the intention of stimulating a broader conversation. I am delighted that he is bringing that inquiry onto an even bigger stage through the pages of this book, inviting you to join him interrogating, debating, disagreeing; whatever it takes to engage as many people as possible in a conversation about how we avoid the pitfalls and enable the very best to emerge.

Our workplaces and workspaces of the future have in the past been both hugely positive, and potentially damaging for some. Our current challenges provide us with an opportunity to frame them differently for the future. Ilse Crawford says about design that it is 'a frame for life; a design that starts with human experience, that prioritizes our well-being and enhances our humanity'[2]. That to me seems like a worthwhile endeavour, and I am delighted that Gary is seeking with this book to encourage us to seize the opportunity to set our ambitions high, to identify the inadequate, to experiment with possibility, and to share our learning with each other along the way.

PREFACE

What this book is about

This is a guide to why we need to, and how to, redesign Human Resources, Organizational Development, and Learning and Development (collectively called people practices in this book) services and processes to be delivered virtually as the world adjusts to far longer-term remote working than ever thought possible, and the prospect of hybrid working becoming the norm for many. In it, we consider how to deliver people practices effectively and efficiently online, and rethink what the people profession could and needs to be as it goes.

This book focuses on what to do now, and how to ensure you are prepared for the future of remote and hybrid working. It will help you rethink what the people profession could be, and needs to be.

When the COVID-19 pandemic hit, most organizations and their people practice teams were forced to work entirely remotely, delivering services in ways previously not fully explored, or even partially explored for many organizations. Many things that people professionals got involved in were previously not considered part of the remit of the profession, but as words like furlough re-entered our language, these teams largely came into their own, providing a different range of services and doing things to keep the organization and its people, on lots of levels, alive.

As the pandemic recedes, it is likely that some form of hybrid working will become normal for almost all organizations, and so we are unlikely to return to the people profession as we once knew it. New priorities, new ways of working and new challenges lie ahead – and although many people professionals, teams and their leaders are up for meeting these challenges, some will face significant barriers.

This book is for you if you want to meet the challenges head on and take big, confident strides into the new world of not just remote working, but hybrid working and delivering people services that could be mostly, or even entirely, virtual. The book is also for you if you are unsure about the future and what to do, and need some practical guidance on how to do things differently.

It contains case studies showing the best sides of our profession in rapidly enabling almost the entire world to work remotely. It addresses overcoming the challenges faced. It draws on research done that shows the scale of the challenges facing organizations and people professionals as we move into the future, and offers insight into how we, and our teams within organizations, can best position ourselves to ensure we and our organizations thrive in a virtual world.

The various chapters contain many insights from leading thinkers, combined with practical case studies from leading organizations and their people practice teams and academic research that showcase what is possible if we reimagine the profession in a remote or hybrid world of work.

It explores the changes that could and should be made to existing people processes, metrics, policies and strategies in order to make them not just 'work' virtually but make a real difference to the employee experience and make the virtual workplace somewhere with real purpose and drive. It explores the role we have to play in managing the transition to new ways of working and set out what role this could be.

Who I am and why I wrote this

In my career, I've done what the world now calls Hybrid Working for a couple of decades, constantly juggling work, life, and more. I understand as much as anyone why getting this right matters to all the stakeholders in our lives – both personal and professional. I was an early proponent of remote and hybrid working, doing it long before technology made it easy and before it became fashionable, and was well-positioned to thrive when it became essential. I've been able to build people teams working remotely and in a hybrid way for a long time.

My business, EPIC, exists as a virtual business, delivering services in a hybrid way since 2017 and also being marketed wholly via social media.

I wanted to write a book to help others in the people profession make significant contributions to organizational direction and performance.

Who you are and why I hope you are here

Some of you will be standalone people professionals or operating in small teams and from a predominantly generalist perspective. If that is you, you may have few people to share ideas with, gain new ideas, sense check modern thinking in your context, and with a CPD budget that may not stretch as far as larger teams' budgets might. It can be difficult for lone practitioners to have confidence to try things in work in a new way. I hope to give you that, and support you in trying out the things you see, hear and learn from other forms of learning.

There is no shortage of strategic output on this subject, but not much that looks at how that works in the places and spaces that most of you and most organizations operate.

Some of you will be people professionals in much larger organizations, who may have a specialism and may support employees based in multiple locations and geographies. It will give you confidence too – your primary driver would be to demonstrate value add and efficiency of your solutions, but you may be stuck with stakeholders who have different ideas and may be short of options of things to try or move towards. You have here a practical guide to help you understand how our remit has changed, quickly and drastically, and how the things you used to do may no longer work – but, crucially, what could take their place. You are no doubt heavily influenced by a growing sense and pace of change in the profession, all of which points towards the realization of having to do things differently – but many of you will have asked the question – where do we start?

Some of you may be from organizations without people professionals – typically small and microsized organizations whose delivery of traditional people services is likely to be done by non-specialists. This may help you to view people services in different lights and reap the benefit of doing so in a hybrid way.

How the book works

The book begins with several chapters exploring the impact that working remotely and virtually has had on people teams, to clarify what has worked and what has not. It explores the remote working journey up to the start of the COVID-19 pandemic, looking at early successes and lessons learnt along the way. It looks at what happened when the pandemic hit and what we learnt from the quick and sudden move to remote working for a lot more people. It explores what the concept of hybrid working is at the moment, and clarify how it changes what we understand as work and working lives, before adding some thoughts on how our use of technology needs to evolve and improve.

The main section of the book looks at specific areas of people practice in turn, looking at case studies, posing questions and offering solutions as to how each could be redesigned to work more effectively in a long-term remote and hybrid future of work. The way we manage the ways that employees join, and leave, our organizations in a hybrid world is examined. It looks at how some of the nuts and bolts of people practice – policies, procedures, contractual documentation and the basics of rewarding people need to change. As we move through the employee lifecycle, the book looks at how employee relations are evolving – what it means to be a leader, what it means to be a team and how performance, disciplinary and grievance situations, and sickness absence among other things are changing. The notion of wellbeing is further examined in terms of how this has now become a core competency for organizations, and how we need to support people differently in creating safe spaces, along with the need to focus in different ways on inclusion and belonging. The book looks at how Learning and development (L&D) has changed, in many ways for the better, embracing virtual classrooms and solutions.

The book's final part looks at the role we need to play in the future, beginning with how we need to help our organizations manage the transition to this future state, including how some of our places and spaces, and the way we view work itself, should evolve. It looks at culture and how we need to protect and nurture the culture in our organizations to protect the future, and examine the changing skillset of people professionals as we solidify these ways of working.

Each chapter has a similar structure (inspired at least partially by Michelle Parry-Slater's book *The Learning and Development Handbook*):

- A shorter read – a few pages for the short-of-time reader who wants a quick flavour and summary of the chapter without getting into the detail behind it.

- A longer read – the detail you need if the shorter read has piqued your interest and you want to go in depth on the issues explored.

- Case studies – stories from the front line, sharing what organizations and their people professionals have done, what worked and what did not. The majority of these are from named organizations, and others will be from clients of EPIC who prefer to remain anonymous – in sharing these anonymous case studies some of the organizational characteristics may have been made more generic to further protect their anonymity).

- Case Study reflections – the main learning points to consider from each case study.
- The Action Plan – in building your practices further, and planning for actions you need to take to move forward on the issues examined in the chapter.

Each chapter concludes with a Sketchnote illustration, superbly crafted and provided by Rachel Burnham (who has also provided the logos for the various parts of each chapter), to summarise the main themes emerging in that chapter. There is also a summary Sketchnote in this section to give an overall route map for the book.

There is a separate section at the end containing the References for each chapter – further and wider reading and much of the evidence behind each chapter, linking to leading thinkers and thinking on the subjects discussed to help you apply the learning from reading this.

I'd love to hear from you as you read the book and/or after you are finished. Track me down on social media – Twitter (@Gary_Cookson) or LinkedIn – and let me know your thoughts and questions.

Happy reading.

Sketchnote summary

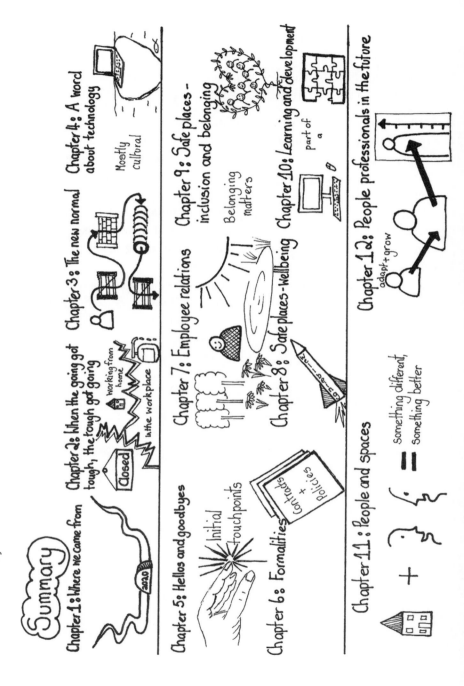

ACKNOWLEDGEMENTS

It would be remiss of me to not first thank you for buying and reading this book. Ultimately while I have enjoyed writing it, it has been written for you – so I hope you enjoy reading it and can use the thoughts within it.

My family – my wife and four children primarily – have been instrumental in my whole life both personally and professionally, giving me inspiration, motivation and gratitude throughout the past two decades. They have believed in me, even if not entirely sure what it is I do, and I am grateful for their eternal support.

A number of people gave me help and advice when I was first thinking about and then starting to plan out writing a book. Specifically, authors and my friends Michelle Parry-Slater, Rob Baker, Katrina Collier and Dr Rob Ellis have been generous with their advice and support throughout, and many of the #HRPubQuiz community encouraged me when I was putting the proposal together and helped me shape it.

A chance conversation with some people at Kogan Page in November 2020 where I said I might like to write a book led me, ultimately, to this point, and the guidance I've had from Kogan Page staff such as Lucy Carter and Anne-Marie Heeney has been invaluable.

Two people have made significant contributions to this book. Siobhan Sheridan's Foreword thrilled me as she is one of my heroes in the profession, and to have someone of her stature comment on and read my work was a delight. And Rachel Burnham's logos and sketchnote illustrations perfectly capture the essence of each chapter and add a different dimension to reading. Without both Siobhan and Rachel this book would have been much less than it is.

Within this book there are numerous people whose contributions to examples and case studies have brought it alive. They have given their time and thoughts willingly and without hesitation. In the order they appear in this book: Eleanor Nickerson, Lisa Tomlinson, Gail Hatfield, Michelle Reid, Nick Atkin, Annette Hill, Nicky Hoyland, Lucinda Carney, Alan Price, Alastair Brown, Liz Dowling, Rebecca Fielding, Morna Bunce, Karen Gilmore, Anna Edmondson, Kirsty Diamond, Jayne Harrison, Cam Kinsella, Sara Duxbury, Kathryn Palmer-Skillings, Jo Brimacombe, Chris Baldwin, Marc Weedon, Robert Hicks, Perry Timms, Steve Browne.

Lots of other people contributed random comments and quotes and to all those mentioned in the book (and all those perhaps not), thankyou for making them. A few more people helped by giving their time to peer review some chapters for me as I went along – and this helped me polish what you have in front of you. In no particular order: Sarah Parrott, Sam Jenniges, Scott Leiper, Alex Killick, Garry Dickson, Helen Marshall, Don Taylor, Helen Astill, Sophie Austin, Krystyna Peterson, Mark Hendy, Sharon Green, Selena Govier, Cheri Brenton.

Thankyou also to many of my clients who have allowed me to anonymously use their experiences, and to my wider network for not just cheering me on along the way but for putting up with my constant mentions of how I'm doing and how it has been going while putting all of this together.

PART ONE

The world we came from

01

Where we came from

To begin looking at what the present and future holds for people professionals and the services we deliver, it is worth reflecting on where we came from and the journey we took getting to this point. The past establishes a good context for many of the issues we now face – they are not entirely new. There are lessons we can learn from our past. It is easy to imagine that our delivery of hybrid people practices, and services began with the pandemic in early 2020, but for many, myself included, it began much earlier than that.

The world's journey to hybrid working is not one that began in 2020, even if the pandemic accelerated things and brought more people into such ways of working. The sometimes-painful lessons learnt in 2020-2021 were, in many cases, already there to be learnt from those people's experiences.

Remote working in the early 2000s from my and many other perspectives was largely done offline and using technology with minimal connection to the rest of the organization. Working mostly offline can appear strange now in our ultra-connected world, and often appeared strange then too. It took time and effort for individuals and organizations to create work that could be delivered remotely, and only a limited number of (mostly white-collar) employees were working even partially from home by 2019 despite technology improving to the extent that it became easy to do so.

Despite the positive experiences many people had and the significant benefits that were being evidenced from delivering people services remotely, the growth of remote delivery of work and people services was slow up to

2020. The equally significant number of barriers – though few were techno-logical ones – often took priority for organizations. There was little, if any, guidance about what to do and how organizations and employees could make their practices work remotely. There was also doubt about what remote employees were doing and a feeling of guilt from many about what they should and should not do. For many, it was becoming apparent that changing the way services were delivered was having implications for organ-izational culture, inclusion, and real estate too.

Research conducted in the 2010s on the impact of remote working on individuals noted many lessons that few would heed before the COVID-19 pandemic. These included the impact of social isolation, and the blurring of work and personal lives. It also explored many of the cultural barriers in place – the attitudes of leaders and managers prime among these.

Remote delivery of people services was something different up to 2020 than it is now – then, it was a chance to work quietly and alone on things, away from contact with other people. Now, with the prevalence of video meetings, remote working has become something different – but there were lessons in these early years that we needed to heed. Those who can manage the divisions between their work and personal lives fared better, and those who can address the perception of remote working from line managers tend to be more engaged and more productive. Social isolation is an issue, but not one that is impossible to overcome with the right processes and technology.

When speaking at conferences or writing articles and blogs in the years leading up to 2020, I've made the following points about what was facing us at that point:

- Not enough was being done to empower people to make small, but signif-icant changes to their work (and working patterns).
- Not enough people policies were flexible enough to address the very different employee experiences that were starting to happen.
- Culturally, not enough organizations were challenging inappropriate views and working practices, or giving employees chances to voice their own ideas.
- Blurred divisions between personal and working lives were there to see, but not enough people professionals noticed this and acted on it.
- The physical set-up of remote working was largely left to chance, creat-ing, or exacerbating exclusion for some groups.

- The whole concept of the working day is something that needed to evolve, and largely did not.
- Not enough was done to look at team dynamics and individual relationships and how to foster these in the right way to allow remote working to be effective.

Put simply, there was plenty of evidence to suggest we should have known what was coming.

The longer read

My own earliest memories of doing any kind of remote working date from 2001. I was working in a large organization doing a peripatetic L&D role, travelling round our various sites across the UK delivering training to our staff. At home my first child was due and being even a couple of hours away from home and at the mercy of public transport was worrying me – as I'm sure it would anyone as the due date approached. I asked my manager if I could work from home and spend my time designing new training sessions and writing reports. I did that for about a fortnight in the lead-up to my first child being born. I didn't have access to my emails or any corporate communication and was, to all intents and purposes, cut off from the organization. I did my offline tasks on my own desktop computer quite happily and effectively from home and saved them to a floppy disk to transfer them back to the work computer when I next got there.

Even a couple of years later this was the only way of delivering my services – even remote access to emails didn't arrive until 2004 for me and up until that point the only thing I could do was forward work emails to my personal email account to access them at home, work on them there, and forward them back to my work email to carry on working on them when back there. In the days before GDPR and greater cyber security issues, no-one worried about the issues this could create.

When remote access to emails arrived in 2004, I began working from home one day a week, delivering my services from there. I was working for an organization that was about 15-minute drive from my house and not at all difficult to get to, and no-one else in the organization worked remotely or wanted to. I remember being slightly ridiculed that I was working remotely when it was easier to come into the office, but I knew what was going to be possible and kept at it. Though remote access to emails was the limit of the available technology, I liked working remotely and I was easily able to deliver my services that way. It just took a bit of forward planning. Knowing all I'd have at home would be email access, I'd have to plan and 'save' work for the remote working day.

Though capabilities and interest in remote working was growing, it was doing so slowly in the wider working population. A survey by the European Commission in 2009 found that only 5.2% of the EU workforce worked at least sometimes from home, and this had only increased to 9% in 2019, with the COVID-19 pandemic imminent[1]. By 2019 the technology was in place to handle lots more remote working, as we saw when most of the world needed to do it just a few months later – so what was limiting the growth of remote working?

It is fair to say some of people's remote working experiences in the early to mid-2000s may not have been very positive, for a number of reasons. Until the wide adoption of broadband and wi-fi technology, using dial-up internet was not always a pleasant experience when trying to work.

It also won't have been something other people knew how to react to. Many of my own friends refused to believe I could be working when I told them I worked from home, simply because they couldn't conceive of such a thing as they'd never done it. I won't have been alone – many early remote workers will have been accused of watching daytime television or skiving – and this is presenteeism in early form. In researching this chapter, I asked for people's recollections and one of my own ex-colleagues surprised me by telling me that, when working from home, she was scared to put her washing machine on in case anyone rang her and heard it and assumed she was doing laundry instead of working. She took her work mobile phone to the toilet with her in case anyone rang, and she wasn't there to answer. This anecdote surprised me because I was the person's manager at the time and such thoughts never occurred to me, but I know the guilt trips many will have felt were real.

From my own experiences, organizations, and their leaders (and I include myself in that) were making it up as we went along in most cases and learning from our own mistakes. I recall having debates with other senior leaders about whether it was right or not to pay employees extra for working from home in recognition of increased costs they may incur (broadband, electricity and maybe more). I remember debating furiously with trades union representatives whether our organizational ban on smoking in the workplace extended to those working in their own home. I recall arguing with an executive who claimed that because an employee, by working from home, was saving 90 minutes a day by not commuting, that they should be working (at least) 45 minutes longer each day on the basis that the benefit should not go entirely to the employee.

In the late 2000s, in my organization we began to measure what percentage of our workforce worked remotely, and the impact this was having on a range of different measures. My own interest was to see what this meant from a perspective of adjusting the way my team were delivering our people practices. We quickly deduced that remote working – and by that we meant people working one or two days a week from home rather than the majority of or all their time – was having significant benefits not just to the employees themselves in terms of their work-life balance and wellbeing, but to the organization in terms of productivity too. With that, I began pushing for more people to do it, and even went as far as to set targets to increase the percentage of the workforce doing this.

In this, I met some resistance – again because the idea was new, and many leaders were unsure how to deal with it. Managers themselves, though perhaps better placed to work remotely, were hesitant to do so because there was a perception that one could not lead a team if one was not **with** the team. This led to some changes in the way we did leadership development to encourage changed mindsets and ways of leading. Some other managers were hesitant to let more of their team begin working remotely because 'no-one will be in the office' and yet, at the same time, the organization was beginning to assess the costs of its real estate and grasp that this changed what we needed in the future – so I was beginning to adapt the physical requirements of the organization as a result of delivering services in a different way.

Culturally we experienced some issues too. When the organization first experimented with VPN access, and brought in smartphones, both around 2010, this changed the behaviour of remote workers (mostly managers) overnight – and not in a good way. Both things had been brought in with a strong and robust business case that set out the benefits they could bring, but instantly this seemed to change people's working hours – I found managers working incredibly late into the evening, and at weekends. No-one had told them, or expected them, to do this – but it had a snowball effect, and it was a challenge to begin to establish new ways of working – something that is equally important in today's world too – left unchecked, bad habits can develop.

The European Commission, reporting in 2020 about the development of remote working, stated that the majority of those who were doing it pre-pandemic were high-skilled professionals and managers[2] and this was the experience in my organizations too. Such workers already used technology to do their work and were employed in knowledge-intensive activities. The Commission also noted that such professionals often performed informal overtime work at home. The high levels of autonomy enjoyed by such types of workers seemed to contribute to a blurring of the divisions between work and life, and as a result, higher levels of stress among such workers. Conversely those in jobs with closer supervision and less autonomy – in my organizations these were customer service roles primarily – were less susceptible to blurred divisions and stress.

Writing in 2013, Acas found that work performance and productivity was slightly higher for partial remote workers, explaining that those working remotely had slightly higher levels of autonomy and control than those working exclusively in the office, and therefore greater levels of job satisfaction and engagement as a result[3]. This tallied with my own experiences at the same time – we found that working hours were elongated for those working remotely, but that this was a personal choice in most cases, with periods of work interspersed with doing personal activities (in my case, the school run, or going for an actual run, and for other people all manner of other activities). Already we were seeing what hit home for many during the 2020-2021 lockdowns – that working remotely changes the concept of work/life balance, and changes working hours and patterns. This has both positive and negative consequences which we will explore as we move through this chapter.

What Acas also noted is that social isolation increased with the amount of remote working[4], and while this finding will not be a surprise to anyone reading this today, it seemed to be a surprise to many as the events of 2020 unfolded. While people professionals largely reacted very well to this, the lessons from the past were there to see and perhaps more could have been done to ready ourselves and our organizations for a future that involved widespread remote work.

The growth of cloud storage changed things dramatically in the early 2010s, enabling access to a wide range of systems and services remotely – in my organization I began (admittedly partially because of squeezes on physical locations) expecting my team to work remotely for two days out of five, and to work wherever they could on those days – that might be hotdesking at another location, working in a coffee shop or at home. To make this work my organization needed to invest in new technology, bringing in videoconferencing facilities to enable remote access to meetings. When I was researching this chapter, many people told me of the early experiments with this, with one person commenting how they were usually the only person dialing in 'from the regions' with everyone else in the city centre office. This is something we will consider in later chapters about coping with hybrid style working – we have had experience of this for over 10 years and need to learn from it. I had some mixed experiences of it – when my third child was (over)due my wife and I were spending a lot of time away from our normal home and this meant that a lot of my work – most of it – was delivered via videoconferencing as I simply couldn't get into the office. By this time, as I'd been doing it for over a decade, it seemed normal.

And yet, my then-organization was perhaps unusual. I moved organizations a couple more times before setting up EPIC and, in each situation, found increasingly unusual views about remote working and remote delivery of people practices. In one organization I was told that remote working meant working at home and at no other location – in case I was needed to come into the office for an 'emergency'. In another organization I was told, unbelievably, that one senior leader felt that I could not possibly be working if they could not see me at my desk. This same senior leader wanted to investigate whether I had a second job, such was their level of distrust about whether I was actively working for their organization while working remotely. In the same place, when trying to encourage my team to work remotely a senior leader told me that we needed to maintain a baseline physical presence to 'man the phones' (sic) despite me explaining, calmly, that the phones could be answered remotely. In a later organization they simply didn't have the technology – if I wanted to deliver my services remotely, I had to carry big, cumbersome pieces of technology back and forth to home with me and even to other sites if I wanted to work there. These experiences are probably ones repeated in many organizations and by many readers of this book.

The concept and practice of remote working changed during 2020. It ceased to be about quiet time to get stuff done and concentrate away from other people (interspersed by occasional phone calls) and became much more about delivering operational services via technology. This had been coming, but not enough were ready.

What did we learn from remote and hybrid working up to 2020?

The period up to 2020 taught us more than we realized at the time and in this section, I will summarize much of this.

We learnt that blurred boundaries between home and work are an issue that remote workers need to overcome, and therefore something that people professionals need to give serious thought to. Acas, writing in 2013, had reached the same view – but said that those who could create the right strategies, such as working in a dedicated room in their home (then not flagged as a luxury but now may be a different situation), and being flexible about when work is done and when they are having personal time, are the most likely to be successful[5]. Our collective experiences in the COVID-19 pandemic reinforced this but again it seemed to come as a surprise to many and is rightly now a focus for many people professionals in terms of guiding and advising remote workers.

In the organizations where I worked, we noticed that those working partially remotely and those who were mobile-based tended to be more engaged and reach higher levels of performance, another conclusion reached by Acas. They also noted the dangers of burnout and social isolation increasing with the proportion of remote working[6] but again we saw many people unprepared for this when the pandemic hit.

I was met with a lot of cynicism about whether remote delivery of my services was real, and workable. I was often met with snide remarks, and in some cases sheer disbelief that anyone could be working remotely. This showed me that many organizational cultures were barriers to effective remote working and effective delivery of people practices. In some organizations prior to 2020, I noticed some significant cultural barriers to making this work.

Some of these are common, but others unique, such as:

- The right policies and processes were in place to enable remote delivery of people practices, but in reality, remote working being restricted to executives or emergency situations and this therefore creating a divided culture.
- The right technology being in place to allow videoconferencing, but only from secure locations, rendering it useless for anyone working at a non-secure location – for example at home.
- Overly cautious IT security arrangements meaning that remote access to systems was clunky, slow, and cumbersome, in some cases taking 20+ minutes to connect.

- Managers putting limits on how many people could work remotely, or how often people could do it – despite the policies not having such limits.

- Managers having narrow views about where remote working could be done from – sometimes specifying that the person's home was the only acceptable place.

- Managers asking for advance notice with justification for remote working, effectively creating a cultural barrier.

- Individuals experimenting with remote working and being penalized for making mistakes rather than being praised for the experimentation and encouraged to continue.

These experiences and barriers, no doubt encountered by many, were commented on in a PM Insight article from 2017. In the article, David Jackson, then-assistant director of human resources at Manchester Metropolitan University, pointed out the need to measure those working remotely via their value added and deliverables, not where or when they work, commenting that the lack of ability to see what remote workers are doing leads to mistrust and false assumptions, and a move away from adult-adult relationships[7].

The barriers that I encountered then had a major impact on me in my later employed positions, and in my last employed role I couldn't overcome them. The cost to me was high – the inability to work remotely and deliver people services in that way made me ill, angry, and created a whole set of personal problems. This led to me setting up my company, EPIC.

The EPIC view on remote working

In this next section I summarize the things I have been writing and speaking about for several years.

- There is something that approximates a perfect day for everyone – but it is rare and unusual. Too often, people don't make efforts to create it, as they are too busy, or don't realize what their perfect day is, or don't know how to create it. Most people's perfect day would include things being great at home AND at work, and letting people make small adjustments to their working patterns, working locations and more can reap huge rewards for all concerned. However, not enough people professionals were actively doing so before the pandemic hit, despite us being in a great position to influence others.

- The demands of modern family life are largely incompatible with the demands of the traditional, face-to-face office working day. People professionals can only realistically influence the latter, and again, not enough were doing so up to the pandemic.

- Organizations who tell their staff how, when, and where (etc) to work are not able to unlock the engagement and discretionary effort they want from those staff. Too many judge people by the inputs – how many hours they sit at an office desk for example, and not by the quality of the output and results they deliver. Too many people policies were too inflexible on this up to the pandemic.

- People often have a very good idea of how they can perform better, and how they can achieve better work/life balance. For some this may be pausing work for a few hours in the afternoon and then working when children are asleep – though there are lots of examples and everyone's needs, and perceptions are different. Not enough people professionals had asked people what their ideas were or encouraged them and their managers to work towards such ideas, ahead of the pandemic.

- Just because technology enables people to work in evenings or at weekends, doesn't mean they should. Doing such things are a personal choice and not to be encouraged or expected by organizations, yet too many managers were, prior to the pandemic, setting bad examples by sending emails late at night or at weekends and being lauded in many organizations as some kind of workplace hero, as if they were working harder or better than those who didn't do such things. As people professionals, our job was to challenge such things – and not enough of us did.

- There are some benefits to a short commute. The precise length will differ for individuals, but it can serve as mental preparation both ways and help to clear people's heads before they re-enter another part of their life. Doing away with a commute altogether by encouraging whole-time remote working brings with it a big danger that work, and life become too blurred, and if we are to encourage whole-time remote working, we need, as people professionals, to help people with those blurred lines.

- If people are to work remotely, we need to help them with the equipment and physical set-up they need. Having worked on a mobile basis for a couple of years, I found it hard to have no storage anywhere, and not having things like a printer or scanner either at home, on the road, or one of my own in an office, made this worse. Up until 2018, I didn't have a fully equipped home office either and while I was able to put this into place relatively easily, I run my own business so of course my circumstances are different. If people are to spend most of their time, or all their time, working remotely, people professionals need to be assessing the health implications of this and ensuring that – ergonomically as well as technologically – things are 'right'. This, again, was something that took many by surprise when the pandemic hit.

• Despite being effectively isolated when working remotely and not necessarily as exposed to chit-chat and informal discussions, staff in my organizations found themselves more productive, and so did I. This was largely achieved by working in shorter bursts rather than one long day and using the body's natural energy peaks and troughs to dictate when one's best work could be done. There's a science to this, something like how professional sportspeople train for events by understanding more about their own brains and bodies and when they are at their best – but not enough people professionals focus on this. For example, I'm a triathlete, and all my races are morning starts. As a result, so is most of my training for those races.

• People working remotely become more keenly aware that work, and indeed life, is about relationships, and staying connected with people socially and emotionally. Do we do enough of that?

CASE STUDY

In this case study we look at an Organization X's hybrid and remote working drivers. We reflect on whether the lessons they learnt give us insight into how we can get this right in the future. Organization X is a social enterprise operating in the northwest of England and has around 1,000 staff. This case study draws on their experiences of bringing in significant amounts of remote working in 2011 and the following years.

The organization began to ask around half of its staff (450–500 people) to work remotely on either one or two day a week in 2011. This was largely due to the organization expanding beyond its real estate capacity and not having enough room to fit everyone in the office on a given day, and there was a need to manage occupancy rates in the short-term. Longer-term it was thought the solution was to acquire or build a new head office, but as this would be several years away, remote working was a viable solution to progress.

Small scale pilots began in early 2011 with handpicked individuals in each team trialling the technology and reporting back on their experiences not just on the technology side but on how it was to be working remotely and away from their manager and colleagues. The managers of these staff also shared their feedback. These initial pilots proved that the technology was workable and could connect people to the organizational IT and telephony systems easily. No other significant adverse effects were noted, so the organization rolled it out to the wider employee base in mid-2011.

Prior to this it had been important to do some consultation with the affected employees, and for the HR team to build a Homeworking Policy because of this. Feedback from the consultation was that most employees were quite happy to work remotely for two days a week, but their trades unions made points about the implications around cost, health and safety and how managers would manage performance of remote workers. There was also feedback from the other half of the employee population that suggested that they were slightly unhappy that they could **not** work remotely.

The HR team built a Homeworking Policy that addressed the eligibility requirements for remote working. It also linked to the existing suite of Health and Safety procedures, particularly around risk assessments on using display screen equipment, workstation assessments and a few other things. It required the remote worker to complete a self-assessment that was then reviewed by the Health and Safety Officer and an IT professional, with some home visits arranged because of this. At the request of the trades unions, specific rules were brought in to cover increased costs incurred by remote workers, though with a requirement for this to be evidenced.

Managers were consulted about their views on managing remote workers. Some expressed concern about having all their team working remotely, preferring only to let the higher performers (who they felt they could trust more to work with less supervision) to do it. However other managers felt there were positives in that they knew their employees may be more accessible if working remotely and get quicker responses to queries as the individual would not be sat in meetings and unable to respond.

As a result of this, the HR team designed and facilitated some workshops for managers with the aim of ensuring that those working remotely were given measurable objectives against which results could be judged, reasonable but not intrusive monitoring, and regular, suitable communication. Communication between remote workers, between the remote workers and their managers and between both and HR seemed to be the most critical aspect to be addressed, so the workshops focused on this.

The other big thing to be addressed before the wider rollout was the impact on the physical office space remaining. Because this was being done to bring occupancy levels down to manageable rates, and because employees were choosing their own remote working days, there needed to be systems in place to adapt to these new arrangements. For example, hot desking was introduced with booking systems for these and for car park spaces, along with improved meeting spaces and booking systems, and clear desk policies.

At three- and six-month points, formal reviews were held with all parties and their representatives. The following themes emerged at both:

- Individuals felt that they had to work more consciously and deliberately, as they couldn't rely on just 'bumping into' anyone or having ad-hoc conversations. There were both up and downsides to this.

- Individuals reported increases in their own productivity, driven by fewer meetings and the ability to choose their remote working days and office days, and in some cases the ability to flex their working patterns.

- Informal conflict between employees had increased, though not formal conflict. The main cause for this was felt to be the lack of face-to-face contact meaning that disagreements were often left unresolved until the next time the individuals were together, and in many cases, this made it harder to resolve.

- The working day had, for most, become extended, though interspersed with time spent on personal activities (for example the school run). Experiences of this were mixed. Some had found this stressful and struggled to manage the divide between personal and working time, whereas others found it enlightening and empowering.

- Managers reported that most individuals were becoming more self-sufficient, able to resolve much lower-level queries without ready access to them as may have been the case if they were within speaking distance.

- From a service delivery perspective, managers appreciated the elongated working day and felt able to deliver better services to customers. At the same time, they felt frustration about the disruption to workflows when individuals could, without notice, suddenly change their working day.

- The Health and Safety team reported a decrease in workplace incidents and accidents though a need for improved general education about ergonomics and (home) office safety.

- The IT team noted that the technology itself was mostly working well. Even in the absence of videoconferencing and video calls, the technology was able to keep people connected to organizational systems and telephony.

- The HR team had dealt with some, but not many, cases of increased costs for remote workers – mostly around broadband connectivity and occasionally around utility costs. However, these were offset by reductions in travel and expense claims. There was also some increased expenditure on the physical set-up of remote and hybrid working, but these were one-offs and not ongoing costs.

- Trades unions noted the creation of a two-tier workforce between those who could, and those who could not, work remotely, which the organization was already keenly aware of.

Following these reviews, small scale changes were made to the remote working arrangements to meet the identified needs. The HR team did work on communication and relationships which addressed some of the interpersonal issues. The organization felt that this had largely been a success and continued to increase the percentage of remote workers in the organization to the extent that, by 2016, around 80% of Organization X were working two days a week remotely.

Case study reflections

- Having a clear reason that is driving remote and hybrid working is useful for establishing the 'why' and helping to persuade employees of the need to do it. The role of internal communications is often integral to making this work.

- A pilot on a smaller scale can be a useful thing to do and can highlight important areas to address before the wider rollout, as well as helping with cultural change in and of itself.

- Consultation with affected employees can help you to understand what worries people and what motivates them about remote or hybrid working.

- People practice policies (a wide definition but anything that affects the employee experience here) should all pull in the same direction and join up with each other but should also not be set in stone to allow for lessons to be learnt and adaptations made, while keeping them people-centric.

- Separate work with managers on things like communication, team dynamics, relationship building and more tend to be effective for improving the experience of remote and hybrid working.

- There will be impact on organizational real estate and this needs considering with those looking at such things, but again from a people-centric standpoint to ensure accessibility and inclusion.

- Job crafting can help to make individuals more self-sufficient and empowered and can also improve the flow of work (as well as the sense of purpose and meaning individuals get from it) and is a key contribution people professionals can make.

- Individuals working remotely may need support from organizations to manage their working day and the divisions between work and personal lives.

- The costs of remote and hybrid working are often offset in other areas, but there may be costs around the physical set-up of remote working environments that the organization may need to pay for.

- Be aware that there will still be jobs that cannot be done remotely and be mindful of the different employee experience in place for those (a subject discussed in later chapters).

The action plan

If you are looking to introduce or increase the amount of remote and hybrid working in your organization, the following questions are worth considering as you develop your plan:

- What experience have you got in your organization of remote or hybrid working from before the COVID-19 pandemic? How can you capture the lessons learnt from this?

- Which roles in your organization could work on a remote or hybrid basis and which could not? How will you manage the different employee experience of both?

- How can you ensure that the people professionals in your organization have got the skillset to be able to guide managers and remote workers on the implications for intra-team communication, developing strong relationships, handling informal conflict and more?

- How can you best work alongside other teams who impact on the employee experience? For example, IT, Health and Safety, Premises (etc) – to ensure that the costs and benefits are properly realized?

- How much will you need to look at job design and crafting to ensure that individuals can get to optimum productivity levels while not encountering unnecessary barriers?

- What will you do to ensure your people policies have the necessary flexibility and links between them to make this work?

- How clear is your understanding of how to help people manage the divide between their personal and working lives?

- How can you help your organization develop a solid 'why' about remote and hybrid working? What would happen if you did nothing?

- What is your best advice to senior leaders in your organization to convince them to actively sponsor and support your planning for a remote and hybrid future?

Sketchnote summary

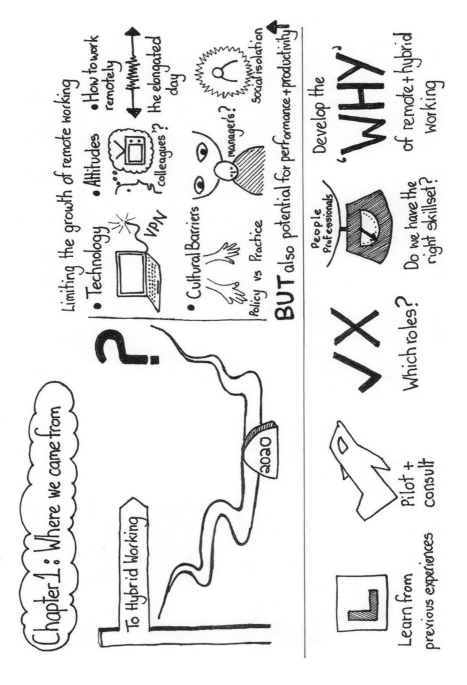

02

When the going got tough, the tough got going

The shorter read

This chapter explores what happened to people professionals as the COVID-19 pandemic hit in March 2020, and how the profession responded, as well as what this taught us. It will give us a good context for what is explored in the rest of this book.

We need to consider the readiness of organizations for remote working. Though the sheer scale of events made it difficult for anyone to cope, some had planned for situations in which they may need to work away from the office, and some had done none.

I can draw some parallels with my own experiences planning for the Swine Flu pandemic in 2009 and have recalled some of the planning I did then and what that taught me and my organization – largely, that we could cope with working in these circumstances, and would be able to if we were faced with similar circumstances in the future. However, not many organizations undertook this level of planning.

Some organizations had the benefit of operations in the far east, in countries where the COVID-19 pandemic was ahead of where it was in the UK and US, and used this knowledge well to prepare their staff. But many people professionals, myself included, were almost blissfully unaware of what might happen until March 2020. The steps I took to protect my clients and my own business when galvanized into action in early March 2020 foreshadowed a lot of what became normal for people professionals as the year continued. People professionals needed to support people and their wellbeing – mental, emotional, physical, and financial.

There are some pertinent examples of how different types of organizations and different people professionals coped with the onset of COVID-19, and note the importance of acting early and decisively, and the impact this can have on organizational culture and ways of working. In these examples it becomes clear that people professionals needed to be open, honest, and transparent with staff, and to take difficult decisions whether staff work remotely or in a centralized, communal workplace. These difficult decisions eventually morphed into critical contributions in other areas – notably organization design, job (re)crafting, home office ergonomics and set-up, and being the prime source of support for employees at difficult moments.

Two case studies from different ends of the planning spectrum show how different perspectives can each aid with eventual success. One took a very long-term approach to COVID-19 pandemic planning and reaped the rewards of this, but the other seemingly did nothing and yet reacted just as well. The contribution of the people profession was critical in both.

The longer read

Was anyone ready?

Looking back at the events of February and March 2020, it can seem like a dream. At the time, it seemed like an entire decade's worth of events happened in the space of six weeks, and so fast did these events develop and change that it was hard for anyone to keep pace with what was happening.

Opening the CIPD Podcast *Business survival in the age of COVID-19*, released on 7 April 2020[1], Nigel Cassidy summed it up well:

> How was your day trying to make sense of ever-changing crisis decisions that you have to make work; maybe breaking bad job news; putting staff on government furloughs or worse; or trying to gee up a scattered, isolated and scared workforce? And yes all this when people managers are worried about their own family's health, about feeding, finances and future employment. Some in HR will be glad that they previously did some disaster planning but we all sense that when this finally eases the world of work will never be quite the same again.

How apt this opening was. And yet despite the sentiments expressed in this quote suggesting that it was chaotic and disorganized for all people professionals, it wasn't. Some had prepared for this – though they were in a minority. Some had actively planned for this – but again in a minority. Even those for whom the COVID-19 lockdown came as a shock had a lot of the necessary things in place to respond well – as we explored in the previous chapter, the technology had largely been tested and proven workable, and the flexibility that people needed had been growing in popularity and use for quite some time.

I recall the Swine Flu pandemic reaching the UK in Spring 2009. In the organization I was in then, this was the cause of some significant panic. We genuinely thought that what eventually happened in early 2020 was going to happen in mid-2009, and we began planning in earnest for it as soon as Swine Flu cases were confirmed in the UK. I remember facilitating several business continuity planning sessions where we looked at the potential impact that Swine Flu was going to have on the organization and mapped out how the organization would cope if potentially up to 50% of our staff were unable to work. At that time too, remote working for our organization was in its infancy – some could have been done, but perhaps not for long. But we built our plans and, more importantly, tested them with a simulated activity that imagined the Swine Flu pandemic had reached a stage where COVID-19 eventually reached over a decade later.

Interestingly, our simulated activities then showed that we could cope, and I was able to learn from the practicing and adjust the areas of people practice that needed adjusting to allow the organization to cope for longer – things like learning and development, absence reporting, and recruitment.

But this plan stayed on the shelf despite the simulated run-throughs. Swine Flu, as we know, didn't go the way anyone thought it might, and my organization and I (and no doubt many others) forgot about pandemics until 2020.

I know we weren't alone in planning that way and as some examples and case studies in this chapter show, this approach tends to pay dividends. When the COVID-19 pandemic hit I tried, and failed, to locate the Swine Flu planning documents I'd built in 2009, and wish I'd been able to review and reflect on what might have carried across well and what might not.

Some people – some organizations – were ready. But most were not.

The oncoming storm

Here we'll examine what was happening in February and the first half of March as the threat of the COVID-19 pandemic grew, and how people professionals responded to this.

In the CIPD's 7 April 2020 podcast[2] David Frost, Director of OD at Total Produce commented on the incredibly rapid change his business had experienced and the types of demand his people and his organization was facing. Frost's organization had the benefit of being a global organization who could see the impact of COVID-19 spreading across the world in their other geographical markets, and so to a degree could monitor developments and plan accordingly. Following Frost, Jaimini Lakhani, Director at Lumiere Consulting, shared how they were working with a client in Singapore in early February 2020 the situation at that time meant a switch to remote work, getting some early learning about the usability of some remote working platforms like Zoom, before everyone was forced to do that.

It is interesting to hear such accounts, and there are many of them – such people professionals were ahead of the curve, and able to take proactive steps to prepare their businesses for what was coming.

My own foresight wasn't as advanced as Frost and Lakhani. I took several flights into London in mid to late February 2020 and was only mildly surprised to see some people wearing facemasks. I attended some large conferences the same month and was not worried about being around large groups of people. At one of those conferences, I was speaking and was ill, with many of the symptoms we now recognize from COVID-19, but it didn't cross my mind not to go, or to try doing it remotely, and nor did it occur to the organizers either.

I had my first piece of work affected by the COVID-19 pandemic in the final week of February 2020, when the person I was meeting had been advised to self-isolate, and we laughed about this and postponed until three weeks later. In the first week of March 2020, I spoke at another event and sat next to someone who had had to close and deep clean their office as they had a confirmed case of COVID-19. Speaking to them, I began to realize the scale of the situation and began my own planning for significant disruption.

In the first week of March 2020, I contacted each of my clients, in the UK and abroad, and advised them of the steps I would take to ensure the safety of any of their staff I met, and any contingency plans I had if I or others were ill or otherwise affected. Much of this involved switching all my work, particularly everything until the end of May 2020, to a remote basis. I also took the time to find out what each of my clients were planning for – as you'd expect, some were making similar decisions and advising staff to work remotely, but others seemed to be stuck, unsure of what steps to take.

I was also asked to give some advice to readers of People Management, and I deliberately echoed advice I was giving my clients and any people professional who cared to ask:

- Support people emotionally.
- Signpost to appropriate self-care advice.
- Adjust work temporarily or permanently to be conducted remotely, or redesign work so that those who are self-isolating could take on other duties if their work cannot be done remotely.
- Review occupational sick pay provision.
- Take steps to combat isolation and loneliness for those working remotely by enhancing and adapting communication, both formally and informally[3, 4].

Later we would see how critical these types of people practices would be for everyone.

When it hit the fan

In our first chapter we explored how remote working had slowly, glacially, increased in popularity and use in the years preceding 2020. Research done in 2020 suggested that the UK government's promotion of working at home prompted by the COVID-19 pandemic led to an eight-fold rise – from 5.7% of workers reporting they always worked at home in early March 2020, to 43.1% by April 2020[5].

But how did we decide to do all this and what were we thinking at the time? The same research points out that the increase was not distributed equally across occupational groups – those in managerial, professional, and administrative positions took up most of the remote working, whereas those in lower skilled occupations continue to work in their usual locations[6] – if such locations were allowed to stay open.

Eleanor Gooding is People and Culture Director at Boost Drinks, who are a private owned SME providing a range of energy and other drinks to the UK market and employing 35 staff in Leeds. Their consumer-facing brand makes the organization feel a lot bigger than the headcount would suggest.

Eleanor explains that she got the nickname Chicken Little before Covid-19 arrived because 'I kept saying "The virus is coming, the virus is coming!"'.

However, Eleanor's views and opinions on what was happening and what the business needed to do were rooted in direct experience. In an earlier part of her career she worked in Vancouver, Canada, and was there when the Swine Flu and SARS pandemics hit. The west coast of Canada is an earthquake and tsunami zone and both individuals and employers are expected to have emergency plans in place. When SARS and Swine Flu arrived, the culture of emergency planning naturally extended to pandemics too.

As COVID-19 hit in February 2020, Eleanor began raising the possibility of having a plan in place in Boost and was able to do just that by the end of that month. Their three-stage plan included:

1   Risk management for the entire business.

2   Communications to the business from the leadership team.

3   Safety precautions for employees.

The things Boost, at Eleanor's urging, did will be familiar to most organizations, but Boost was doing them two to three weeks before most organizations:

- Education about hygiene.
- Workplace signage.
- Provision of hand sanitizer.
- Additional cleaning.

Significantly though and in advance of any government advice on such things, Boost increased their occupational sick pay, giving additional payments to anyone who had exhausted their standard allowance. This reflected an ethos that the government and most organizations eventually came around to – to support people and provide them with financial reassurance if they could not come to work. Boost actively decided to not just follow government guidance, to not just protect their business but to keep their people safe and well as one of their guiding principles.

In addition, Boost ensured that the technology was ready for the entire organization to work remotely – giving each person a laptop and improving their home connectivity where needed and sent out regular updates to the whole company from mid-February onwards. By the time lockdown came to the UK, the Boost leadership team was meeting several times a week and had implemented a company-wide rota to ensure that face-to-face contact was minimized, and the move to 100% remote working went smoothly. It was helped by the People and Culture team doing remote working risk assessments and providing equipment such as chairs, desks, lamps, first aid kits, risers and monitors to anyone who needed it.

When the government announced the furlough scheme, Boost had felt it may not need it, but ended up furloughing a very small number of staff largely to protect the mental health of those staff and made an early decision to top up the salary levels to 100% again to provide better levels of support.

What we see in the Boost example is an organization acting early, and acting decisively, focusing on the right things that people professionals can and should be doing. Boost weren't unique, as we will see with other examples, but it shows how a little forward planning and the right principles embedded in that planning can eventually shape the prevailing way of working and culture in an organization.

David Frost was able to take a similar stance. Benefitting from having a base of operations in Italy, who entered lockdown two to three weeks ahead of the UK and US, he and his colleagues were able to see the early impact of isolation on employees and could take steps to introduce more informal catchups and focus on the social side of being an employee. Frost also noted that their Italian colleagues described three stages of enforced lockdown – the first 7–10 days where it is a novelty and people enjoy it, the next 7–10 days as people normalize it, and then after that, some 14–20 days in, people begin to feel social isolation and seek company[7]. What Frost was seeing in his Italian colleagues was what Gooding was able to predict would happen in Boost, and what most people professionals then came to realize in late March and early April 2020.

What became clear to those delivering people practices in March 2020 was the need to be honest, open and transparent with employees about the reality of life and work during the developing COVID-19 pandemic. For many people professionals, doing this while operating under considerable pressure of learning about new legislation and regulations, handling large scale consultations and organizational changes, while looking after their own emotional and mental state, was a challenge.

Lakhani commented that she encountered many people professionals showing incredible creativity and innovation, prompting their organizations to focus on organization design issues such as highlighting core activities and critical decisions and people, dealing with streamlining anything that could help with what could be life or death decisions[8].

Jane Smith began her role as a Global HR Manager at the beginning of March 2020, with pharmaceutical operations in the UK and South America. She describes anxiety being present in the organization in her first week. The organizational response to the growing COVID-19 pandemic was entirely the responsibility of the HR function which she headed. She spent the first half of March ensuring that the organization had the right policies, both internally and externally facing, to give flexibility and enable speed of decision making if necessary.

In giving advice to and consulting with staff, even before government advice said that it would be necessary, Jane realized social distancing and hybrid working would be the most appropriate response. The entire workforce was split into two shifts in two locations, and those who could work remotely did so. This created the physical space and distance needed, and was in place by the middle of March 2020, a full ten days before the UK went in lockdown, working well during this time and relieving some of the anxiety.

When lockdown came to the UK, and the furlough scheme was announced, Jane had one overriding aim – to keep people safe. As she had responsibility for the operational response to the COVID-19 pandemic this flowed into almost everything the company did. She decided to top up the governments furlough scheme to full pay but was determined to use it only where necessary as she was concerned about the mental health implications. Overall, the organization only furloughed 10% of its employees. To keep this per cent low Jane led some work redesign processes, at speed, to ensure that most people could do most tasks at home and where that wasn't possible, to give them other organizational duties that could be done remotely. This latter initiative meant that employees were grouped into temporary task forces instead of their usual teams, and she designed projects for each task force to work on.

Jane also began redesigning her people policies and processes so that things like pay were not affected by anything going awry in the process, and in the final week of March 2020 implemented specific well-being initiatives to support mental health, as well as introducing daily employee communication, having laid the groundwork for both several weeks earlier.

Jane's example is not an unusual one, but she was fortunate to be able to get so many of her employees working remotely and to redesign work to keep them productive and away from the potentially damaging effects of furlough. Steve Browne, Chief People Officer at LaRosa's Pizzeria, was not in such a position, partly through circumstance and partly through choice: 'Our field folks are (not working remotely) because that's how we need to do the work – the pizzerias, the call centre, the bakery and manufacturing plant and the office. We remained minimally hybrid, not because of policy though. It's because we want to be there in person to model that we support our field folks who don't have a choice. Remote and hybrid working works for white collar roles but not so much for blue collar ones.'

During this period, most people professionals were faced with difficult decisions, with consideration not just given to wholesale organization redesign and keeping things as normal as possible, but also, sadly, to large scale furloughing, and mass redundancies. I was asked on several occasions in March 2020 to advise leaders on how to mitigate the need to make redundancies either ahead of or at the expected end of the furlough scheme. I noted at the time that all the available options came with downsides but that a sensible move for all people professionals and leaders would be to ask staff for ideas about how to manage and cope, and indeed many of my clients did just that and were surprised by the creative responses to the situation.

It was a tricky time for most people professionals, with even the UK government predicting that around 20% of the UK workforce could be absent because of the virus at the peak of the COVID-19 pandemic. With that in mind, organizations had to be agile, and needed their people professionals to be agile too. The CIPD, in a press release early in March 2020, advised that: 'Employers must place the health and wellbeing of staff at the heart of their contingency planning and response. We recommend that businesses are as generous with their sick pay and leave policies as possible, both to support staff health and wellbeing, and to minimize any impact on their pay'[9]. Already in this press release we see the role of people professionals beginning to shift and reform. The CIPD were also at the forefront of lobbying the government in the eventual creation of the furlough (etc) schemes.

The prime focus for people professionals, at least in the UK, as March 2020 progressed, seemed to crystallize into the following areas, as we have seen from our examples and from my own experiences:

- Strong and effective communication to staff, with a focus on how the staff are being kept safe.

- Basic workplace safety advice.

- Supporting individual mental health concerns.

- Reviewing working practices to ensure maximum flexibility, and to put the right things in place to minimize staff presence in the workplace.

- Working with business leaders to redesign work and teams to enable some functions to continue as normal and staff to be flexible enough to change duties at short notice.

A review of press releases issued by the CIPD in March 2020 gives a good insight into how they viewed their own role and that of people professionals changing. From the issuing of guidance on how to put staff health and well-being at the heart of organizational responses early in the month, through to lobbying the government to provide more support in mid-month, to later in the month when they began giving advice on how to work effectively remotely, they clearly saw the role of people professionals taking on a new slant.

There was one thing different though by the end of March in the UK that made remote working more difficult for many – home-schooling. As a father of four myself I had my own challenges but was lucky enough that both my wife and I run our own businesses and can control a lot of our demands. For others it was not as easy, and I found myself giving lots of advice to individuals and organizations on how to reconcile the seemingly irreconcilable demands of home-schooling and remote working. For many families these demands fell disproportionately on women. All of a sudden, having the right setup and equipment to effectively work remotely, something many people professionals had spent time and energy ensuring was in place for many staff, was not enough – when there may be several people all needing to work or be schooled, at the same time, potentially in the same room and using if not the same equipment then at least the same Wi-Fi, became a significant issue for people professionals, myself included, to wrestle with and advise upon.

The CIPD commented on home-schooling and its impact in a press release from 19 March 2020: 'Employers must accept that there will be disruption and that working parents will struggle to be as productive as normal. Employers need to make allowances for this and take a flexible approach, especially for people with younger children who will inevitably need more care. With many schools looking at remote teaching, parents will have to juggle their work with helping their children to access school activities. There may be limited space and limited equipment to manage both parents and children working from home each day. There will be disruption'[10].

Disruption is one word for it. In my own house alone things got incredibly pressured, but the advice I was giving other people professionals and my clients focused on the need for understanding, for empathy, for flexibility and above all for showing of vulnerability. Suddenly, I was advising others to work when they could around their home-schooling responsibilities, and not necessarily the other way around. Suddenly, I was advising organizations to let remote working parents to complete their duties in evenings and at weekends if necessary, or to accept them completing less duties for a while. Suddenly, I was advising people to embrace the fact that they had new 'co-workers' and to involve them in their working lives. In that vein, some of my children appeared on video calls with me, and even when not, could be heard somewhere in the background. Such things became commonplace, and it was for the people professionals to largely encourage this in the workplace, something few saw us doing when the month began.

My clients responded to things hitting the fan in a mixture of ways. One, an events organizer, decided to mothball the entire business, and used the government furlough scheme and other support to hibernate. My advice to them was largely about furlough. Another, a professional qualifications provider, transitioned entirely to remote delivery and remained so, so my advice was around how to upskill their staff to operate in such a way. A third, took an extremely flexible approach, changing staff roles and duties and having a mostly remote but occasionally hybrid approach to work. My advice there was about how to redesign jobs and the organizational systems. Within these three examples we see a microcosm of how organizations, and their people professionals, made choices that shaped what the reality of remote and hybrid working was to be like.

When the going got tough, the tough most certainly got going.

EPIC reflections – what did the crisis teach us about the role of people professionals

The onset of COVID-19 in March 2020 highlighted the importance of some aspects of leadership and management that soon became part of what people began to call 'the new normal', and which we explore more in our next chapter. Many people began to realize the importance of being connected to others, and to take a genuine care and interest in their wellbeing. Many leaders and people professionals began to realize that looking after the wellbeing of their people was becoming one of the core competencies needed in organizations, and many were also grasping how technology could be used to develop and share such practices. Peter Cheese commented that 'sometimes you need a crisis to jolt us all into a different way of thinking'[11].

To me this period reinforced that many of the barriers to delivering great people practices in organizations were not necessarily about technology, but about culture and leadership, which again we will explore in later chapters. That it took a crisis of this magnitude to make the majority realize this is disappointing, but it ultimately brought the importance of connecting with our people and helping them in different and more human ways to the fore.

As most people professionals know, businesses that are struggling will often need them to make tough choices and potentially enforce job losses, but what we learnt in March 2020 was the different, more human, ways to do this, including not doing it at all by using the furlough scheme and in some cases re-hiring staff who had been let go immediately prior to the furlough scheme being announced. A client of mine, using associates to deliver learning and development workshops, decided at the point of furlough to offer each of them an employed position to avoid them seeing the loss of income that many of the self-employed seemed at that point to be facing – employed positions gave greater individual protection and security. My client didn't need to but wanted to – they saw the human side of the situation and wanted to deliver people practices in a different way. Peter Cheese, in the CIPD's 7 April 2020 podcast, talks about doing the right things in the right way, and therefore retaining the trust of people[12] and this came through very clearly for many organizations. Ethical decisions came to the forefront of what many people professionals were asked to, and needed to, do.

This shift in what the people profession focused on was not new at all but wasn't as widespread as it became in March 2020. The technology brought much of this into focus as it forced us to deliver our people practices in different ways, but instead of losing our humanity in doing this, many of us found and embraced it. For many people professionals, March 2020 saw some major learning about what work is, and about what was important in how people deliver their work. Everything became so interconnected both within and between organizations, and people professionals seemed at the heart of this. Organizations became, almost overnight, communities of practice.

This seemed set to carry on, imprinted in the collective memories within organizations, behaviours and mindsets changing and making it hard to go back to how things used to be. One of the main challenges though was maintaining this – in my own planning I had worked on the effects of

COVID-19 lasting three months, worst case scenario – and when that was proved an inaccurate prediction, things began to unravel for many.

Earlier in this chapter we had an example from Jane Smith's organization and noted how agile and flexible they were. However, the downfall to being so agile was that when the COVID-19 pandemic didn't show signs of stopping, and every decision was being made in that crisis/chaos zone, the workload for Jane Smith's people was being continually increased – because they would do something but then the situation would change overnight, and the organization and its leaders were being pulled in a different direction.

In this organization, Jane and the rest of the Leadership team were carrying the largest burden. Many were burnt out, and there was no sign of anything easing.

While this organization handled the initial crisis well, and many people involved thrived on the chaos – they quickly came to realize that that was unsustainable for individuals, so interest from employees started to wane in what the organization was doing at the same time as burnout approached for those leading it. The various regulations, and sustained health concerns, were tough for Jane to manage, and this echoes how many people professionals experienced working life as the situation continued. However, for some it was a good opportunity to refocus on different priorities.

Lisa Tomlinson was Head of People at Fircroft College near Birmingham in March 2020. The College provides a range of specialist education to people with specific learning needs and had a strong focus on inclusion and wellbeing which it did not wish to lose because of lockdown and remote working and were doubly concerned that such things could lead to greater exclusion (for example digital exclusion).

Lisa's focus was to ensure that no member of staff felt isolated, and she tried through her people practices helping them maintain a sense of structure and routine. She also didn't want a one size fits all approach to technology, so made a conscious decision to let people pick their own technology (both software and hardware) based on their communication preferences and working styles and made heavy use of low- and no-tech solutions such as phone calls and outdoor meetings (within government guidelines). No piece of software or hardware was mandatory for anyone to use.

Lisa decided to heavily reduce the organizational learning and development budget but used that to top up its wellbeing budget. Far from reducing learning and development though, if anything it increased – with a lot more informal interventions and a significant increase in Yammer use to curate resources and materials to enable individualized learning. A similar thing happened with wellbeing resources and materials, and this helped shift the view of her people professionals being the provider of things like wellbeing and learning and development, towards everyone else taking responsibility for them.

It was difficult to see how things would pan out and how long the shift would last for, and making long-term commitments became a difficult thing to do for many people professionals. However, in all of that, behaving sensibly and ethically became even more important than before for organizations, and this is where people professionals came into their own. To come out of this with any kind of good organizational reputation, the people profession needed to use its powers for good and look after the people who they wanted to look after the business when the COVID-19 pandemic receded. The risks were clear – those who didn't do that could find they didn't have a business when it was all over, new normal or not.

There are two case studies in this chapter, both looking at aspects of people practices planning when the COVID-19 pandemic hit. One organization did a huge amount, and the other did none. We will explore the impact of both approaches.

In this first case study, we see how one organization took steps to prepare its people and people practices for a COVID-19 pandemic and enforced long term remote working well before 2020, and look at the lessons learnt from such planning.

In the second case study we look at a different organization who did hardly any level of planning for the impact of the COVID-19 pandemic and how this shaped the delivery of their people practices as everything hit the fan.

CASE STUDY ONE

Gail Hatfield is the People and Resources Director at Energy Systems Catapult (ESC), which has 175 staff in the Birmingham area.

ESC, like my own experiences with Swine Flu, had a business continuity plan that focused specifically on flu-type pandemics, albeit theirs was constructed much more recently in 2018, enabling them to do some full testing of both this scenario and some others that could require shorter-term but similar modifications (for example buildings inaccessible due to heavy snowfall).

When ESC did a full run-through of their pandemic business continuity plan in 2018, they modelled what would happen and fully simulated many aspects of the COVID-19 pandemic. In their models they planned for up to 50% of staff being absent through sickness or unable to fully work because of home-schooling and reviewed how their people practices and the whole employee experience stood up to such things.

Gail learnt that most of their people practices were not sufficient to cope with a pandemic. For example:

- The organizational absence reporting system completely fell over. Its absence categories didn't include self-isolation or shielding, and it could not cope with the sheer volume of activity coming through.

- IT capability meant that not everyone could remote work at the same time – there were bottlenecks which severely limited capacity at set times.

- The laptops available for staff were partially locked down, meaning that staff could not freely download apps that they needed to access parts of their work, and in particular external sites.

- Staff often had mobile phones but no chargers, or vice versa.

- There were no support mechanisms for staff mental health and wellbeing.

- There were not enough cleaners, cleaning equipment and good hygiene practices in the offices.

As a result of this, Gail and her team ensured that from an IT perspective, extra VPN ports were arranged, and that all staff had mobile phones and laptops (and chargers) that offered flexibility and freedom. To avoid unnecessary panic this was spun to staff as business as usual – IT upgrades and the like.

Gail's team also changed their absence reporting process so that this was done into the HR team as a central point, with HR then triaging calls and notifying the appropriate people.

In December 2019 as one employee holidayed in Japan, that employee learned of COVID-19 and that prompted the organization to again review its pandemic business continuity plan, several months before any other UK-based organization did so. From an equipment perspective Gail felt that they were prepared, but not from a customer or service delivery perspective, so legal professionals were engaged to review and insert force majeure clauses in customer contracts. Gail herself wrote a risk paper on COVID-19 in late January 2020 advising the organization to adopt A and B shifts and some other aspects that later became necessary for many but was told not to share this thinking or advice for fear of causing panic. She later re-presented this paper in early March 2020 but again many people felt she was panicking, made worse by her team telling people on a regular basis to take their things home with them in case the building was locked down the following day.

To Gail's surprise, people complied with this. This gave her the confidence in early March 2020 to build the communications hierarchy and templates to deal with the COVID-19 pandemic accelerating. Then on 11 March ESC ran an event in London and had a significant number of no shows, all citing the COVID-19 pandemic as the reason not to attend, and this seemed to galvanize the rest of the organization into action. Gail and her team were faced with an influx of employees wanting help to get set up to work remotely and worked tirelessly to achieve that by the end of 16 March, a good week before the government enforced it. During these days, Gail's team delivered crash courses on Microsoft Teams, which the organization had had for years but had not been used, and everything moved to virtual delivery, something Gail described to me as 'very clunky at the start'.

At various points in this journey Gail was, understandably, concerned for her reputation but trusted what she calls her sixth sense. She knew that if she followed the business continuity plan, itself based on the principles of the organization, she would be on solid ground. This proved true, as the modifications they made to absence reporting, and other processes such as productivity data analysis, held up very well indeed and enabled smooth transitions to be made. The additional support for those self-isolating or off sick, including mental health support, also proved prescient.

ESC could not access the furlough scheme because of the nature of their funding streams, so this meant that in their pandemic planning they had already made plans to redeploy people into other work quickly. What it did mean though was a temporary halt to a very large recruitment campaign as there were concerns how this could translate to a remote setting, and the team needed to do some process redesign and mindset shifts before this could work effectively.

Looking back at it, Gail feels that 'people thought I was crazy' in doing full pandemic simulation activities across the organization in 2018. However, people remembered it and this helped to lower their anxiety levels when the real COVID-19 pandemic hit. The organization had also built lots of useful contingency budgets – Gail on wellbeing, the IT team for long term remote working, and this meant these could be accessed and used quickly.

CASE STUDY TWO

Michelle Reid is the People Director at the Institute of Occupational Medicine, with 90 staff, most based in Edinburgh with a handful in Singapore. Michelle had been arranging the delivery of a leadership development programme based on David Marquet's intent-based leadership theories and considers the delivery of this in the year leading up to February 2020 as critical preparation for what was to come as it helped leaders to build trust with each other, giving them toolkits and ways of thinking that proved helpful in the COVID-19 pandemic. Michelle herself spent much of her time in Singapore during this period, who as a country were around six weeks ahead of the UK in the COVID-19 pandemic, so she had first-hand experience of masks, hand hygiene, mandatory testing and more well before her compatriots did. The organization also requested that she self-isolate on her return to the UK in mid-February, which she found confusing.

Unusually for the type of organization, it carried on much as normal until the UK lockdown was announced, with no COVID-19 pandemic or remote working planning having taken place. Michelle and the rest of the leadership team felt that their inherent flexibility and stock of research and exposure knowledge would allow them to cope no matter what came their way. Michelle was aware of some in the organization, in the know about infectious disease and exposure control, being very concerned, but largely paid them no attention, with the only action she took being a cursory look at contractual documentation to see if there was any clause around layoffs and short time working – and noted that there wasn't.

Consequently, when the UK lockdown was announced, Michelle felt that their entire business would have to close, and aside from her own individual financial concerns she had concerns about the financial viability of the business, whose value came from the knowledge and skills of its employees.

Following this, Michelle facilitated a full day leadership team meeting to do some initial planning, and then they brought as many employees as possible in for a face-to-face meeting, with others dialling in remotely. At this meeting Michelle and other leaders were open and transparent about the situation, sharing what they knew, how they were feeling, and what they didn't know. They told the employees that to safeguard the business and their employment that contractual change was needed, quickly, and put in place rapid consultation processes. Within 24 hours all employees had agreed to clauses around short time working and furloughing, and 75% had gone onto the furlough scheme. The rest, including all senior leaders, agreed to work at 80% capacity for 80% pay. Michelle ensured that any staff working remotely could take anything they needed home from the office, without question, and ensured that she put in place daily communication summaries, which lasted for nine months without exception. The organization deliberately over communicated, and felt that worked, recognizing the importance of early and continuous engagement of their people.

Within a few days, the organization realized that they could bring forward parts of their strategy to work on with the space and time created. Things like digitalization, and business process re-engineering, became new priorities for Michelle, who was the only people professional who remained working. Aside from those big strategic priorities, the only parts of Michelle's usual duties that carried on were the contractual change processes, basic administration and checking in with people.

The organization took the opportunity to balance its books and restore some financial resilience while the pressure was off for delivering its projects. Quickly, they realized they had people who would be critical for research into the COVID-19 pandemic, for example epidemiologists and other healthcare experts and engineers, so could change their business model to offer frontline NHS services. Michelle herself took on some operational delivery responsibilities, particularly around business process re-engineering, blending them with her existing people practices, which had become entirely digital, doing away with wet signatures on documents and going completely paper free overnight. The experience allowed her to demonstrate the value she could bring to the organization beyond transactional people practices and honed her skills not just in looking after people but their performance too, and taught her that she had skills in communications, marketing and more. Along with the entire senior team, Michelle was able to re-craft her own role during this time.

There were a number of lessons learned according to Michelle:

- Initially they relied on communications coming from one person – the Chief Executive – and this created some bottlenecks as well as not fully empowering other leaders. The organization eventually rectified this.

- Michelle would also do more on wellbeing earlier than she did, recognizing a focus on social contact and team development being needed.

- She feels the organization could have done more to recognize its 'heroes' early on – those coping well with extraordinary circumstances – and improved its approach to recognition.

- The organization knee jerked around the furlough scheme and put some people on it who neither wanted or needed to be on it and should have given this more thought at the time and particularly as the weeks turned into months.

- Some people practices stopped completely as the lockdown in the UK was announced – leadership development, executive coaching, learning and development, recruitment, and employee relations. While Michelle thinks this was a sensible reaction in the first week, by the second week it was becoming clear to her that these should resume, but it took too long for that to happen.

Case study reflections

- In the first case study:
  - Stress testing your people practices can give a good insight into how they will cope with massively different volumes and types of activity, and under different circumstances.
  - The employee experience when working remotely touches on more than just the remit of people professionals but may need people professionals to bring together sometimes disparate stakeholders to ensure that this experience is a positive and straightforward one.
  - Sometimes, people professionals can be a lone voice, advising the organization on a course of action that seems unpopular or unnecessary. When we are that lone voice, we should not go quiet – if anything we should continue to speak up.
  - When organizations change rapidly, we need to provide more wellbeing support for people within it.
  - The benefits of forward planning seem to speak for themselves if the plan is flexible enough to be adapted accordingly. People professionals are fortunate to work with resources – human beings – that are long-term in nature, and forward planning is most definitely possible with human beings.
- In the second case study:
  - Going with the flow and trusting the people in organizations to do the right thing, even under difficult circumstances, can also reap rewards for people professionals.
  - When crises arrive, organizations and their people professionals need to consider both short- and long-term consequences of decision-making and try to balance both.

o Such crises can change the nature of the roles we do as people professionals, and we may well find that we are in demand in other areas of the business due to the strong level of transferable skills we have.

o In extreme circumstances, cutting back on people practices is a knee-jerk reaction at best, when in fact it is better for the entire organization if such practices continue and are maybe even increased in scope.

The action plan

If you and your organization are headed into, or pitched into, a crisis or set of extreme circumstances, and you want to get through it effectively, the following questions may help you prepare appropriately:

- Can you update your business continuity plans, and test them out fully, so that you are aware what impact the scenarios envisaged in them will have on your people practices?

- If your organization has bases in other countries, what and who can you listen to, to ensure that you are ahead of the curve when it comes to events beginning to sweep the globe?

- Given that rapid large-scale change wreaks emotional havoc with many people, what can you put in place to provide support for those affected by the changes?

- What aspects of your people practices are fixed in stone, and which can be flexed according to circumstances? What are those circumstances and how much flex can be achieved?

- How can you increase your visibility and credibility in the organization so that senior leaders not just listen to your views but actively seek them out?

- What is your relationship like with other departments who impact heavily on the employee experience, such as IT, and Facilities? Do you or can you work together to promote a better employee experience, and could you do some joint planning for extreme circumstances?

- How can you ensure that jobs are flexible enough to be re-crafted at speed to give people flexibility and focus in extreme circumstances?

- How much of your people practice is about culture and relationships (and leadership) versus how much is about compliance, policies, and procedures? Is this the most appropriate balance?

- How much forward planning do you do (or do you need to do) about your people? Do you know the knowledge and skills they have and could use in different circumstances, and where some may need more, or less, support? Do you know what things you could start for them or stop for them to make their experience better in a crisis?

- What is your best advice to senior leaders in your organization about how they can better plan for emergency situations?

Sketchnote summary

Chapter 2: When the going got tough, the tough got going

The Value of:

Contingency planning

stress testing

People Practices

Being Flexible

Listen + Learn

from early experience across the world

Different Experiences

Working from home

CLOSED furloughed

A and B shifts

in the workplace

visible + credible

People   IT   H+S   Premises

work together

Policies

Review + Flex

All round support

Redesign work practices

focus on core activities

for wellbeing

03

The new normal?

The shorter read

The phrase 'the new normal' is one that both encapsulates our situation well and can inspire derision in equal measure. However, it is a unique situation and one that affords us as people professionals a real chance to make a difference to our organizations.

For many, living and working remotely raised big challenges around managing the divide between work and life, technological issues and, most obviously, being isolated from other people. Although the research existed before to tell us about these challenges, the latter concern has become a very big issue for people professionals to wrestle with. There have been some innovative ways of dealing with this, but challenges remain. Some of these challenges were magnified by technology, but just because we have the technology, doesn't mean we should use it for everything.

The new normal also made almost every organization confront some 'truths' around what work is and where and when it needs to be done, to the extent that the majority of organizations and employees now want to include some element of remote working in their working lives, in a hybrid approach. There aren't many who want to remain fully remote though. Our organizations are likely in future to have different groups of employees working fully in the office, in a hybrid way and some fully remote. We need to design people practices that can create a consistent experience across these different ways of working.

We need to ensure that we design communication and engagement differently in our organizations so that no-one is excluded, and that isolation is minimized. We need to work on resetting team relationships and culture so that the rules of interaction are well established and agreed. We need to work with the leaders in our organizations to understand how and why their role has changed and how they need to act and behave differently.

This comes with challenges of its own though. Some of the physical spaces we work in are simply not fit for purpose. Some of the technology isn't either. Our people need upskilling (or reskilling perhaps) to be able to learn in different ways and share knowledge more effectively. Individual and collective wellbeing needs to be a top priority for organizations and sometimes hasn't been. Leaders themselves may be a significant barrier around how inclusive they need to be and the different skills they need to operate in this new normal.

We need to keep our organizations people-centric, building connections with and between people who don't see each other as often as they used to. The nature of engagement is changing, and our people practices need to change with it. The way that teams communicate and make decisions needs to be different too in order to get the most from our people.

There's a lot to do.

The longer read

What even is 'the new normal' and do we want to escape or embrace it?

The phrase 'the new normal' can divide opinion – some feel it describes the situation we find ourselves in well, but others have tired of it and consider it a cliché. However, the COVID-19 pandemic brought with it some significant, long-term changes to the way we live and work and therefore to the way people professionals need to act.

The phrase initially described the reality of life in the early days of the COVID-19 lockdown as people tried to make sense of what was happening and to create new routines, new patterns of work and life in what was a frightening time. Along with phrases like 'in these unprecedented times' it became something that signified how the world had changed but that this wasn't going to be something that blew over quickly.

Soon many began to tire of the situation and the restrictions it placed on them, and the phrases that expressed these bore the brunt of some of that frustration. People understandably wanted to go back to how things were, or move on to how things will be, and using the phrases that reminded people of how long COVID-19 was dragging on was, in itself, a frustration.

Nonetheless, the pandemic **did** continue longer than anyone thought possible and the ways of working we adopted in a hurry in March 2020 are largely still with us – people working remotely, people working in a hybrid way, and other people still working where they always used to. Great changes were wrought upon a great many people in March 2020 and the world created then is mostly still the reality for many and will continue to be.

So, what kind of world is it? It is one that has both significant advantages and disadvantages in perhaps equal measure. In the *2021 State of Remote Work* report (Buffer, 2021)[1], these were explored for those people forced to work away from what had been their usual workplace.

Listed as the top advantages were, in order:

- The ability to have a flexible schedule.
- The ability to work from anywhere.
- Not having to commute.
- The ability to spend time with family.

However, the top disadvantages, clearly linked to these, were, in order:

- Not being able to unplug.
- Difficulties with collaboration and communication.
- Loneliness.
- Distractions at home.

When you put those two lists together you begin to understand the unique nature of working remotely and the challenges that face people professionals and line managers in pivoting to these radically different ways of working. In previous chapters we've explored how many organizations began to embrace remote working and how many individuals appreciated the benefits it could bring – but it is important to remember that most of this happened when both individuals and organizations could choose to do it, not when a global pandemic forced them to do it.

Regular in-person interaction with other human beings is something that most people took for granted until it didn't happen anymore. Socializing is a core purpose and need (reflected in some of the lower levels in Maslow's Hierarchy of Needs) for all of us – and our ability to do this has huge implications for our mental and physical health.

A 2018 Neuroscience report found that when researchers removed mice from what was their highly social structure and put them in isolation away from that group, the mice's brain cells showed signs of atrophy caused by lack of social interaction.

Put simply, when the mice were removed from their social structure, their brain cells started dying off (Psychology Today, 2017).[2]

As many discovered in the early days of the pandemic, isolation and loneliness in humans can be just as detrimental as this example. And while longer-term remote workers had largely found ways around this, such as working in coffee shops, spending time at co-working locations or other places, during the pandemic most were deprived of even these options. Individual homes became workspaces, with all the strengths and weaknesses of that home as a workspace, and people were mostly prevented from meeting face to face with the colleagues they had come to rely on more than they realized.

Early in the pandemic I advised my clients to be aware of this, to encourage social engagement, and to encourage people to use their exercise opportunities to help combat the loneliness (as well as reap the cardiovascular benefits). Even taking calls in an outdoor space (e.g. garden if available, though even access to that led to exclusion for many) would help, and for that my clients needed encouragement to **not** use video calls for everything – 'just because you can, doesn't mean you should' became a mantra for me advising other people professionals on how to cope with what the world had become.

It also became obvious that longer-term remote workers had got used to the ergonomic needs and demands they faced – and that those forced to adopt full-time remote working had little or none of the same set-up. I had got used to working remotely for two days a week for around twenty years but hadn't really invested in any equipment that would really make this a comfortable situation up until the pandemic forced me to. What made the difference for me was that I'd worked very well remotely for twenty years or so but nothing had prepared me for having to share that remote working space with four children and a wife all trying to do their stuff remotely too. I know I won't have been alone in finding compromises in the short-term to make the situation work.

So, we were plunged, headfirst, into 'the new normal'. But it is clear from the Buffer survey that, if it is done well, remote working leads to significant advantages. The enforced and extreme nature of it during 2020 for most employees meant that many of these advantages were experienced alongside the disadvantages. However, it forced many individuals and their organizations to confront some previous, longstanding and wrongly held, 'truths' about the nature of work:

- That the best way of working is done in five shifts of eight hours (often 9am-5pm).
- That the optimum working week is around 40 hours to achieve what needs to be done in each job.
- That people need to live close enough to their place of work to be able to get there on any given day.
- That work had to be done in one physical space in one location.

Confronting these 'truths' was often painful for many but helpful for all and helps us with what we need to consider in this chapter. As the CIPD stated in *Flexible working – lessons from the pandemic*[3], 'the impossible turns out to be possible after all'. As many as 63% of employers planned to introduce or expand the use of hybrid working, but also noted similar challenges around enforced remote working to do with employee wellbeing, unsuitable work, unsuitable home circumstances, insufficient or outdated technology, and, notably, line manager capability.

In 2015 I gave up a permanent desk in my place of work and began splitting my workplace across not just home but potentially three or four offices as well as other social spaces like coffee shops, and being able to work at any of those locations at any time I wished. I immediately benefitted from a reduced commute and the flexibility to choose my work location, which made me more flexible in meeting customer demands and able to build better working relationships with a wider range of people than I'd have been interacting with in just one location.

This meant I was more reliant on technology, but was able to use that to be more connected to the various locations I could work at and felt like I was more accessible to this wider range of colleagues as a result. I began working in coffee shops more and more often and noticing other people (from different organizations) doing the same, and I appreciated how this made me both more interactive with strangers but also more productive. It also made me realize that I needed to work in short sprints or bursts to be most productive, interspersed by times when I did personal things.

I also realized that I needed a commute, perhaps just 15–20 minutes but something to give me a physical break in-between work and life.

Speaking in April 2021, during the CIPD podcast *Building back better post-pandemic*[4], Polly McKenzie, Chief Executive of Demos, said that most people found remote working a generally positive experience and want to continue it in some form, while benefitting from a return to the office. So the challenge for us as people professionals is to build something that enables people to get the benefits of both ways of working, while recognizing, as David D'Souza points out in the same podcast, that many people don't have a choice about where they work – some never have and some never will[5] – the challenge here is to be inclusive in the way we build this offering, that we now call the hybrid model of working, and to develop people practices that create the best experience for all aspects of that and for all involved.

Exploring hybrid working and where it is going

If our organizations adopt hybrid working, we need to be really clear what we mean by that. Is it work from anywhere, any time or is it set days a week at home? Is it something that applies to **all** employees or something that only applies to some (but by definition the organization itself will have a hybrid model)? As people professionals we are well-placed to help the organization and its leaders answer these questions and no doubt many have, but many others will be struggling with it.

Many commentators predict that hybrid working will be the inevitable future. Chris Herd shared on Twitter[6] and at the International HR Forum in June 2021, that the large companies he speaks to are intending to cut their real estate by around 50-70% through non-renewal of office leases. Touching on the issue of burnout he made the point that the enforced nature of remote working has obscured many of its benefits and exacerbated many of its drawbacks, and that this will be less of an issue with designed hybrid working. He asked if we remember what happened to companies that didn't embrace the rise of the internet, implying what could happen to those who don't embrace hybrid working. However, despite Herd's views, a survey by Understanding Society in 2021[7], showed that 88% of UK workers feel that they want to work in the traditional workplace for at least some of their time. The office isn't dead yet, but it is clear that we won't be returning to the 'old normal' just yet – with one article suggesting that up to three-quarters of workers would accept a pay cut if they could retain remote working for a few days a week[8].

The reasons for the desire for hybrid or remote working may be obvious. The Leesman Index (2021) gathered information on over 180,000 remote workers in 90 countries and compared their level of productivity and happiness with those in the workplace prior to the pandemic. The average happiness score of those in the workplace – 63%, with the very best being 78%. The average happiness score of those working remotely during the pandemic – 82%.

Simply looking at happiness though doesn't tell the whole picture, and nor does looking at productivity either. People do need some level of face-to-face interaction and in many cases crave it. Full-time remote working appears something that isn't attractive to many people at all, and so our people practices have to be able to operate across the different types of working situations we will face in the future – fully remote, fully face to face and hybrid.

To look at why fully remote isn't attractive we don't have to go far. There is plenty of evidence that when we are around other humans we find it beneficial and energizing. Rowers found their endorphins doubled when around others[8], and people who sang together found the same[9]. Somehow, then, we must enable all the benefits from all these types of working and interactions to be present no matter how an individual works.

So, based on the research so far, what do people need to do in a hybrid workplace future?

- Avoid simply duplicating the physical workplace remotely. There must be something noticeably different about the experiences in both places to give them both some attraction.

- Give proper attention to the set-up of their remote workspace (in 2021, Chris Herd predicted a rise in personal injury claims if this is not done[10]) – working at home now and again may not be an issue, but potentially for years several times a week would – although that may lead to some exclusion and organizations will need to work to address this.

- Invest in not just communications technology but specifically communication skills – remote working often requires a greater proficiency with both reading and especially writing.

- Increase focus on internal networking events and conferences to help encourage in-person relationships and make these a good reason to come into the physical workplace when they happen.

- Utilize marketing skills that already exist in organizations and which are used to cultivate external communities (remotely) to create and nurture internal communities (also remotely).

- Provide more choice to employees over when and where they work, trusting them to make the right choices without building onerous processes around such things. At the same time, it is important to manage expectations that some roles may not have the same degree of choice as others do.

- Help managers to understand that what employees do is more important than dictating when and where the work needs to be done, and reflect these stances in the organizational culture, encouraging and consciously building opportunities for collaboration.

- Focus on inclusivity in people practices and organizational culture to ensure that every employee feels that they can contribute to the same degree.

As a result of all of this, there are implications for how we need to design and deliver people practices, so let's explore those.

Why we need to do people practices differently

The previous section ended with some broad areas we need to focus on, but while many of these things seem obvious, some of the other areas may need further explanation as to why they need to be different or enhanced in a remote or hybrid work environment.

COMMUNICATION AND ENGAGEMENT

It seems obvious that communication and engagement would be a challenge with managing remote employees, partly because we lose the informal, ad-hoc chats that you might get if you just wandered by someone's desk, but I believe it is more than that. Relying primarily on text-based communication and video calls, it can become harder to sense meaning and purpose in the communication signals.

I'm sure you've reacted badly to a text-based communication or even a video call, only to discover later that your reaction was an over-reaction and maybe even mistaken – I certainly have. This is based on the philosophical concept of Hanlon's Razor – 'assume ignorance before malice' when communicating with others. Hanlon's research was based on thousands of years of primal programming causing us to assume many communication signals are threats before anything else – a version of the fight or flight survival instinct. How does this translate into the modern world? Well, if you send something in a message that could be viewed as a 'threat' (some feedback, a question, any kind of criticism) then the recipient could assume negative intent even when you've not intended any – but without the non-verbal cues to help us discern intent, this isn't surprising.

It is easy to feel left out of things when working remotely, particularly if others are in the office but even when those others are working remotely too – because you can't see celebrations, how your opinion is valued or even noticed, ad-hoc social events like going for a drink after work, it may feel as if you're less visible working remotely and have less access to key decision-makers in the organization. As a result, your engagement suffers. As people professionals we need to put things in place that combat this.

TEAM RELATIONSHIPS

You'll be familiar with the well-known model by Tuckman (1965) on team development – Forming, Storming, Norming, Performing (and, in later versions, Adjourning). Many of us will have helped leaders work through this with their teams, but what many teams didn't realize when the pandemic hit in March 2020 was that every team went back to the beginning of this model, no matter what stage they were at previously. The pandemic hit the reset button, and unless teams worked to re-establish their shared sense of identity then this may have been lost. Many teams carried on in the same way they did when co-located, simply switching their existing relationships to a virtual footing, without perhaps realizing that they had an opportunity to redraw team relationships and responsibilities.

As an example, in co-located teams, the rules of how the team members interact are often implicitly understood – part of the culture perhaps – things like etiquette around meetings, emails, phone calls and the like. But in a remote or hybrid environment these are not necessarily the same and need explicitly stating, or re-stating.

TEAM LEADERSHIP

If individuals and teams are still managed on how long they are working for then we are missing something. The focus of leaders managing remote or hybrid teams needs to be on results and outputs (and working out whether these are because of people working longer or not), and this in itself should lead to leaders beginning to use their time and skills in different ways – more of a problem-solving and empowering style of leadership than task-focus. Many leaders will be able to cope with this, but many will struggle – and another key role for us people professionals is to enable this skillset.

Leaders of remote or hybrid teams need to work harder at communication to keep everyone informed of significant events. They need to help people collaborate and review each other's work and give each other feedback so that communication is not exclusively funnelled through the leader. They need to encourage the sharing of performance information and agree how this will be developed and feedback given on such matters.

Leaders of remote or hybrid teams need to work harder at recognition – ensuring individuals and teams feel valued and encouraging team members to do the same with each other, keeping people connected as a team and keeping workflow on track.

They also need to create routines – for individual and team meetings, and other processes, and encourage the sharing of information across the team. They need to notice what is happening within the team, reading between the lines of communications and picking up on what isn't being shared or said. They need to be more social than ever before, increasing rapport and easing communication and feelings of isolation.

In an article he wrote for HR Magazine in 2017[11], Nick Atkin (then Chief Executive of Halton Housing Trust, but now Chief Executive at Yorkshire Housing) wrote about how to encourage leaders and organizational culture to be different in a remote or hybrid working environment. Atkin had been pushing Halton to adopt remote and hybrid working for many years at this point. Reviewing the article now, it seems very ahead of its time and very prescient in the way Atkin makes points about the way leaders need to adapt and sharing thoughts that resonate with us some years later as we wrestle with making remote or hybrid working work.

Atkin said that 'for some the workplace is about being seen, characterized by a culture of presenteeism and distrust', but that at Halton they were already working 'from a default position of trusting everyone and treating them as adults'.

Showing considerable foresight, Atkin stated that 'work is something you do, not somewhere you go, which means you don't have to be in work to be in work. Our approach is based on flexibility and agility. The office should be somewhere people come to collaborate and spend quality time'. He noted that the line between work and home life was becoming increasingly blurred and provided a range of digital devices to help people manage all aspects of this.

This approach was already, back in 2017, paying dividends in terms of staff retention. One of Halton's staff had moved from Cheshire to South Wales but had been able to stay with the organization, working remotely for nine days out of every ten. It also had effects on the organizational real estate, saving money on office costs but allowing employees to claim back the costs of getting themselves set up to work remotely. This approach also had benefits in terms of reducing staff absence and increasing engagement.

Atkin also noted that this changed organizational culture around recruitment too: 'We recruit for attitude and not skills or experience because we've found that you can train people to do most things, but you can't generally change how they think or fit in with a culture. There are uncertain times ahead for the UK, but also lots of opportunity. That's why at times like this we have increased our investment in training to increase the capability of our people to adapt.'

Barriers we face in helping organizations adapt

Making this work will not be easy. We must consider how feasible it is for this type of remote or hybrid working environment to be sustained over a long period of time, particularly without the imperative provided by the pandemic. Research done in 2020 suggested that 43% of UK-based jobs could be carried out at home for an unspecified period, with similar proportions for other developed countries (Felstead and Reuschke, 2020). There is perhaps evidence that this proportion is not equally distributed across the regions and across job types, but it seems clear that there is sufficient desire and feasibility to make remote and hybrid working greater in use than it was pre-pandemic.

We need to consider some of the main barriers and challenges that people professionals face in shaping this world of work.

OUR PHYSICAL SPACES

We know from earlier in this book that many employees did not, and do not, have the right homeworking set-up and we have noted the implications of this. It is perhaps not enough to give guidance on the right set-up, but we need to consider remote working exclusion here – some people simply don't have the right environment no matter the equipment we could provide them with, and this is something we have to address as a barrier to making remote and hybrid work more effective.

By the same token many organizations will face challenges redesigning their current workplaces to take account of shifting needs from employees – with more modular, flexible spaces encouraging networking and collaboration being seen as more useful – but even that may be beyond the resources of some smaller organizations.

PEOPLE

We have explored how prolonged isolation can impact employees negatively, and many surveys do report that most employees miss the informal, ad-hoc conversations and interactions that they were used to in the physical workplace. Leaders have a challenge in ensuring that these take place, be that physically, digitally or both. Social events and individual check-ins not just between leader and employee, but between employees themselves, will become more important. Some organizations have scheduled recurring, 15–30-minute virtual meetings which are for anyone to attend at any time and have a coffee break with whomever else is there – recreating something of the ad-hoc serendipitous breakthrough chats that people miss.

Elsewhere in this chapter we've looked at some predictions of where remote and hybrid work is going, and we have noted the risks for organizations of not following this curve. To attract and retain the right employees will require significant organization (re)design work to shape the right culture that engages these employees. We will have cohorts of employees who want to or can only work in the workplace, and some who want to or can only work remotely, alongside those who want to do both. Finding systems and processes that operate well across these populations is a challenge for people professionals which we explore in later chapters of this book.

Creating similar experiences for these populations is a real challenge. Microsoft have put in place systems where everyone has the same view of meeting participants and the same access to information and whatever is being worked on, and relying more on social cues such as emojis and GIFs to convey emotion and reactions (Forbes, 2021) – in essence, designing interactions as if no-one is in the room, even if they are. But Microsoft are a company you'd expect to be able to do all of these things and have the latest and shiniest technology – many other organizations may struggle, so again we'll explore this in a later chapter.

LEARNING

The importance of knowledge management for many organizations is well-evidenced, but there is danger that if people don't see each other as much face to face that some of the tacit knowledge that helps organizations to function may be lost. Learning has become more individualized and digitalized during remote working and there is a challenge for people professionals to harness knowledge management in different ways, and to provide learning opportunities that encourage networking and knowledge sharing.

Some learning technology already helps with this, for example allowing employees to display their credentials and areas of key knowledge on an intuitive system, enabling others to search them out and even automating the initial contact. The principle behind this is sound – but again many smaller organizations could struggle to access this technology.

On a related note, we may need to be providing some learning and development that specifically helps people deal with the after-effects of the pandemic and enforced remote working – some kind of 'dealing with survivor syndrome' learning that specifically addresses the impacts of the individual and shared experiences we have each had.

WELLBEING

A study found that 69% of employees working from home have experienced symptoms of burnout. Many larger organizations with a higher level of resources have been able to put things in place that have helped with this, but some smaller organizations have struggled. Technology and data can help here – there are settings in many email and calendar applications that can automatically shorten meetings for example and analyse working habits, but these are not well utilized in many smaller organizations.

More than that though, wellbeing has moved from being a benefit to being a management capability, which firmly repositions it within the realms of leadership development programmes and less as something delivered as part of a reward offering. Organizations and leaders will need help with this, especially in a remote or hybrid world.

Safety, no matter where the workplace or employee may be, is a priority. Some technology solutions will help here but may be beyond the reach of some smaller organizations. However, they will still need to have a system to manage the number of people in the workplace at any one time and perhaps to verify their current health status (things like vaccinations, boosters, recent tests and more – though such things are proving difficult and controversial).

PEOPLE LEADERS

Many of the things discussed above pose challenges for our people leaders. This represents a shift in how people are managed, developed, communicated with and much more. Leaders who have relied on being able to see people in order to judge the effort being expended will no longer be able to do that, and although that may have changed when most people worked remotely, a challenge for us is to ensure that old habits do not creep back into leadership practices as the hybrid workplace takes off. Polly McKenzie, talking in a CIPD podcast in April 2021[12], suggested that many leaders are now actively considering what outputs and outcomes they need from each person, and welcomed that, but that's been during a pandemic – can we sustain that and embed that?

Leaders also need to focus on how they create inclusive people practices – David D'Souza, in the same CIPD podcast[13], comments on identifying talent being a challenge and I agree with that – he asks how do we ensure that we are giving voice to and developing/promoting the right people in a remote or hybrid working environment, and not just focusing on and responding to the noisy voices? We face challenges here, and in how leaders bring people into their teams and help them to learn about the culture if the new employee isn't wholly in the physical workplace with them.

There are also challenges in using the right communication tools. Email, for so long a staple of workplace communication, may no longer be the most appropriate tool for leaders to use when communicating with people in a remote or hybrid environment. Very rarely, for example, do we tend to use emails in our personal lives to keep up with what friends and family are doing, and we have something akin to a hybrid situation with those groups in that we both see them face to face but largely connect and communicate virtually. We use other methods to lead those groups and will need to adopt similar methods with our leaders in our organizations and the groups they lead.

Keeping organizations people-centric

As we have noted in the previous section and throughout this chapter, the challenge for people professionals in a remote and hybrid working world is to keep our organizations and what we do people-centric. It may seem that some organizations, preparing for a remote or hybrid world, are adopting a digital first approach – but that doesn't equate to being digital exclusive. Again, I'll paraphrase a quote from the film *Jurassic Park* – 'just because you can, doesn't mean you should'. This means that we must remember, in this technology-driven world, that people professionals' prime role is to support, nurture and engage the people who work for our organizations. The CIPD describe this as championing better work and working lives. There are some questions we need to consider if we are to keep our organizations people-centric.

HOW DO YOU BUILD CONNECTIONS WITH AND BETWEEN PEOPLE WHO WORK IN A REMOTE OR HYBRID ENVIRONMENT?

I am often asked this and usually respond by advising to find things people have in common, something they have shared interests in. Think about the way we build relationships online via social media, which are often as strong as or stronger than the bonds created in person – these are mostly based heavily on shared interests, and we all have examples of people we have never met or meet very rarely who we feel like we know like a close family member. The shared interests are likely personal things – sports teams, places lived/visited, favourite television shows/films, shared pastimes. It is easier to build connections with and between people on social levels than on any work-related level. We need to ensure that people find out about each other in ways that don't involve talking about work. Some of my clients have encouraged employees to set up clubs based on mutual interests.

Some of the best team development activities blend online and offline challenges, getting people to work together to achieve their goals in a healthy competition. The same is true of work-related challenges that involve collaboration and potential doses of gamification – they encourage people to work together and bond as a team. We need to find ways to do more of this in our organizations and we'll explore some ideas in a later chapter of this book.

WHAT DO WE NEED TO LOOK OUT FOR AROUND ENGAGEMENT OF PEOPLE WORKING REMOTELY OR IN A HYBRID WAY?

Again, this is a common question I'm asked by clients. People tend to leave a virtual wake behind them and that's something we should notice. We have to be careful of reaching a conclusion from any isolated piece of data and triangulate as much as we can – but we should be noticing what people say and how they say it, and things they don't say. We need to notice the outcomes they achieve versus the apparent effort involved in achieving them. We need to notice what is said about other people in the team by the team. We need to notice the contributions people make and the ones they should make but don't. We need to notice interactions between people and how they play out. We need to notice if people work excessive hours or in an unpredictable pattern, and we need to talk to people about what is happening for them, what is on their mind, what steps they are taking to look after themselves and what help they need with that.

That's a lot for any leader to notice and it's no surprise that many will miss things that could be spotted around engagement, motivation and well-being. But if we are to keep our organizations people-centric then it's something we must do. We may need our leaders to provide explicit permission and encouragement for non-work topics to be discussed in meetings and for people to have fun together, otherwise it may not happen. If engagement and motivation come from being human around other humans, we need to not just allow it to happen, but prompt it to happen.

HOW DO YOU MANAGE DECISION-MAKING AND COMMUNICATION IN A REMOTE OR HYBRID WORLD?

This is another question I am often asked. This is a question of balance – too much communication, such as back-to-back meetings and people trying to do emails while in or in-between meetings, as well as keeping up with internal social media channels, is a bad thing and prevents work being done.

Not enough communication, with people being left to their own devices and no check-ins happening at all, is equally bad.

Jo Owen, writing for Kogan Page in 2020[14], suggested that we need to agree clear rhythms and routines about how to communicate and plan, and to keep communication fast but informal. Owen goes on to give some suggestions how to do this and we will explore those and other suggestions in a later chapter.

This style of working will mean that we inevitably need to change the way leaders make decisions in teams, to become more consultative and democratic in the way they make decisions, and will change the way we develop plans, becoming more collaborative and exploring ideas at a much earlier stage – avoiding a 'tell' approach to team leadership.

In an earlier example we looked at how Eleanor Gooding, People and Culture Director at Boost Drinks, helped prepare that organization for the pandemic. I also asked her how she kept the organization people-centric while they were working in a remote and hybrid world.

Boost were clear at the outset of remote and hybrid working that they needed to get the work done as it was what would keep the organization afloat. They were also clear that remote and hybrid working could be disastrous unless people found the right routines, motivators and set-up. They gave people advice on how to prepare for their working day and how to structure it, saying things like:

- Pretend that you're at work and get dressed instead of crawling to your laptop in your pj's.

- Structure your day. Use lists and tick things off as you go along.

- Take breaks.

- Eat & Drink.

- Get up and move.

- If something's not working for you try different things until you find what works.

- If you have a super-productive time of day, schedule your 'solo' work at that time.

Boost were also conscious that many employees were juggling home-schooling responsibilities while remote working and were open and honest that no-one had a magic formula on how to make that work, with everyone's circumstances being unique. Keeping things people-centric again they advised to set realistic expectations and to realize that no-one is alone in juggling the different responsibilities and being explicit that the organization understood the need for flexibility, empathy and even alcohol!

Boost were well aware at the outset of the pandemic that it could last for some time and asked people to prioritize their own and their families' mental health, reminding employees that Boost owed them a duty of care and would notice if they were struggling and not able to make changes, asking them to communicate how they were feeling and what was causing that (such as a child having a bad day).

Gooding told me that they told employees they could deal with most situations in the short term but would not countenance employees being stretched beyond reason and working evenings and weekends on top of home-schooling challenges. They encouraged children to attend work meetings and to be part of the Boost family. She was also aware that people would get lonely and gave advice to take time to socialize.

Adopting the 'just because you can, doesn't mean you should', principle, Gooding told employees to be mindful of boundaries – just because the technology may show someone as free, doesn't mean that they are available for a meeting, and to avoid judging how people spend their time on and off technology.

The company was also ready to hold people accountable for looking after their own health and wellbeing. They gave good advice on getting set-up correctly to work remotely, giving information and equipment and advice on how to get this working right, and told people about the importance of scheduling breaks into their day, both from screen time as well as from work itself, and to remember to exercise. Interestingly, they also gave nutritional advice to their employees, advising on the need to stay hydrated, snack sensibly and eat well in general.

A considerable amount of thought went into giving people information about their mental health, and Gooding reinforced with employees that the company considered it a strength when people knew when to seek help, and that they considered it time well-spent if an employee took time to look after their mental health. People were encouraged to talk – to each other, online and offline, and to the Leadership Team – about anything they wanted to.

Boost's example is one of a company that stayed people-centric and has continued to be that way. We need more organizations like that. But unfortunately, there are a lot of stories in the press about company leaders wanting their employees back full-time in the office. This is largely driven by fear, of not knowing how best to capture the benefits of remote and hybrid working, and of not understanding enough about how people practices can allow such ways of working to thrive. As Polly McKenzie said in the CIPD podcast from April 2021[15], wellbeing and productivity are not in opposition – happy staff are much more likely to be successful and effective at work. If such staff are made happy by being able to work in the physical workplace, remotely or some hybrid blend of both – then we need to respect that, and provide them with people practices that can help to make that a great experience for all.

CASE STUDY

In this case study we look at how one organization adjusted their people practices to cope with remote and hybrid working as the pandemic hit, and what they learnt from that. Following this we'll consider the implications this has for us as we progress through this book, as this brings into sharper focus some of the issues we need to address if we are to deliver people practices better across a remote and hybrid workforce.

Annette Hill is the Director for People at Hospiscare, providing specialist care to those with life-limiting illnesses across Mid and East Devon. They employ nearly 300 staff but have a similar number of unpaid volunteers, and when the pandemic first hit, they made several decisions about what to do – clinical and estates based staff stayed on site, their retail outlets closed and the staff were furloughed, and almost everyone else was sent to work remotely.

The People team at Hospiscare were, prior to the pandemic, a very paper-driven and manual process operated service, with little technology in use for any process, despite having access to some. Annette described it as highly transactional and centralized, with lots of processes being controlled by and accessed through the People team, with limited use of self-service technology.

I asked Annette to summarize the issues she encountered in moving to remote and hybrid working and how she addressed them:

- Initially they severely cut back on their learning and development offering so that it focused on compliance-led training only. As a result of this, and because it was heavily clinically focused, Annette's team relinquished control of almost all learning and development, which has now gone into Operations.

- The pandemic exposed many leaders in the organization as lacking confidence in how to do some basic leadership and management tasks – what Annette described as basic functional activity. In response the People team arranged some virtual management training (the word management is deliberately used here instead of leadership to show the focus of the intervention).

- As the People team were to deliver this management training, Annette realized that the level of skill to design and deliver such training in a remote way was very low and had to put things in place to upskill her team rapidly.

- Given the nature of the labour market in which the organization operates, workforce planning and succession planning became a higher priority, and a greater focus has been placed on Apprenticeships as a result.

- The organization had previously disbanded its Staff Council due to a lack of agenda items from staff. Annette realized that this needed resurrecting and so set this up again in a virtual format. It was replaced by a group called Staff Voice, which was similarly lacklustre. To combat the way it had gone wrong initially, she arranged for it to meet more often but for shorter durations, and found this resulted in more focus and better engagement. Pleasingly it also seems to have brought many people's leadership qualities to the fore and she has been able to identify talent better because of this.

- In response to staff beginning to raise issues of loneliness, isolation and poor mental health, the organization started a Feelgood Friday newsletter, which was entirely crowdsourced in terms of content from staff and volunteers – people began sharing book ideas, television and film suggestions, recipe ideas and more. Annette also put the organization through The MIND Wellbeing Index and arranged some mental health first aid training.

- The nature of the manual and paper-based processes became an issue for Hospiscare, who relied on things like wet signatures on documents and contracts, and Annette quickly had to find workarounds for this – email confirmations at first, with things like Docusign following later.

- The lack of use of technology ahead of the pandemic meant that rolling out app-based services became tricky and required a lot more thought than it might have done if people had been face-to-face. Some of the apps could not handle the complex nature of things like self-rostering and some types of flexible working, so work still needed to be done manually by the People team.

- Disciplinary (and similar) procedures moved to a virtual footing and were not wholly successful, with issues around who else might be 'in the room' (for example some were helped by people not visible on camera) and attendance at virtual meetings. Written representations were increasingly used, and while some parts of the process worked well remotely, others did not, and Annette is considering how best to make that work using a blend of both face to face and virtual methods. Annette found that those who knew they were going to face bad news preferred for this to be done virtually instead of face to face.

- Recruitment initially paused but then moved virtual too, but the organization is only just starting to attempt processes more complicated than straightforward interviews and presentations, as they start to learn how to manage this virtually, for instance running a virtual recruitment fair on Zoom.

- Annette is now very aware that people's sense of priority in terms of pay, rewards and benefits is changing, but has not reached a conclusion about what she or the organization can do about this. She has used an app-based staff questionnaire to find out 'what matters to you at work' so the data can be used to develop the employer value proposition (EVP) for different staff groups.

However, one unexpected positive consequence of not being in the office was that the People team, who were used to being regularly and frequently interrupted with minor queries and having to be gatekeepers for all kinds of basic processes, were suddenly freed from these burdens. Communications became a lot more deliberate and planned or switched to email and digital means instead of face to face, allowing the People team to focus far more on things like wellbeing and engagement – so the pandemic has shifted the focus of the team considerably.

Annette used a four-box model devised originally by Helen Bevan to help analyse the impact of the pandemic on the organization's people practices.

TABLE 3.1

LET GO:	RESTART:
WE'VE BEEN ABLE TO STOP DOING THESE THINGS THAT WERE ALREADY OR ARE NOW UNFIT FOR PURPOSE	WE'VE HAD TO STOP THESE THINGS IN ORDER TO FOCUS ON THE CRISIS BUT THEY NEED TO BE PICKED UP IN SOME FORM
• Relying on paper employee files and other documentation.	• Job evaluation project completion, implementation of revised job descriptions and pay modernization.

(continued)

TABLE 3.1 (Continued)

• Doing lots of printing.	• Consideration of annual pay rise.
• Paper based communications with volunteers.	• Performance management discussions (which needed modernizing anyway).
• High volume of classroom-based training. (Some is still necessary).	• Review of organisational values.
	• Staff surveys and pulse surveys.
	• Staff Engagement – i.e. Staff Voice.
	• Recruitment.
	• Work Experience programme.
	• Stonewall Diversity and Inclusion work.
	• Leadership Development Programme.
	• Updating people policies.
	• Development of next stages of (HR system) roll out.

END:	**AMPLIFY:**
WE'VE DONE THESE THINGS TO RESPOND TO IMMEDIATE DEMANDS BUT THEY ARE SPECIFIC TO THE CRISIS	WE'VE BEEN ABLE TO TRY THESE NEW THINGS AND THEY SHOW SOME SIGNS OF PROMISE FOR THE FUTURE
• Furlough of 2 team members, and the rest working remotely entirely.	• Electronic documentation.
• Shortened Disciplinary process.	• Experimenting with workflows and other process automation.
• Cancellation of some of the L&D programme.	• Virtual L&D.
	• Virtual onboarding and induction.
• Performance management discussions moved from twice to once a year.	• Virtual team meetings.
	• Use of Zoom, Teams, Skype and other communications technology.
• No external classroom-based L&D.	• Weekly wellbeing newsletters.
• Produced guidance for managers to use, e.g. what to do if staff need to self-isolate, how to use furlough scheme.	• Virtual occupational health appointments.

Hospiscare analysis of the impact of the pandemic on people practices, reproduced with the kind permission of Annette Hill

As you can see from this helpful structure, the move to remote and hybrid working had a major impact on Hospiscare's people practices, and forced them to fully reassess what they wanted to do as a team and how they wanted to deliver services.

Case study reflections

- Organizations with small teams of people professionals can often have a largely transactional focus and may have built up unnecessarily bureaucratic and heavily administrative processes over many years – while they are ripe for transformation, there needs to be a burning platform for this to happen.

- People professionals will often not be able to cater for the entire organization working remotely or in a hybrid way – there may be some employees always in the physical workplace – and so having processes that allow for working with these different groups and experiences is key.

- If managers are heavily reliant on face-to-face support from people professionals, moving that support to a remote setting may expose significant skills gaps for those managers.

- Not all people professionals will have the skillset to design and deliver their services in a remote or hybrid way and may need upskilling themselves.

- Shorter and more frequent engagement and voice mechanisms seem to work better in a remote and hybrid environment.

- Crowdsourcing some aspects of internal communications also seems to work well and helps to keep people connected.

- Moving people processes to a remote setting will inevitably require some level of investment in automation and workflows, and the systems organizations have in place may not be fit for purpose any more.

- Some aspects of employee relations processes work better remotely, but others do not – and it may be easier to treat each case on its merits.

- Moving recruitment to a virtual footing may stifle creativity in the process if the staff managing it are not confident in operating virtual processes.

- A highly transactional people practice team in a face-to-face environment is likely to find that it becomes less so in a remote or hybrid environment and may speed up its transformation into something different… something better.

So if we want to become something different and better as people professionals, let us see what we need to consider in doing so.

The action plan

In what we have called 'the new normal' during this chapter we have explored some of the things we need to ensure we get right if we are to keep our organizations working remotely or in a hybrid way. Questions for you to consider if this is on your agenda:

- How can your organization, without the imperative provided by the pandemic, sustain working remotely or in a hybrid way? Think about the practical and the business issues here – and whether these apply to all, or just some, employees.
- What is your workforce saying? Have you asked them?
- What is the definition of hybrid working for your organization, and is there a universal definition or one that may differ according to job role and area?
- What are the potential inclusion issues that could arise from the implementation of longer-term remote and hybrid working?
- How will you ensure that people remain connected on a social level and are given appropriate encouragement and practical support to look after their own health and wellbeing?
- Do senior leaders (who may have other priorities and perspectives) believe remote and hybrid working is the best business model to pursue? If they don't, and you do, how will you gather the evidence needed to persuade them?
- What need would there be for smaller-scale trials and pilots of hybrid working before rolling it out to a wider population?
- Will the choice about remote and hybrid working be made by the organization on behalf of employees, or made by employees based on their individual preferences?

- What kind of guidance and support could you give to individuals working remotely on how to get the right physical set-up of their remote workspace?
- What contractual consultation and internal communication is needed to make a longer-term change to remote and hybrid working?
- What considerations do you need to make around upskilling not just people professionals but all employees around specific skills they will need to thrive in a remote or hybrid work environment?
- How will your approach to internal communications (and community management) need to change?
- Have teams that do or will work in a remote or hybrid way been supported to reset and redraw their team culture and ways of working? If not, how will you do this?
- How will you support leaders to understand the differences in demands and expectations of their role?
- What is your best advice to senior leaders in your organization to ensure that they fully consider whether the organization should embrace more remote and hybrid working?

In this chapter we have looked at what we now consider to be 'the new normal' and noted the ways that technology has shaped this for many. In the next chapter we examine technology in more depth to see what is happening with it and because of it.

Sketchnote summary

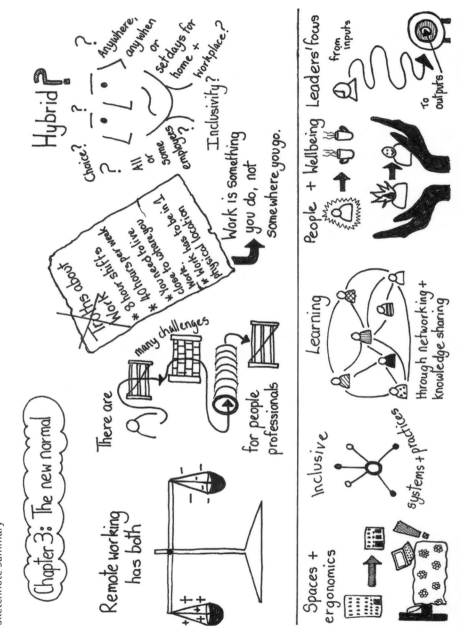

04

A word about technology

The shorter read

I wonder if the pace of change in people technology is matched by our ability to evolve our people practices and the skillsets of people professionals? As we begin to get used to working in a remote or hybrid world, we will be making more use of different technology to deliver our people practices. We are used to using technology in our personal lives to automate many things, but less used to doing so in our working lives, and therefore there are challenges ahead for many.

This isn't about automating everything and relying on technology to deliver most of your people practices – just because you can, doesn't mean you should. There is no one size fits all approach, and you must carefully pick your way through what's available to find what works for your organization.

Many organizations have made unfortunate, rushed choices when it comes to people technology, and have suffered some level of disengagement as a result. That isn't irreversible though, and there are many things that organizations can put, simply, into place to make digital transformation work – and rarely are these things about the technology. Buying and install-ing the right technology is less than half the battle – the majority is cultural, and what we as people professionals are good at doing.

The technology itself also needs to evolve, otherwise many of the down-sides we have encountered won't be resolved. Many people have struggled to disconnect from the 'always on' technology but the technology itself could help with this if we have made the right choices and if we have the skills to use it.

The future of the people profession is heavily influenced by the growth and evolution of technology. There will be some level of automation that will come for everyone, and that will mean we as people professionals need to further evolve. We will need to understand our organizations in different ways and see the way people technology changes the employee experience. We will need to be more comfortable with finding and using data to make decisions. We will need to be OK with a deluge of information at our fingertips and find ways to filter and use this better. This will be a challenge for some.

We also need to be aware of the downsides of too much use of and reliance on technology and find other ways of helping ourselves and our employees to manage the impact of this.

The longer read

We are now working in a heavily remote or hybrid world, but the reality is we've been living (and thriving) in such a world for some time now. We are used to using technology to automate many of our household tasks, but even in our personal lives many of us only use a fraction of the available technology – and the same is true at work too.

We could do a lot more with what we have, and what is coming. We will look at what has been happening to people technology and what may happen to give us a good context to explore some of the much more operational changes that we could make in later chapters. There are so many things that could be done remotely, but not all of them should – remember that.

In the case study at the end of this chapter we show some data collected by BrightHR on some of the more transactional changes they have seen in the use of their people technology. However, what is clear from my own research is that there is no one size fits all approach – every organization and every individual will have different needs for their people technology, but still need to harness it to help them work smarter, more effectively, to collaborate and learn together.

Nicky Hoyland is the Chief Executive of Huler. She believes that the nature of work in every organization has changed, but that many leaders still have constraints in how they think about it and how people think about working in the office.

She believes that organizational use of and design of office space needs to change due to the changes in how we use technology and the changes in the way people work – for example large conference rooms should ideally not be used to host one person making a video call, and many offices are still largely based around a one person one desk layout, making collaboration difficult. Even the equipment in offices may need to be adapted – note, not upgraded – for example we will need far more cameras placed in workspaces, and for these to be multi-directional and at eye-level. This is a challenge for many organizations though.

Hoyland's company has also seen growth during the pandemic, but she feels this was largely a forced acceleration. The implications of that are that many companies bought what they needed in a hurry, and without properly going through the normal due diligence process. This means that their technology comprises a lot of disparate systems, and technology that isn't necessarily fit for any long-term purpose. This, to me, is the equivalent of going food shopping in the supermarket when you're ravenously hungry – you end up with things you don't really need and maybe aren't even good for you!

Hoyland believes that many people have reached a point of cognitive overload – working remotely or in a hybrid way is mentally and emotionally challenging enough as it is, without adding lots of new technology into the mix. Many of her organization's clients have needed help finding out what all the systems do and how to use them – so their level of cognitive load is already high before they begin to use them properly. This means that there is a big need for organizations to stabilize their technology usage before they enhance it.

In the above example we clearly see that there are issues about whether organizations have the right technology (as well as the right spaces, something we touch on in Chapter 11). Research conducted by Microsoft and the CIPD in 2021 showed that the 49% of employees said their organization had upgraded people technology, but that one-third of employees feel that they don't have everything they need to work effectively remotely. Interestingly, there was a disconnect in the survey, with many leaders feeling that staff were well-equipped, whereas the staff themselves felt differently[1].

This gets me thinking about digital transformation and whether enough organizations have considered the forced acceleration and adoption of people technology during the pandemic in the same way as other simultaneous digital transformation journeys. I suspect not.

What makes digital transformation work?

In my experience I've worked in organizations where digital transformation has worked well, and in others it hasn't. I've been able to observe lots of common factors in this, which I've summarized in Table 4.1.

TABLE 4.1 Common factors in the success or failure of digital transformation

Where it has worked	Where it has not worked
It involved everyone who was affected by it.	Top down change managed by a small group of people.
It addressed the elephant in the room – the fear, the pain, the frustration and the emotional side of the change – people being actively encouraged to discuss their emotional views on the change(s).	People being told off for expressing negative views about the change(s).
A burning platform that could be used to fuel the desire for change, to help people understand what was happening and why it was needed.	Change that lacks any kind of imperative.
Explaining the benefits to all stakeholders – it isn't just about efficiencies or needs must.	New technology being sold as an efficiency that could lead to reducing staffing in the future.
Involving people in shaping the future, getting and using their ideas.	Leaders assuming they know what is best for their staff, and not asking for their views.
Promoting the technology as aiding collaboration not creating competition – using the data it would create for the greater good and to enhance communication.	Using the technology as a way of creating silo thinking, and competitive and often-divisive cultures.
Seen as an ongoing task, a way of life meaning constant evolution.	A temporary, one-off activity with an end point and a team that disbanded once the technology was installed.
Use of change agents to spread the cultural change virally in organisations – people who live and breathe the new technology and set good examples.	Reliance on senior leaders telling people this was for their own good.

(continued)

TABLE 4.1 (Continued)

Where it has worked	Where it has not worked
Encouraging experimentation and the making of mistakes, and rewarding/recognising those who do experiment, are patient, seek help or help others try new things.	Punishing mistakes, and ignoring those who show interest in using the technology.

What seems apparent here is that buying and implementing the technology is perhaps less than half the battle. The bigger battle is always cultural and about people. I've used Nudge Theory without realizing it in some organizations to get people adopting new technology – for example news about a merger being released only on a new internal social media app, which immediately got people using it without having to go through a lengthy launch process for the app.

Organizations who want to make the most of their new (or existing) people technology do need to put effort into finding the right technology and for the right price but need to be clear on their reasons for doing it and put just as much, if not more, effort into ensuring the culture supports and encourages the adoption and greater use (and more appropriate use of it).

Lucinda Carney is the Chief Executive of Actus, a provider of people technology. She has seen a huge growth, as have many such providers, in demand for the technology. She feels that the forced acceleration noted by others has broken many paradigms about the use of such technology and remote working. As examples she talks about how digital learning and development has taken off because the technology allows it to be broken down into manageable bite sized chunks that can fit into the working day but still be as interactive and engaging as face-to-face learning. However, what she does note is that many people technologies are not the most effective at delivering this.

Carney reports that the growing use of the technology has exposed many managers as lacking some of the basic skills of management, which is a theme commented on by others in this book. Again, this shows that implementing the technology is perhaps only half the battle, and that there is more that people professionals need to do other than just helping to select the right technology – there are elements of organization design, cultural change and more to consider too.

How does people technology need to evolve?

Nicky Hoyland, when I interviewed her, talked about organizations needing to give people responsibility for managing technology themselves and making decisions on how best to work with the technology. She explained that the technology will be able to record how this is done and could even prompt people to disconnect if a certain limit or type of activity is logged.

You will have seen horror stories in the media about some unscrupulous employers using technology to spy on their employees – here the technology is the same, but the challenge is to use it for good instead of evil! This may mean we need to draw up individual and collective agreements, with boundaries, about how to use technology around our working times, and setting expectations of how and when people can be contacted and how and when they may respond, while allowing for individual circumstances to be factored in.

The Huler platform that Hoyland's company provides offers a way to bring together all the personal and professional apps that an individual may use but giving direct shortcuts to the tasks individuals need which would avoid them having to navigate through various menus and folders to get there. It can also automate many of the routine tasks around things like onboarding and offboarding (discussed in our next chapter), and when certain working time limits are reached, it can recommend turning the work-based applications off while continuing to allow personal use of the apps on the platform.

This type of platform sounds very forward-thinking and perhaps gives an insight into where people technology may be heading, but from speaking to people in researching this book, very few feel they have got the right technology in place now (or perhaps the right culture to support it). Almost every piece of software or app in use has some limitations. A good example of this would be people using third party apps such as Miro, Mural and Jamboard for team thinking and collaboration simply because hardly any of the people technologies organizations have purchased have such capabilities.

It is clear to me that the people technologies we have need to continue to evolve and are not necessarily fit for purpose. Many organizations will not have the right technology for their needs and have been using something generic (for example a Microsoft package) that may suit many but not all in their organization and has significant limitations. Having the right people technology won't create engagement however, but not having it is likely to reduce engagement – people technology isn't a motivator, it's a hygiene factor.

That said, people technologies can be used to enable and deliver some motivators. For that we need to stop using the technology as a mere communication tool and begin using it as an engagement tool, offering genuine two-way communication across the organization, and making it easy for people to find information to make decisions that would aid their productivity and level of satisfaction in their roles.

Most organizations have technology that could help but haven't invested the time in making it easy to use, making it cohesive and ensuring it gives a great experience to those working in perhaps complete isolation. Many organizations have features that are useful, but not necessarily in the same pieces of technology – during the research for this book I came across people in recruitment roles who needed to manage applicant tracking and collaborate with their colleagues but needed two or three apps to do this. That doesn't seem to be the most effective use of time or technology.

On the converse, I've come across organizations taking a lower-tech approach to achieving some of these things and making good use of texting apps to encourage collaboration – though while this is cost-effective and simple, it again divides the focus of the user across different apps. We need to consider whether what we have in organizations is helpful, or in fact a barrier to what we want to achieve.

Where is this heading in the future?

One way of answering this question is to say that there is no one size fits all approach, and that would be correct – for some organizations introducing better people technology may mean nothing more than digitizing the employee files and timesheets, but for others this may mean full digital transformation of business models and practices, and redrawing team boundaries.

It is also important, from a people practice perspective, to remember the mantra 'just because you can, doesn't mean you should' – not everything we do needs digitizing. A helpful approach may be to adopt the 80:20 rule – 20% of your processes take up 80% of your time, so focus on digitizing those. The drive for digitization of people practices has been something long advocated by many, with a report from Phase 3 back in 2011[2] advising on the need to do this to streamline what we do and reduce administrative burdens, as well as some wider business benefits. I'd question whether this has fully worked given that over a decade later we are discussing similar things.

We can contrast the way we have slowly updated our people technology over the last decade with similar evolutions in our use of technology in our personal lives. Our smartphones, smart home hubs, online everything are light years ahead of where they were a decade ago, but we can't say the same for our use of people technology.

That, though, is not the fault of the technology.

In the CIPD's *People Profession 2030, A collective view of Future Trends*[3], the CIPD suggested that digital and technological transformation would be one of the main trends impacting the people profession and it is easy to see why, and how this has been kick-started by the experiences we have had in the pandemic.

There are clearly some demographic changes driving some of this, such as generations entering the workforce who have grown up using social media to communicate with their social circles and to collaborate with school and college peers (I've lots of stories about my teenage children's use of Snapchat that could illustrate this well), but this isn't the only driver. However, the CIPD's report details a range of other trends shaping the world of work, and poses the question – is your current people technology ready for these changes?[4].

I don't think it is.

A decade or so ago we could hide behind the significant upfront investment and hardware/infrastructure required to host different bits of people technology, but cloud storage and hosting has removed this barrier. The development of smartphones and the ubiquitous nature of these has also removed many individual barriers and concerns. But organizations may still need to audit what they have, what each piece of people technology provides and where it may lack functionality.

We don't need to look too far to find examples of how it is predicted that all routine physical and mental tasks will be automated and performed by machines, however the people profession has historically not been good at predicting and embracing the future, and we need to be, otherwise other functions will take those decisions for us.

The implications for people professionals

To really make people technology work for us, and not against us, we need to understand our organizations more fully, and have a clear idea about how various things flow around and through it:

- People – understanding what happens to people as they move into, through, up and out of the organization.

- Performance – understanding how we define performance, how we know when it is happening, how we reward it, support it and if or how we penalize its absence.

- Information – understanding what information people need, how they get it and what they do with it.

- Work – who does what, where, when and how.

Technology exists that will help us with that, but not all people professionals have access to it or perhaps know how to use it or what to do with the information if they get it. Perhaps we need to use this knowledge to help redesign the entire nature of work and the organization, but perhaps it is a less complex solution that is required. Either way, we have a fantastic opportunity to use people technology for the greater good.

Laura Ryan, Director of International HR at Dropbox, talking to HRD Connect in 2021[5], summarized how this worked at that organization. When answering the question 'if we had the opportunity to start again with a blank page, how would we redesign our work life?', she also considered how to give flexibility but with human connection and collaboration, amongst other dilemmas. In the article, Ryan explains how Dropbox has redesigned physical spaces, as well as embracing asynchronous working by allowing staff to design their own working schedules and adopting a 'virtual first' mentality. But Dropbox are a large multinational corporation with a good number of resources and people professionals – the ideas sound great, and exciting, but for many organizations some of these things are simply out of reach and not achievable (or in some cases, desirable). We need to take a more practical approach to this and help those in smaller organizations with less resources and fewer people professionals to achieve similar things. We need to embrace the opportunities afforded by new people technology and not be afraid of it, provide flexibility and empowerment, have clarity about ways of working and communicating – in essence, redefining work – but not always in radical ways that make working life unrecognizable from how things have been.

What we may see is evolution, not revolution. And even that may be scary. As Nicky Hoyland explained to me, it is perfectly OK for us, as people professionals, right now, not to know what is happening or where we are going. So, if that's you, you're in good company.

What skills do we need?

The ability to manage technology is now more than a nice-to-have for people professionals, it is a core competency. With that comes the ability to use data and interrogate it, but also to see patterns and trends in it and in ways that avoid data bias.

We need to start using people technology systems like many in organizations use customer relationship management (CRM) systems. Such systems have loads of data about customer interactions and needs, and we can now replicate that for employees. How do we know our employees are doing OK unless we have data to help us with that? How do we help our employees to disconnect unless we have data that shows us they aren't currently doing so effectively?

We need to consider the employee experience but potentially begin segmenting the focus of this. A minority of organizations now have roles with titles like 'Head of Remote'. I'm not recommending this specifically, but we need to have a focus on what working remotely or in a hybrid way is and having someone focus on it may be a good thing.

Deloitte commented in 2021 that we need to stop doing digital and start being digital[6] and this is good advice. It is not enough to think that putting in a market leading brand of people technology will be enough. The world of work we are in requires us to think differently and behave differently, upskilling people's digital skills, enhancing internal communications, and avoiding automation for the sake of it, remembering that we are dealing with human beings here with all the mental health issues that we have seen come to the fore in the pandemic.

In learning and development, we need to consider the very real skills gaps that many organizations face, and simply moving our content to virtual delivery may not solve those skills gaps. Michelle Parry-Slater's excellent book *The L&D Handbook* covers the behaviours needed in learning and development in great detail and makes similar points – it is not just about the technology here, it is about how we act and behave as people professionals.

Using data better

I once listened to Clive Woodward give a talk at a CIPD Conference, as far back as 2015, and he talked about how he revolutionized England Rugby by bringing in data and technology to analyse the way players performed, behaved and acted while playing. I remember thinking then that the sporting world was years ahead of the business world in the way it did this, but perhaps by now we have caught up somewhat.

What was interesting though was how Woodward really pushed for the front-line staff (rugby players) to develop their own IT skills and analytical skills to review their own and others' performance, as opposed to this being something the manager or coach did solo. In my own training and sport, I am all over the data I have about myself. I use it to improve what I do, to set myself targets and to motivate myself. I can't imagine training or performing without it. But how often do we see that in business?

Woodward started using technology to look at the game and performance in a different way, and sometimes began using it instead of looking at actual video footage. He broke down the whole game of rugby into just seven areas and began capturing the knowledge of every person involved in the team in each of the seven areas. This is knowledge management at its most basic, but also being enhanced via technology. These are things we have the skills to do, and the technology to do, now in our organizations, but have we the confidence?

All this is well and good, but could this lead to people professionals being overwhelmed with data? How do we cope with this? At another CIPD Conference, Dave Coplin from Microsoft suggested the following techniques:

- Skimming. Learning to quickly scan the deluge of information we get to get a broad understanding of it without going into detail.

- Snacking. Learning to be able to dip in when appropriate and not spend too much time-consuming digital information.

- Multitasking. Learning to do other things as well as obtaining information digitally.

Our problem is that we will be faced with potentially unmanageable sources of data in every aspect of our personal and working lives, but if we can manage that then we can make our lives so much better. It is possible to make our working lives much better through more targeted use of people technology – the data, if we can find it and listen to it, will be able to tell us how people are feeling and therefore make a huge difference to how they perform.

Several years ago, I analysed what my then organization was doing in terms of people data, and concluded that it wasn't doing much. Our data wasn't being actively sought by the organization to drive better decision-making and improve performance. It was static, retrospective and didn't go much beyond benchmarking in terms of analysis. Up until that point I'd prided myself on my team's ability to extract mounds of data that was then published to lots of people, until I realized those people didn't look at it thoroughly.

Part of the issue then, and now, is that many people professionals aren't in the profession because they're good with data. We are good with people, not numbers. In some later organizations I was able to use management information analyst roles not just to own the data and its production, but to draw conclusions and offer insights. This helped us to move towards modelling, root cause analysis, scenario planning and then predictive analytics, and link all of this to risk analysis and strategic planning for the business. The drawback to all of this was the perception that the organization had to be of a certain size to justify such a role, and that role was rarely filled by someone from a people professional background – although that could be, and sometimes was, a good thing!

I think, though, having a data analyst in your team is only half the solution. We need to understand what the problem is we are trying to solve with improved analytics. What are the most important things the organization needs to focus on, and which interventions would have the most impact on these things?

At a data analytics conference I attended back in 2015, questions were asked about what aspects of culture impede customer service, and what we can do to improve innovation.

People attending the conference mentioned things like including an analysis of complaints or compliments data against specific groups of the workforce, maybe at an individual level, to look at what your best performers do to influence customer satisfaction, or what the worst do.

Others suggested looking at recruitment data and where you found your best performers, and whether certain recruitment sources provide better performers than others. You'd also want to explore the link between recruitment and performance data, and absence/performance and behavioural data.

The overall conclusion from this was that people professionals need to find data correlations and use them to start a wider dialogue and build credibility. The technology will give us that. We shouldn't, though, rush in throwing statistics at the organization without having some context and understanding the organizational problems first. A quote attributed to Voltaire (though later popularized in the Spider-Man comics and films) 'with great power comes great responsibility' – and this means if we have the technology, we need to use it in the right way.

If your people team has a relative lack of analytical skills, you could do it well regardless by harnessing their innate curiosity. Your team could get involved in brainstorming correlations in data, generating hypotheses and go looking for data to support or disprove them.

Ultimately with predictive analytics we could get to Amazon-style customization of jobs and work for employees, with work and work environments tailored to produce high performance based on how we know performance and engagement has been generated in the past. We have seen how some of this could work in the forced remote environment of the pandemic – perhaps now is the time to bring this to life?

The downsides of too much technology

The concept of cognitive overload works on the principle that our brains have a finite processing limit, and one that is easily reached. When we are using technology, we are increasingly susceptible to this, with many of us now recognizing things like 'Zoom fatigue' as a real thing. This is because on video calls we are receiving information on lots of different levels and our brains can't always keep up with what the right thing is to be focusing on. This is made worse by the temptation to multi-task throughout and the numerous distractions while on video calls, and our brains can sometimes make bad choices as a result. When using technology, we reach cognitive overload far quicker than when we don't, so one role for people professionals is to help with that.

We need to help people manage their working time, and to disconnect when they need to – going as far as to help them work out when that is. The right to disconnect has been promoted a lot in recent years but seems almost incompatible with the concept of truly flexible working, something explored in Gemma Dale's book Flexible Working in more detail. The technology can help us do that, as our case study later in this chapter begins to explain. Around that we as people professionals need to be helping organizations to define working time as a concept – something like the Work/Life Manifesto that Zuora have developed, talked about by Marc Weedon in the CIPD podcast from May 2021[7]. This works on the principle that the commute, love it or hate it, gave us a defined start and end to the day that has largely disappeared for many remote workers, and helps individual employees define a start and end to their day. It covers avoiding back-to-back meetings, and many email programs will now allow you to set meetings of 25- or 55-minute durations to give you at least something of a break between them.

People professionals can help with some of the ergonomic and safety issues of using technology almost constantly through the day. Later in this book we discuss ergonomics, but here we need to consider things like physical strain and psychological strain that come from prolonged exposure to display screen equipment. We must give better advice about such things.

We could also help managers and individuals with job crafting, something explored in Rob Baker's excellent book Personalisation at Work (2020), encouraging them to redesign jobs so that the workload and type of work is interesting and varied enough to avoid constant technology use and give enough breaks between tasks to help avoid cognitive overload.

We can use the technology to create discussions around all these things, whether for managers, employees, or both, where they have a safe space to discuss these issues and share ideas about how to use technology more effectively and with a positive impact on mental health and more. Some of the tips are likely to be about using technology less (for example Zoom calls without the cameras on or using text messages instead of Teams channels) and this should be actively encouraged. As people professionals, we should be active in such discussions to influence the messages being sent about what is expected and what is important.

Ultimately though all of this is a fine line and is shaped by organizational culture and resources, and more besides. What we have explored in this chapter are some of the issues surrounding our use of people technology, and some of the predicted ways in which the technology could help us – giving us a good platform (sic) to explore in later chapters of the book as we move on from the 'why?' and 'what?' to the 'how?'.

CASE STUDY

In this case study we look at how a people technology provider considers the way the industry is heading and the trends that they have been seeing in terms of use of their products by people professionals and their organizations.

Alan Price is the Chief Executive of BrightHR, and Alastair Brown is their Chief Technology Officer. Bright launched in 2015 to provide people technology solutions for small to medium sized enterprises. Their headquarters is in Manchester, and they have a small but growing workforce.

Unsurprisingly, Bright have seen a big change in the way organizations use their products in the last few years, and accelerated due to the pandemic, as the data they share in Figure 4.1 shows.

We can see in Figure 4.1 the slow but steady growth up to Q1 2020, and the impact of the immediate onset of the pandemic and the first UK lockdown where some people practices were temporarily paused, but then how quickly organizations adapted to the changed environment and began embracing semi- or fully automated people processes at a rate of growth not previously seen.

Price commented that many of their customers see people practices as transactional – they are small to medium sized enterprises, sometimes without a dedicated people professional or with a small number of such people. In such circumstances the main driver for purchasing Bright is to automate as much of the transactional people processes as possible. Typical examples include:

- Digitizing employee files.
- Digitizing the holiday planner (which most people still like to see visually) and process for requesting and authorizing leave.
- Digitizing the work rota and the process for arranging working patterns.
- Making the legal compliance side of people practices easier.

In essence, Bright's clients are aware of problems they may have, but need to access a ready-made solution. Usually within their client base there is little understanding of people analytics and the insight that can come from this, and a general reluctance to spend time working on such things – so Bright aim to make such things simple for their clients.

FIGURE 4.1 Volume of people practice activity in BrightHR software

Growth of usage of BrightHR functions

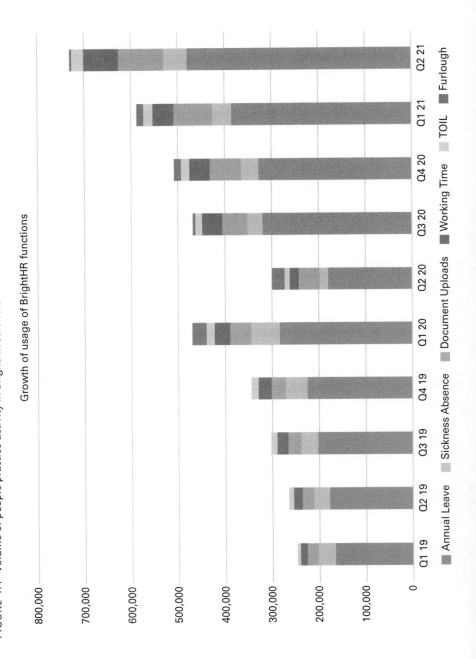

Bright clearly saw a huge growth in the demand for self-service functionality and automating many of the basic people practices in organizations using workflows. In addition to those shown on the chart earlier in this case study, there was an upturn in the usage of their technology to manage working time and handle check-ins (using their Blip technology which just requires a smartphone and a QR code). There was also a growth of interest in e-learning (on basic health and safety and the foundations of good people practices) particularly for micro-enterprises who would traditionally have relied purely on face-to-face learning.

Bright began developing more workflows for returning people to offices and handling furlough requests, but also found themselves increasingly developing policies on remote and hybrid working for their clients, advising on internal communications, and creating guidance on using different devices for work.

Bright noticed that the impact of the first UK lockdown in March 2020 was much more significant than any subsequent lockdown, as if many organizations did what they needed to in the first lockdown and didn't feel as affected by the next one.

WHERE DOES BRIGHT SEE PEOPLE TECHNOLOGY HEADING?

Both Price and Brown see some obvious trends that are happening in the people profession which people technology needs to be mindful of, and vice versa:

- Lots of people technology has traditionally required technical support, but there is a reducing need for this in the future as the use of it becomes more intuitive and people's skill levels increase.

- There is a real need to simplify internal communications channels, with lots of different media and places for this to happen currently, often working against some of the organizational intentions.

- Many of their clients would benefit from some use of artificial intelligence (AI) chatbots to handle basic people practice queries. This is driven by people policies often being too lengthy and written in sometimes inaccessible language for many employees to understand when working in isolation.

- People processes will become more efficient because the technology that can and will now deliver them will increase people's expectations of speed and simplicity.

- While presenteeism has taken on new forms in a remote or hybrid world, other problems related to the use of technology such as elongated or extended working hours have become apparent, and most people technology doesn't do anything about that. It needs to prompt disconnecting. Apps such as Blip can check when people are working, but Bright's experience is that the data held in such systems is not being used to show whether people are approaching burnout levels. What they are seeing is that the initial data is used – device logged in or not, and when – but no interrogation is done of that beyond noting that it is there and looking at compliance and legal issues.

- Many people technologies don't cope well with the increase in the need for wellbeing support, particularly around highlighting the data that they already hold which could offer useful insight. Bright are building features that start to alert managers if the working time data around their people shows an issue around wellbeing – they consider AI and machine learning perfect for automating this and are aiming for it to draw on lots of other data around engagement.

- As online learning and development has grown significantly, many people technology systems have been found wanting – while many have learning and development modules, they are not as intuitive as standalone learning management systems (LMS) are, and this has priced many small to medium sized enterprises out of managing such things effectively. People technology is going to have to adapt to make this more accessible.

- As onboarding and inductions have moved mostly or entirely online (something discussed in the next chapter in more detail) many systems have not kept pace with this but will soon do so.

- There are now more problems with workplace scheduling and rostering as people's working patterns evolve and take on inconsistent shapes, and the technology will become more complex in responding to this.

Case study reflections

This was an interesting case study which drew on lots of knowledge about how technology is being used by people professionals and looked at how these trends may continue in the future. It poses several issues for people professionals which are summarized here:

- Our people policies need to be a lot simpler, likely shorter and much easier to access as the technology will demand and force such things.

- We need to simplify our approach to internal communications because the technology has created multiple, potentially confusing channels.

- Many people professionals still need to use evidence and data more and make links between business data and the people data that we already have and have increasingly easy access to. Many people professionals lack skills around predictive analytics, and much more could be done with the technology if these skills were there.

- The technology gives us access to data about how and when people work, which we may not have had face-to-face, but we need to use it more.

- Many of the things we feel we lack when working remotely, such as walking around the office and sensing the mood, can be achieved digitally – the technology is there according to Bright, but people professionals often lag behind on spotting patterns in the data that they already have, and mostly fail to share this data.

- As a profession, we have been often led by technology rather than the other way around, and we need to be driving its use and evolution. For most of Bright's clients, now, this isn't happening – however, most of their clients simply haven't had the technology for long enough to be confident of using it correctly and suggesting improvements to it.

The action plan

If you are considering how to make more or better use of technology in delivering your people practices, here are some questions to consider:

- Review what people technology you already have – how fit for purpose is it?

- What are your top five to ten most important people processes (i.e. the ones that take up the most time, or have the most visibility)? Focus on using technology to improve these, as opposed to trying to automate everything.

- How much does your office space need adapting to cope with increased use of technology?

- Where could you strengthen your approach to cultural change to help the adoption of new technology?

- How will you use people technology to help employees manage their working time and avoid burnout?

- Where do you need to learn more about the organizational 'flow' to see where technology can have the biggest impact?

- What data do you have about your employees that would be useful to help manage those working remotely or in a hybrid way? And what data would you like to have?

- What is the skill level of your people professionals in handling and using data? Where could it improve?

- How will you manage the risk of cognitive overload for employees?

- What is your best advice for senior leaders in your organization on the use of technology to aid, and not hinder, the remote and hybrid working experience?

Sketchnote summary

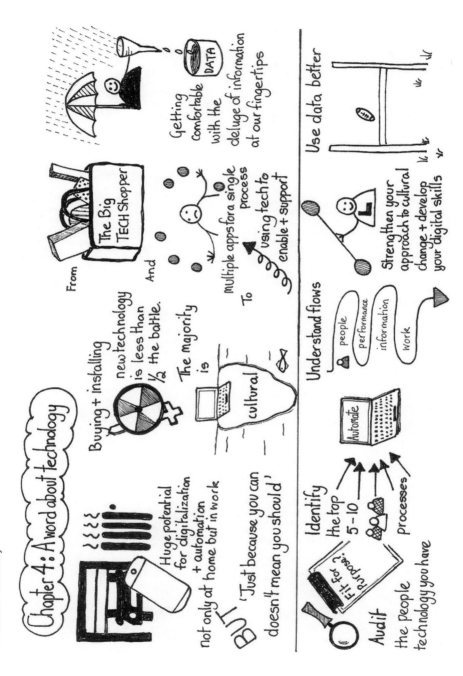

Chapter 4: A word about technology

Huge potential for digitalization + automation not only at home but in work

BUT 'Just because you can doesn't mean you should'

Buying + installing new technology is less than ½ the battle.

The majority is cultural

From The Big TECH Shopper

And multiple apps for a single process

To using tech to enable + support

Getting comfortable with the deluge of information at our fingertips

DATA

Audit the people technology you have

Fit for purpose?

Identify the top 5-10 processes

Automate

Understand flows
people
performance
information
work

Strengthen your approach to cultural change + develop your digital skills

Use data better

PART TWO

The world we are in

05

Hellos and goodbyes

The shorter read

There are lots of top-quality books on how to handle recruitment more effectively, and I'd recommend those by Katrina Collier (*The Robot Proof Recruiter*), and Matt Alder and Mervyn Dinnen (*Exceptional Talent* and *Digital Talent*). As a result, we don't need to look at how to do recruitment better per se. We do, though, need to look at the challenges of recruitment (and onboarding, inductions and offboarding) in a remote and hybrid world and looking at examples and good practice tips on how to overcome them.

A theme running through the chapter is getting the initial touchpoints for the employee experience right and doing so in a human way. If we are entering, or ending, a long-term relationship with an employee, then we must do that in a way that is helpful, but also now in a way that works just as well remotely as it ever could face-to-face.

A general theme for this book is the need to be more human in a digital world, and this is especially true in recruitment processes. Automation and artificial intelligence can really help such processes but can also take away the much-needed human touch.

For example, video interviewing can be problematic for many, with difficulties in assessing body language, digital anxiety, technological barriers, and logistical issues all causing concern. There are many practical solutions to these. We should future-proof recruitment processes so that they are looking at potential needs and using technology in the right way. We must also cope with either increased, or reduced, volume of applications because of a remote process, and examine some preparation you could consider making the overall process smoother for everyone.

Our case study in this chapter focuses on how one organization that handles large volumes of recruitment managed to transform their processes almost overnight, what barriers they faced, and what they learned as they overcame them.

From an onboarding perspective, processes that can be done remotely really do help but the sequence in which you may need to do the various aspects of this phase may need to change. There are practical elements to ensure are right, such as the delivery of equipment and the set-up of the remote and virtual workspace. Even more critical are the socialization opportunities that need to be carefully created to build personal relationships and reassure the new starter that they have made the right decision to join your organization. There are some useful tips to begin the relationship building process and what to do if impending new starters are finding it difficult to separate themselves both physically and emotionally from their last employer.

With inductions, we need to consider these as no longer being one off events, but longer processes, taking months in some cases, and being driven by the employee in a self-directed learning way. There are several things you could consider enabling remote induction processes to be a better experience for all concerned.

Finally, with offboarding, we need to consider how to keep a positive relationship going with remote employees who are leaving, noting the potential issues with emotional separation from employers. We also have a changing role in managing communities of ex-employees (or alumni), and must consider how to keep engagement high among remote employees who are leaving or who have left. We could heed several suggestions on how to manage the security and knowledge management risks of remote offboarding.

The longer read

Recruitment

The starting point of the employee lifecycle is the recruitment and selection process (shortened hereafter to recruitment). It is the first active touchpoint in the employee experience, where the employer and employee first make purposeful contact with a view to entering a long-term relationship. It is something that is important to get right.

I helped my son apply for an apprenticeship position with a nearby large employer in mid-2021. I say helping, I mean doing the application for him. It was the first time I'd used any kind of online application for well over five years and this one was shockingly bad.

I thought I'd finished the application but when I didn't get an email confirmation, I logged in a day later to find that the system had now 'opened up' more sections to complete, without telling me or him, and that the deadline had been shifted, again without telling me or him, so that there was only an hour left to complete the application.

The application form wasn't mobile enabled so bits couldn't be seen on the mobile screen that needed completing, and the error messages that appeared when the form was attempted to be submitted just said 'incomplete fields' without saying which they were. They were, of course, the fields that couldn't be seen on a mobile screen, but it didn't point us to them.

The role was an entry-level position, but the application process had lots of questions you'd expect to be asked of a senior leader which as a result had to be left blank. The form also needed multiple documents uploading but only had space for two uploads.

Technical support and the recruitment team both had email contacts, so I emailed them and the auto response said expect a response in around 48 hours, despite there only being one hour left to deadline. The technical team did respond around 24 hours later, to say that the recruitment team would be in touch. They never did get in touch.

And then after submission they asked for feedback on their application process and whether I/he were more, or less, likely to want to work there based on this process. I'm afraid I told the truth at this point.

We must be better than this. When was the last time you road-tested your candidate experience? Was it like my son's experience of applying for a first job, or something more human and intuitive?

The candidate experience really matters. Glassdoor report that 72% of those who have a bad candidate experience will share their experience online, and LinkedIn report that 87% of those with a good candidate experience will change their mind about a company they had previously viewed negatively[1].

The Covid-19 pandemic forced most organizations to change the way they manage recruitment, but this shake-up of purpose and process has consequences for retention also. As we see in this book, employees are beginning to want different things from their employers, and if organizations can't or won't give those to them, then they are increasingly susceptible to advances from other organizations who can and will. Remote working has increased the 'mobility' of employees, who can now consider employers a lot further away than previously, and therefore the concept of competition in the labour market takes on a whole different nuance.

Remote and hybrid working changes the purpose and process of recruitment, and we need to consider this in more depth. Organizations need to focus much more than before on their employer brand, and to sort out the candidate experience (so that it isn't like that of my son).

To make this work, we need to have a human first approach, as Katrina Collier and Liz Dowling explained to me in the research for this chapter. We need to build trust with candidates and ensure that the process is easy for managers to run (as it is not usually a regular or large part of their role), and that the business is organized enough to manage a recruitment process at the given time and won't put blockers in place.

Many organizations and people professionals will have used approaches such as video interviewing and assessments perhaps for the first time during the Covid-19 pandemic, and many employees will also have joined organizations remotely, without having met those they work with in person. For many, this will have worked well. For others though, it will have been a difficult and fraught experience. We will now examine many of the challenges and solutions to making remote recruitment work.

Eleanor Gooding is People and Culture Director at Boost Drinks. We first looked at Gooding and Boost in our second chapter, but here she tells us about their experiences of doing remote recruitment for the first time.

'What we tried to do was approach things as normally as possible – still giving any new starters as normal a Boost experience as possible. The Covid-19 pandemic and the need to hire without the ability to meet face-to-face was completely alien to us so it forced us to do things differently.

We had the ability to use video interviewing already built into our HR software and so we learned how to use that, and we will never go back now. That gave us the ability to have a 'first round' of interviews with way more people than we could if we were doing them face-to-face. We shortlisted candidates who applied and then we asked them to prepare and answer four video questions – always decided by the hiring manager (with guidance and support from the HR team). We do not focus on skills and experience in these video questions – they are always a focus on the cultural fit, the ambitions of the person and so on. We want people to show us who they are, what makes them tick etc. From this we then went on to do a second interview with –two to four candidates.

This already felt different, like a big step forward for us. We have not embraced technology as much as we could over the years, but we wanted to – so this fitted right into that agenda. It also gave us the ability to really get the hiring managers and sometimes even other people involved in the interviews.'

Video interviewing issues

THE CHALLENGES

The technology itself may be a barrier for some people who may not have the technological capability or capacity to handle what organizations expect them to. Knowledge of how to use the technology appropriately and to its maximum potential can be limited in some hiring managers and even recruiters.

Video interviews require much greater focus on processing facial expressions, body language and tone of voice. A German study from 2014 found a delay of just two seconds on a video call can create a negative view of the person speaking[2]. Technical difficulties can happen at any time, and there is often a great degree of nervousness on the part of the candidate that outstrips any nervousness they may experience in a face-to-face interview.

The nervousness may come from a unique context for the candidate, for example caring or home-schooling responsibilities, or an environment that is subject to interruptions from children, deliveries and more.

The speed that some people speak at is not conducive to effective video interviewing, and their choice of words and diction is not always appropriate to engender full understanding in the interview. Those with strong accents, or with speech impediments, may find video interviewing a particular barrier, and the latter may prefer telephone interviews which may work better with any hearing aid technology.

The flexibility that remote and hybrid working gives employees means that it is quite likely that their working pattern may not match those of the recruiter, causing scheduling difficulties for the video interviews.

In 2018, according to LinkedIn survey, 63% of employers said, back in 2018, that one of their biggest interviewing issues was the inability to identify soft skills. This becomes harder in remote recruitment processes due to the fewer opportunities to connect with candidates.

The questions themselves that are asked in a remote interview need to be appropriate. For example, questions like 'tell us what you know about our company?' can easily be Googled in the moment.

Remote recruitment can often take longer than face-to-face recruitment, so digital fatigue is an issue for both candidates and recruiters and staying online can be exhausting.

THE SOLUTIONS

Question whether every interview **needs** to be a video interview – could it be a phone call or – whisper it – a face-to-face meeting? Connecting with the applicant across different media may be very helpful for you both and may also help with any necessary reasonable adjustments.

Consider the video interview being asynchronous (particularly if scheduling difficulties present themselves). This means the candidate pre-recording their interview based on some pre-shared questions and you as the recruiter reviewing these separately. Give the candidates sufficient time to give their answer – longer rather than shorter timeframes will elicit better quality responses.

Plan out what the recruiter will need – apps or windows open in readiness for screen sharing, files ready to send to or share with the applicant, documentation you need to complete available and ready etc. In the same vein, tell the applicant (in advance) anything they need to have ready. Providing training to hiring managers on tone of voice, language and diction, and pace, may become very important in building rapport and understanding during a video interview. Likewise, providing all parties with clear guidance about how to use the technology professionally, including how to appear on camera, audio quality, device and app choices, and what to do if things go wrong would also help.

Prepare candidates on what to expect – what software will be used, anything they need to download or test access to.

With fewer opportunities to experience the non-verbal cues that you'd get in a face-to-face situation, you must consider your questions carefully. Using strengths-based interview questions may help you get a better insight into individual skills and ways of working.

Giving the candidate more time to settle into the interview and acknowledging their unique context out loud and discussing specific things that are concerning them may be very helpful. Encouraging the candidate to blur their background (and you do the same) may help deal with some of the nerves.

Planning technology use will only minimize potential issues so far. Thinking of alternatives for candidates placed at a disadvantage by technological limitations, such as doing a phone call, will enable a smoother and more effective experience for all. Giving both the recruiter and candidate some backup options if technology fails will be helpful for both. It is also worth explaining to those recruiting that a candidate's inability to have the right technology in place for the (one off event) selection interview doesn't mean that they are not right for the organization, and organizations need to educate themselves about this. In the same vein, there are many people who are not comfortable speaking on video calls, and for whom this creates anxiety – managers should be educated that this is not a weakness.

Create and use questions that use the technology appropriately. For example, ask candidates for jobs that will use organizational systems to choose a piece of software or a website they are familiar with and demo it via the remote platform, testing their ability to use systems and give clear instructions.

Schedule appropriate breaks in between candidates and perhaps within each candidate interview if there are distinct parts to it. Create breakout rooms where candidates can relax and (potentially) network with other candidates and existing employees, without the pressure of being assessed.

Use the full functionality of the chosen technology – for example Chat as an informal method for people to seek help in large group exercises, breakout rooms for group discussions, screen sharing for delivering presentations.

Workforce planning

THE CHALLENGES

Mervyn Dinnen, speaking on the HR Chat podcast in 2021[3], outlined that one of the main challenges he sees is that jobs are evolving so quickly because of remote and hybrid working that we need to be recruiting not for what the job is now, but for what the job will be in a year or two's time. Dinnen explained that this means making hiring choices about people who can do the job that it will be rather than the job it is now.

The Covid-19 pandemic forced many organizations to consider how to perform jobs when the people themselves may not be around, through using technology and undertaking business process re-engineering.

THE SOLUTIONS

People professionals need to talk more to business leaders about the way those leaders see the organization, and its key jobs, evolving. They need to be close to IT professionals to find out where technology may disrupt jobs in the future in the organization, and close to external stakeholders to consider what requirements may need to be met in the future. Then when jobs are advertised, they can be 'future proofed' and as a result it is more likely that someone 'future proofed' will be appointed as opposed to hiring someone who can do the job as it is today.

Explaining the corporate culture

THE CHALLENGES

An entirely remote interview doesn't really help the candidate get a feel for the corporate culture in the same way as walking around the office might.

THE SOLUTIONS

It is worth thinking about how the corporate culture is expressed remotely. For example, the communication tools used, the way people share information both on social and work-related levels, and what the experience of working remotely is like – considering the various touchpoints that the new employee is likely to experience and explaining these to the candidate.

Some of this can be achieved prior to the interview. Social media platforms can really help your employer brand solidify and stand out. Some clients of mine have used social media to share images of teams working remotely and communicating and collaborating with each other in remote or hybrid teams.

The candidate needs to be able to assess the culture to determine whether they feel they will fit into it. We should consider what any new starter would want to know about a new organization and the likelihood of 'fit' within it, and front load as much of this as possible.

A recorded video walk through of the physical office would also be a helpful thing to try.

A friend of mine was successful in obtaining a new role and was negotiating her salary and start date, only to be asked by the hiring manager what dog she had. My friend didn't have a dog and asked why this was being asked. It turned out that the organization was dog-friendly and encouraged its employees to bring their dogs to work. My friend was allergic to dogs and ended up withdrawing from the process. While this is a face-to-face and not remote example, it illustrates the importance of clarifying the culture up front.

Increased volume of applications

THE CHALLENGES

The ability to recruit from anywhere for a remote role and the turbulent labour market means that many roles are seeing a considerable increase in the volume of applications, and this can make remote recruitment a time-consuming process.

THE SOLUTIONS

You can be much more specific in the job advert and other literature explaining what the job is all about, so that realistic expectations are set and unsuitable candidates filtered out. With remote working being one of the key attractions for many candidates, explain clearly what this means and whether it is set in stone or not.

Use technology to automate key parts of the process such as interview scheduling and large parts of the background checking done on candidates.

Video interviewing can offer significant time-savings, as our Boost example showed, allowing organizations the chance to assess lots more candidates in a shorter space of time, and therefore increased volume is not necessarily the bad thing it may seem. However, if it is a problem, then consider advert placement – going for a niche job board may be a good move as opposed to a mass-market job board.

Decreased volume of applications

THE CHALLENGES

There are plenty of other roles where there is a distinct lack of talent applying for roles, particularly in the geographical area near to the employer.

THE SOLUTIONS

Consider having several different recruitment processes. Some entry-level positions may be more easily filled on social media compared to mid- and senior-level positions that may require a more nuanced approach. And remember that geography is not the barrier it once was, so if there is no-one near to the office, advertise purely for remote workers and stress the flexibility of remote working.

We may need hiring managers to start to think like product managers. The job, in this instance, is the product, and they have to sell it – Liz Dowling and Katrina Collier explain this as needing to create a roadmap for the hiring manager and show them how to think differently about attracting people to want to work for and with them.

Onboarding

In this section we will use the term onboarding to define the period between acceptance of offer and first day of employment. Some people call this period pre-boarding or merge it together with the induction period and refer to both as onboarding, but for clarity in this book onboarding is something in between acceptance of offer and start of employment. For some people this may only be days, but for others it could be many months.

In their book, *Onboarding*, published in 2019, authors Christian Harpelund, Morten Højberg and Kasper Ulf Nielsen share that one quarter of new employees leave within the first year, almost one quarter leave in the first 45 days, and one in twenty don't come back after their first day. While some of the blame for that will be in the induction process (which we look at later in this chapter), an effective onboarding process can minimize the risk of these early exits and is a critical period for any new starter.

Much of effective onboarding was already done remotely prior to the Covid-19 pandemic, but this was largely the compliance-led people practices designed to perform background checks on new employees. These background checks continue unaltered in our new remote world – but while they serve a good purpose and must be done, they're not exciting processes and don't tend to create engagement in employees, which is what you need to be using the onboarding phase to be doing.

The onboarding phase is critical for beginning the process of engagement and should involve line managers as well as people professionals – at all costs avoid leaving the employee alone (aside from the background checks) until day one, as huge opportunities could be missed. And just because we are working more remotely or in a hybrid way, doesn't mean these things are less important – in fact they are even more so. But we must change how we do things.

Gail Hatfield is the People and Resources Director at Energy Systems Catapult (ESC), which has 175 staff in the Birmingham area. We first looked at ESC in the case study in our second chapter.

Before 2020, ESC had done welcome lunches and social events for their new employees, and these had to stop, and everything went remote. They didn't have any formal policies on remote onboarding (or remote induction) and left managers to work things out for themselves, with largely positive results. Managers seemed to sense that social relationships were of utmost importance and, without prompting, went out of their way to ensure new employees felt part of the team before they started.

One lesson learned was that the provision of equipment to new employees was a bit messy, and left until the very last minute to arrange, which caused a few problems. Now Gail's team ensure that this is more proactive and have repositioned this to take place at an earlier stage in the process, such as when the offer letter goes out.

ESC's experience is not unusual in the lack of formal process for remote onboarding. It is often left to chance but should not be. Boost Drinks (see earlier example in the recruitment section) create an onboarding plan for each new employee, but admittedly have a low volume of these. However, this provides some level of structure to the process, ensuring that each person has the right set of virtual meetings created, the right equipment delivered to them, and that a home office risk assessment is undertaken. Boost have been able to ensure that some elements of the onboarding are done face-to-face – invites to the office, even if not fully occupied, to collect some branded merchandise and equipment double as opportunities to look around and say hello to people before they start, even if most of the onboarding phase is remote. However, entirely remote onboarding processes can work well.

At VIOOH, Liz Dowling is the Head of People and talked to me about their approach to remote onboarding. In essence, everything that could be automated, was automated – workflows were created in Slack and other apps such as ZenDesk to create smooth and efficient processes for the entire onboarding phase.

Dowling considered all of the touchpoints in the pre and onboarding phase, which is good practice, and used external IT and home office providers to get equipment, swag and furniture to new starters as early as possible. All documents were available on CharlieHR – cloud based HRIS to avoid the need for any physical documentation. She also focused on building social relationships as much as possible, which is something ESC's line managers also did, realizing the importance this had on creating a sense of belonging whether that be via cohorts on Slack or virtual meetups. VIOOH were also clear with new starters about their hybrid working model and what support and equipment is available to help with this.

COVID-19 provided an opportunity for VIOOH to review their onboarding process by embracing automation and creating access to the right knowledge, information (factsheets, explainer videos, new starter hub), time with key people and invites to regular virtual socials and more. This created the expectation, carried over into the induction phase, that VIOOH's focus is on developing an inclusive, values-based culture and building connections from day one with fellow VIOOHers on a personal level is at the core of how the business operates. Their company value #teamviooh states, we are stronger together as a single and unified team. We collaborate, respect each other and value diversity.

SO HOW DO WE GET THE MOST FROM REMOTE ONBOARDING PHASES?
Here are some top tips:

- Build the anticipation. There may be no such thing as over-communicating in the onboarding phase, and the new employee needs to know that their impending arrival is prepared for and being looked-forward to by all concerned.

- Connecting people. Setting new employees up on the communications platforms that their team-mates use **before** they join is important so that everyone can introduce themselves and start to build relationships. Helping the new employee identify things in common with existing employees is important (for example this may be following sports teams, liking certain activities or hobbies, or sharing a passion for travel, and lots more).

- Buddying up. Decide who will be responsible for sharing information and helping the new employee in their induction phase and ensure they have made contact before the new employee starts.

- Creating a welcome pack. Lots of this could be generic – links to online resources, policies and procedures, and more. However, it could be specific to each job – explaining what equipment and software they may need and explaining how these will be obtained.

- Clarifying the set-up process. Explain what equipment will be sent and when to expect it – and what to do with it. Explain what logins are being created and when they will be activated and any action needed on the part of the employee (such as downloading software, password creation and more).

- Induction clarity. Provide details on what the induction phase will look like – include links to key meetings, a clear agenda and timetable.

- Remote working expectations. Explain what the culture is, and expectations are around using things like headsets, ethernet vs Wi-Fi connections, blurred virtual backgrounds, cameras in meetings, other people in their location (such as children). Their experiences of working remotely elsewhere may be quite different!

- Frequently asked questions. Think about when you first started your job and the things you wish you'd found out beforehand. Then put that stuff into a document to help the new starter.

Finally, consider that if the new employee has been working remotely in their last job, that the process of separating – emotionally and physically – from their last employer and joining you may have some problematic elements. For example, they may have left their last role on a Friday and start with you on the Monday – but from their perspective they are sat in the same chair in the same room of the same house, perhaps using the same personal equipment (which may bring data protection issues into the spotlight) and having the same view out of their window. For many people, it will seem like the same job! I would strongly recommend calling out this elephant in the room and addressing it early on – it is not necessarily a bad thing and can be helpful to bring in experiences from other places, and to retain links to past employers too – but the new employee needs to know that their new employer **knows** about these links and difficulty separating and is willing to work with them to create new and more productive relationships. We will look in a bit more detail at this in the offboarding part of this chapter too.

Inductions

Across my experience, most induction processes focus on the formal aspects of a new role. I think the informal aspects are perhaps more important, and crucial in developing the high engagement levels linked to high performance. Such things shouldn't be left to chance.

Remember the last time you joined a new organization. Friendship and building relationships are likely to be the main thing that made you feel settled in the organization. This can be made more difficult by working remotely – but it doesn't have to be. There are plenty of good practice guides on how to handle the more informal aspects of the induction process but in this section, we will focus on how this needs to operate differently in a remote or hybrid working environment.

In essence, I'll encourage you to think of induction as no longer being an event, but a process. It isn't something that has a defined end point and something that takes people away from their work – it is their work and is ongoing.

Gail Hatfield at ESC also feels that the informal aspects are important. She explained that some of these things happen easier in a remote environment – for example the inhibitions one feels walking up to a new starter to introduce oneself (or vice versa) don't seem to be as prevalent in a remote world – as the initial introductions are digital.

ESC's induction process used to be a face-to-face event mostly about information provision, and Hatfield found that this was rarely memorable. The remote version is a longer process, self-directed learning delivered in the flow of work, that lasts up to three months. This change has forced ESC to really think about what is essential on day one, and they concluded very little was.

Interestingly, ESC's new remote induction process has been attracting interest from existing staff and they have opened some of the learning opportunities to those staff.

Elongating the process is a good move. There are obviously some key meetings and people to meet, but to avoid overwhelming the new remote worker these should be limited in their first week. Their line manager and team-mates should be the bulk of these, and should be as informal as possible, focusing on relationship building rather than learning about the job. This distinction is important – imposter syndrome often strikes in a new employee's first few weeks, and they need to feel reassured that the organization is confident they can do the job, so focusing less on learning the job will help with that. Including the new starter in virtual social activities can help with relationship building and improve communication, as well as reducing the sense of isolation new remote employees can feel. Here, the technology can help as almost all communications technology have instant messaging functions, drawing on the intuitive 'likes' and reaction functions on social media to show how individual contributions are landing.

Many organizations already have buddy systems, and these can work well virtually – but the choice of buddy is even more critical. Choose someone who embodies the organizational culture and who can share the way things work and help the new employee to fit in. The buddy should be comfortable using all kinds of communications technology, and open to learning from the new starter too. This may well mean that the buddy isn't someone from the new starter's immediate team since the geographical proximity between buddy and new starter is no longer an issue.

In the meetings between line manager and new remote employee, focus as much on emotion and how the new starter is feeling as how they are shaping up to perform. The technology should help the delivery of praise and recognition, letting the new starter know that their contributions are being noticed and valued and giving them something tangible as they tick things off their new to-do list. The manager needs to focus on reassuring the new starter that they aren't working in isolation, and that they are there to help them understand what is expected of them.

Further down the line, there will be more meetings needed – but these could be listed for the new starter to arrange when they are ready. Because these will be more spaced out and initiated by the new starter, they are likely to be more valuable and effective when they do happen as the new starter is likely to schedule the introductory meeting for a time when they would most benefit, as opposed to it being forced on them in their first few days and instantly forgotten.

If the new starter is working predominantly at their own home, it is worth showing understanding of the unique challenges this can create and explaining that things like childcare and other interruptions are to be expected and embraced, not hidden away, and that the new starter has freedom to decide how best to learn what they need to learn, at their own pace.

Many of my clients have begun using both gamification, and virtual or augmented reality, to enhance the virtual induction process. Gamification can add some fun to the process to boost engagement and foster social connection if a new starter can collaborate with other new starters in completing the tasks. Stephen Baer, writing for Forbes[4], suggested some of the following gamified activities as part of a remote induction process:

- An organization chart scavenger hunt.
- Reviewing tasks in a project management system.
- Tests on people practice guidelines and policies.
- Icebreakers to learn more about new colleagues.

Virtual or augmented reality experiences can provide a very different experience, though clearly come with some resource implications. However, if it can replicate the physical office in a virtual way, it can help new employees to come close to a genuine workplace and cultural experience.

The hints and tips above should help you create a more immersive and effective remote induction process.

Michelle Reid at the Institute of Occupational Medicine had a very paper-based induction process when the Covid-19 pandemic hit, with no online elements. While overhauling this was necessary, in the initial days of the pandemic in 2020 she focused on keeping things simple.

She noticed that the biggest change was having to make the regular checking-in more deliberate and conscious, and this created more of a procedural feel to their new remote induction process.

Some of the problems the organization's new starters encountered helped her think differently about the remote induction process. Ensuring new starters had the right equipment and technical knowledge became important, and that they have the right physical and ergonomic set-up all became important. While in a face-to-face induction process these would have happened during the first week, in the remote induction process these had to be moved to the onboarding phase. Additional e-learning packages were created to help impending new starters to learn what they need to know before day one arrives.

As we have explored in this section, remote inductions can work well – but there is often a more conscious and deliberate approach needed. One anonymous contributor to this section reinforced this – they were helped by having existing relationships with their new organization and colleagues before they were recruited, but still found it hard. Issues such as not having the right equipment before day one, and getting socially up to speed in a small, close-knit team, as well as having a different working pattern to most of their new team, all contributed to the difficulty. After a year in their role, they benefitted from a 'state of the nation' type of review – something akin to a mutual probationary review – which enabled them and the organization to review the entire induction process and determine whether they wanted the employment relationship to continue (which they did). Further down the line, they feel part of their team and organization, but echo the need to be more proactive and focused at making remote induction processes work.

Lifting and shifting your face-to-face induction process won't work. Create a new, unique remote induction experience.

Offboarding

The process of offboarding begins when the employee hands in their notice and in theory ends on their last day of employment, although as we'll see in this section, it may be more ongoing than anyone thinks with remote workers. Like onboarding, it is a phase that can last for days for some people, and many months for others. Nonetheless it is equally important to get right, as mismanaging this phase creates considerable reputational and business risks that could easily be avoided.

This is, of course, true for anyone who leaves an organization, not just remote workers, but there are unique complications to remote offboarding that we need to consider before looking at how we make this phase more effective. We need to consider offboarding from two perspectives – the operational one, and the emotional one.

At Boost Drinks, Eleanor Gooding has found that offboarding is not the same. Social events can take place virtually, and have done, but Gooding says, with some justification, that it isn't the same as standing around giving people goodbye hugs or watching them open a card or present. Managers can still do leaving speeches and things can still be delivered to people's houses, but as Gooding points out, long-serving employees may find that logging off and closing their laptop after potentially decades of service will be anticlimactical and, certainly, less than ideal.

The Boost insight focuses on the human element of offboarding, and this is replicated in other organizations. For example, Michelle Reid, People Director at the Institute of Occupational Medicine, overcame some of these barriers by using PayPal and Kudoboards where people could write a message, post a picture or a Gif – this meant that goodbyes didn't need to be location or time specific, and could involve collaboration from a wider range of people. These are important aspects which need to be considered, but before we get to those, we need to look at more process elements, for example dealing with the security loopholes and inconsistency around what happens and when (for example when equipment is returned, when access to systems is removed).

Many organizations now have a dedicated offboarding portal managed as a collaborative effort between the IT and people practice functions. This would include guides on how to return equipment and remove software, and guides on how to virtually hand over responsibilities. This may also include what things the employee is allowed or permitted to take with them or retains ownership of – apps like Huler can create 'collections' of resources, links and more, and allow employees to take them with them when they leave, retaining access to the Huler app but only the collections that are personal to the employee. For things that do have to be physically returned, providing the employee with labelled files and boxes and access to a courier service, and guidance on what documentation to be confidentially disposed of, are a big help too.

The bigger risks are around knowledge management, security, and engagement, so we will now look at minimizing each in turn.

Knowledge management risks

Important offboarding tasks around transfer of knowledge and handover of tasks can often be left to chance when working remotely because the employee can't be seen every day – in a face-to-face environment it is difficult to not notice if someone is preparing to leave, but remotely it is easy to forget about this. Scheduling frequent check-ins to talk specifically about handovers and knowledge transfer should be encouraged.

Most remote workers will have inbuilt audit trails of their main work by virtue of completing it online but talking about these audit trails and how to follow them is important.

You will probably already ask departing employees to document their main tasks so that it is easier for the next person to learn how to manage the tasks, but you could now go further and ask the departing employee to specifically think about how a person brand new to the organization as well as the tasks and potentially to remote working would learn the nuances of the role.

Security risks

Many teams are at risk from organizational data being transferred outside the organization without them knowing. This could be the departing employee forwarding files to their personal email or uploading them to a personal account. Such things can be prevented with the right IT security limitations, and this should now be part of the offboarding process if the risk is significant enough.

The departing employee will have access to important and sensitive organizational information, and their passwords should be retrieved at the point of departure and then changed as soon as they leave to prevent data breaches. Again, this should be part of the offboarding process, and all parties should be aware that this will happen, and when it will happen.

The IT team should also be able to update email distribution lists so that the departing employee is not invited to meetings that are due to take place after their departure, or where future-focused information is shared that the departing employee has no use for.

If there are any residual risks then ensure that your process includes post-termination agreements (that the employee may already have signed) such as confidentiality, restrictive covenants, and the like.

Engagement

As explained in the examples earlier in this section, leaving remotely can feel quite impersonal. Kudoboards and Padlets can help by creating walls of appreciation and asking colleagues to record short videos can also help, but only go so far. We need to work harder with remote employees who are leaving to ensure we keep engagement as high as possible. How do we do this?

Regular and short virtual check-ins between line manager and departing employee are crucial, as are those between the people practice team and departing employee. Some of these will cover traditional exit interview ground, but unique to the remote working experience you should be asking for feedback on how this has felt.

On a more social level, it may be appropriate to set up a leaving celebration. This may involve post-work drinks where people share happy memories, or a leaving remote dinner where all are eating similarly themed food. I've seen an ex-employer surprise a senior leader leaving with a well-rehearsed virtual 'flash mob', which created a very memorable goodbye for the individual in question. In this example, this was tailored to the individual and their tastes, and this is important to bear in mind – not everyone will appreciate that, but they might appreciate something more in line with their preferences.

Some may not like a fuss being made, but gifts and packages delivered on their day of leaving or a few days later, personalized to the individual, are likely to be well-received and help to maintain the relationship beyond the leaving date. Keeping positive relationships in a remote world is even more important, as we will now examine. The people who leave your organization are your brand ambassadors and there are things you can do to help maintain positive relationships.

Gail Hatfield, at ESC, found that remote goodbye meetings were quite stilted. She found they couldn't be as spontaneous as their face-to-face equivalents and were more impersonal. They felt facilitated, like any online meeting or training session, and people tended to defer to the most senior person in the meeting, creating a slightly unnatural feel to the event. It was also easier for people to ignore such invites to virtual meetings, whereas face-to-face it is hard to avoid or ignore a large crowd gathering around someone's desk.

As a result, these remote events have not really worked. Hatfield is in the process of creating quarterly face-to-face leavers' events where anyone who has left since the last event would be invited, though she has also noted that individual leavers are creating their own leaving events – both remotely and face-to-face – instead of these being driven by the organization.

ESC's example considers a point we made in the onboarding section of this chapter, that the emotional connection between departing individuals and their employers remains post-termination. In a remote world this is even more apparent. When people move to a company where they may still be in contact, from a networking perspective, with their ex-employer, it may feel like they have not left at all. We talked earlier in this chapter about emotional and physical separation, and we see this with remote offboarding. Functionally, process-wise, the remote offboarding phase can be made very effective and efficient. Emotionally, it doesn't work.

However, I don't think that's necessarily a bad thing. People leave operationally but if they remain friends with ex-colleagues they don't leave in any other sense – they become alumni. And this means people professionals take on a different role – we need to become community managers. Alumni management – community management – becomes more critical in a remote world. The whole remote employee experience becomes quite different, something we will explore further in later chapters.

CASE STUDY

In this case study we look at how an organization that manages high volumes of recruitment coped with an almost overnight switch from face-to-face to remote recruitment processes, and what they learnt along the way.

Rebecca Fielding is the Founder and MD of GradConsult, a graduate recruitment consultancy based in Sheffield that works with clients globally. In March 2020 GradConsult was faced with flipping their recruitment processes supporting dozens of SMEs and hundreds of candidates from face-to-face, to remote, in less than 48 hours. This was achieved, and created real benefits – considerably reducing costs, and improving feedback from candidates and clients too. Diversity of new recruits has improved too as geographical barriers have been removed. Since then, they have been operating almost entirely remote recruitment processes, and have learnt a lot in this time.

Technology can cause anxiety for many people, so GradConsult ensured that all candidates had offline contact details for those involved in the recruitment process in case anything went wrong. They also wrote detailed candidate briefing packs and included friendly personal videos to help the candidates feel well informed and as relaxed as possible. The briefing packs included links to allow the candidates to check out the platform being used in advance. On the day before the interviews, the team made personal phone calls to each candidate to check their readiness and answer any questions.

Fielding was aware of how digital anxiety could cause performance issues for candidates, on both emotional and technological levels. Their team ensured that recruiters called out this elephant in the room and reassured candidates that such things were normal, and they were being assessed on their skills and not their technology. Recruiters talked openly about the anxiety that remote recruitment processes could create, and signposted candidates to tips and techniques to use beforehand. She noted that this anxiety didn't focus on older generations, and many younger candidates were just as nervous. They also offered alternatives such as phone calls for those who needed reasonable adjustments and for whom technology such as video interviews would be a barrier.

From an effectiveness perspective Fielding says the early signs are that remote recruitment offers comparable validity (while noting longitudinal predictive validity is yet to be confirmed) and experiences to face-to-face recruitment for both the candidates and recruiters, but only if certain things are in place. One is that the recruiters themselves need to be briefed on how to use the platform properly, and how candidate performance may look and feel different in a remote process compared to face-to-face equivalents (for example what good looks like in a virtual group discussion may not be what good looks like in a face-to-face group discussion), and so the way they assess performance needed to be adjusted.

The overall volume of applications was greatly increased and GradConsult made use of pre-application assessments and rich content to reduce the number of unsuitable candidates for roles, but Fielding offered a note of caution on the use of technology to automate some parts of the process – it needs to emphasize the individual employee value proposition, create genuine human connection, use diverse role models and be future proofed as far as possible – what works today may not work tomorrow.

In the video interviews and digital assessment platform Fielding found that giving candidates time to settle in and some quiet time and space (possibly with cameras off) to compose themselves was a learning point – this took time that initially they had not planned for, so made the process slightly longer. This had the knock-on effect of making it difficult for the recruiters to be online and concentrating for so long. So, looking after wellbeing, maintaining energy levels, and creating breaks away from the screen, was just as critical for recruiters as it was for candidates.

Case study reflections

While GradConsult are handling a higher volume of recruitment than many organizations, their lessons learnt are relevant to all. Some key reflections from their experience:

- Remote recruitment can be considerably more effective from different perspectives – financial, diversity and inclusion, and the overall candidate experience – but there is much to consider.

- Digital anxiety can cause real problems for all parties in the process and needs to be carefully considered – there are lots of things that can be done to help, but a human approach and calling out the emotions involved is helpful.

- The technology should work well but have backups available for those who need reasonable adjustments.

- If run well, remote recruitment offers comparable validity to face-to-face recruitment methods – this is helpful in convincing any doubters you may have in your organization. Key to this is ensuring those running the remote processes are well-trained and confident on the software being used.

- The qualities being assessed are likely to look and feel quite different in a virtual setting – so those running such processes need to consider this in advance and adjust their assessments accordingly.

- Technology can help speed up and automate some of the remote recruitment process but be careful how this is done.

- The actual video interview itself is likely to take longer and need more time allocated to it to allow for breaks, settling-in and to avoid digital fatigue.

The action plan

If you are looking to implement remote recruitment, onboarding, induction or offboarding processes in your organization, here are some things you need to think about:

Recruitment

- What is your candidate experience like for those applying for roles at your organization? Have you road-tested it recently or asked recent recruits how their experience could have been improved?
- What other mediums do you have to use if your preferred video interviewing process is unsuitable or is a barrier?
- How could asynchronous video interviews help you?
- What would you include on a checklist or guide for those running remote recruitment interviews in your organization to ensure they are prepared?
- What would you include on a checklist or guide for those attending remote recruitment interviews to ensure they are prepared?
- What implications does taking longer for a virtual interview have for your recruitment processes?
- What could your software do to help create a better, more engaging candidate experience for virtual interviews?
- What disaster recovery procedures do you need to build?
- How can you future-proof your recruitment so that you are recruiting for what roles will be in two to three years' time as opposed to what they are now?
- How can you position your employer brand up front to candidates to better explain the culture of working (remotely) in your organization?
- What impact could automating parts of the remote recruitment process have for your organization?
- What is your best advice to senior leaders in your organization about how they could benefit from changing recruitment to cope with more remote and hybrid workers?

Onboarding

- What bits of your face-to-face onboarding and induction process need to be brought forward to ensure the remote onboarding process is smoother for all?
- How will you promote and push socialization opportunities for remote staff during their onboarding phase?
- What do you need to include in a remote welcome pack?
- How will you explain the often-hidden cultural trip hazards in your organization during the remote onboarding phase?

- How could you help new remote workers to get a sense of separation from their old employer?
- What is your approach to senior leaders going to be to convince them to play a more active role in onboarding remote and hybrid workers?

Induction

- What implications does extending your remote induction process have?
- What things are **really** critical on day one for a remote worker, and what could be left for the remote worker to organize themselves?
- If the new starter's buddy doesn't have to be in the same team as them, who is the best person for this to be?
- What aspects of your remote induction process could be gamified, and what impact would this have?
- What is your approach to senior leaders going to be to convince them to play a more active role in the inductions of remote and hybrid workers?

Offboarding

- What asynchronous collaborative technology could you use to enable people to say goodbye to remote employees in different ways?
- How could you use a dedicated offboarding portal, and what could be automated through it?
- How will you handle the knowledge management and security risks of remote employees leaving?
- How can you retain some engagement and connection with remote employees once they have left?
- What is your advice to senior leaders in your organization about how offboarding of remote and hybrid workers needs to work?

In summary, we must do these things differently and better for our remote and hybrid workers, building the process of engagement before they arrive, enhancing it when they do arrive, and ensuring that the separation, when it happens, is appropriately managed also. In our next chapter we continue through the employee lifecycle to look at contractual terms and conditions, pay, benefits and other formalities.

Sketchnote summary

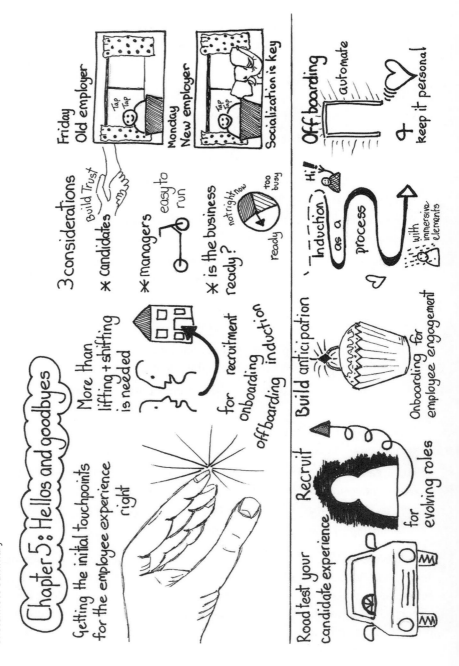

Chapter 5: Hellos and goodbyes

Getting the initial touchpoints for the employee experience right

More than lifting + shifting is needed

for recruitment
onboarding
offboarding
induction

3 considerations
  Build Trust
  * candidates
  * managers — easy to run
  * is the business ready?
    not right now
    too busy
    ready

Friday Old employer
Tap Tap

Monday New employer
Tap Tap
Socialization is key

Induction as a process
with immersive elements
Hi!

Offboarding
automate
keep it personal

Road test your candidate experience

Recruit for evolving roles

Build anticipation

Onboarding for employee engagement

06

Formalities

The shorter read

There are many practical issues that need consideration as we move more employees to remote and hybrid working arrangements – things like whether to (and how to) change any contractual terms, what policies and procedures may need updating or overhauling, and whether to change any pay, benefits, and rewards.

With contractual terms, it is important that we consider whether there is a need to change anything at all, and if there is, whether there is a path of least resistance that can be followed to minimise any potential risks. There are of course several routes to achieving contractual change if it is deemed necessary and considering the use of pilot schemes may smooth the path to this but may also create some problems around custom and practice over time.

Depending on how existing contractual terms are worded, discussions may need to take place around things like place of work, particularly where that may involve working abroad, and making it clear where the employee is expected to be based and on what kind of pattern. Hours of work will also need to be looked at, with employees needing to balance increased flexibility with the demands of service delivery and a greater responsibility for managing their own working time.

Confidentiality clauses need to be more explicit about the risks of having company information at remote locations, and even the use of company equipment will need to be looked at in different ways to accommodate potentially quite varied use of such things.

Expenses will need to be managed carefully, and the nature of claiming for and accessing such things will inevitably change. So, too, will health and safety arrangements, with different responsibilities around reporting and managing safety issues and processes.

From a policy and procedure perspective, we will likely see bigger and more obvious changes even if they're not captured in changes to contractual terms. Ideally, we will all work within adult-adult relationships but that isn't always possible. Different types of policies may need to be adapted or changed to cope with people working remotely. Now is a good time to review these and set the tone for the future.

There has been lots of publicity about some large organizations considering whether to reduce pay for remote workers and there are considerable risks in doing this which will be covered in this chapter. However, there are differentials becoming obvious in a total rewards sense between remote and on-site employees, so the whole package of reward does need looking at.

For example, some benefits and rewards are only available to those working on-site, and the provision of such may need to be reviewed. What could we give remote workers in place of this? There are many useful and practical things you could consider, given that the cost of introducing them should be offset by less take up of on-site rewards.

The importance of recognition and praise as a reward is something that cannot be overstated, but even this takes on different forms in remote and hybrid working. Line managers ability and willingness to notice and recognize good work is increasingly important in that type of working arrangement. Again, this will be explored in a later chapter, but the scene is set here.

The longer read

Contractual terms

If employees are beginning to work remotely or in a hybrid way on a more permanent basis, and if jobs are being advertised as such, then it is important to ensure that the contractual terms are reflective of such arrangements. It was entirely understandable and necessary that, in the COVID-19 pandemic which forced remote working on many people, that such contractual changes and terms were left unaltered as no-one could predict how long such arrangements would last. Now, however, we have the luxury of time, opportunity, and a lot of lived experience to draw upon. We need to consider which terms must change, which could change, and which new terms may be needed, along with how to successfully make such changes.

First let's consider whether contracts do need to be changed if adopting a remote or hybrid working model. Feasibly, if contracts are worded flexibly enough, no changes may be required, or the changes may be implemented entirely by non-contractual policies and procedures. Clearly, the path of least resistance is the one I'd recommend and possibly the most commercially attractive one too.

One could also consider varying contracts by agreement, given that many employees will be the ones requesting remote and hybrid work. This would be a recommended approach too but relies on all those affected giving such consent. Consultation is the next approach to consider – to negotiate such changes with a view to reaching agreement, wording such new or amended clauses in ways that allow for future flexibility and refinement. Finally, termination and re-engagement exists as an option, but is risky and exposes any business to potential claims of unfair dismissal. My own research suggests that there are very few employees who would object sufficiently to a hybrid working model to reach that point – such methods are more likely for organizations that are moving their entire workforce to full remote working.

A useful way of gaining support for such changes is to run pilot schemes or trial periods, something I used to do successfully in many organizations when introducing something new and untested, something that senior leaders were unsure about. There is something about calling it a pilot that gets around initial objections and offers the chance for all to learn lessons and refine plans as things develop and evolve. Piloting remote and hybrid working contractual arrangements and changes is likely to achieve similar results and smooth the path to eventual agreement by most of the workforce, as well as allowing the business to review whether it is something that works and is sufficiently future-proofed. It also allows for trial and error to take place, something that most people would accept and embrace in their working practices.

Be mindful though that where informal changes, with nothing written down, are implemented that these don't become custom and practice, as this would make it difficult to change expectations in the future.

What contractual terms need looking at?

Here we will look at some of the main contractual terms that you need to consider and the issues that may arise when implementing remote or hybrid working.

PLACE OF WORK

This one seems obvious, doesn't it? However, depending on how this is already worded, the clause may not need any adjustment. One such clause I wrote in a previous employment was 'You are liable to serve at any of the company's establishments, or from a mobile or home base'. This would have allowed for remote and hybrid working – and indeed it did, because many including myself operated that way. However, it may not have been detailed enough to cover some of the specifics that may arise with more permanent and widespread use of such practices.

For example, in a hybrid working arrangement it may be necessary to specify how often the employee may be expected to attend the office (e.g. a minimum expectation of a certain number of days per week/month/year). This expectation would clearly differ for each employee or role, and what causes that to differ may need to be set out along with circumstances which could lead to a change for either party, and any exceptions to the normal pattern – for example special training sessions in the office, or lockdowns forcing full remote working.

You may also need to set out what may happen if the employee's home location really isn't suitable for the type of work, or if they move house to a location that isn't as suitable.

WORKING ABROAD

The nature of remote working means that this is now a distinct possibility for some employees. When writing contracts many years ago I included a clause that employees would 'not be required to work outside the UK for any continuous period of more than one month' and the reasons for that remain valid today, though the clause may need tweaking.

There are tax, immigration, and employment law implications for anyone working abroad that they and their organization need to consider. I'd encourage getting specialist advice about this, and even informal arrangements like working in a holiday home abroad may give rise to complications around tax, visas, and local employment laws.

If someone wishes to move abroad permanently and remain as a remote worker, this may cause even more difficulties as there could be no guarantee that any employee would **never** need to attend the physical workplace, and logistically this would be a lot more difficult if living abroad.

HOURS OF WORK

Every contract will contain such a clause, but as many will have noticed during the COVID-19 pandemic, stating rigid working hours are no guarantee that these are the hours that will be, or could be, worked. However, as contracts must state the normal working hours and days of the week employees are required to work, a clause should be worded in such a way that reinforces the need for variations in these and explains under what circumstances variation may occur and how much variation can be tolerated. Some of my clients have adopted some core hours where they expect remote or hybrid workers to be contactable, but outside that allow the employee to set their own hours.

With a view to the Working Time Regulations remote or hybrid employees must be more responsible for self-regulating their own hours and rest breaks, and for managers to take a step back from closely monitoring these, encouraging adult-adult conversations and relationships to deal with issues. The requirements around Working Time may need to be made explicit in the contract for remote and hybrid workers as well as in relevant policies.

While there may be separate rules around annual leave, the ability of employees to carry over unused annual leave (more than the minimum requirements set out in the Working Time Regulations) may also change. Some of my clients have attempted to help employees avoid burnout by removing the ability to carry over any annual leave, and this would need explaining too.

CONFIDENTIALITY

Most contracts will include a clause around confidentiality, although this is by no means universal among employers or for all job roles with any employer. However, with the onset of more remote and hybrid working, confidentiality takes on different perspectives and, if not already made explicit, should now be.

Breaches of confidentiality may be considered gross misconduct, and this should be made clear to employees, and they should be given guidance on what information needs to be kept secure and how to manage the security of the information.

If employees are using their own devices to access organizational systems, then there may need to be coverage of how such use may be monitored, and to make the employee clear about what can be viewed and accessed by the organization.

Remote and hybrid working may mean sharing working space with non-employees. This may mean not just other people seeing confidential information, but to potential listening devices such as other people's smartphones and home hubs like Amazon Alexa. Giving employees guidance on how to address such security concerns is likely to be helpful.

USE OF COMPANY EQUIPMENT

Most contracts will also cover the provision of company equipment for any worker regardless of whether they work face-to-face, remote or hybrid. This is likely to clarify that anything made by or stored on the equipment remains the property of the company, and that such equipment and anything made by or stored on it should be returned at the end of the employment. Does permanent remote or hybrid working change this?

Yes, it does. The equipment will need PAT testing and arrangements made for this to be done regularly – this is likely to mean adding in a contractual right for organizational workers to enter the employee's home to install, maintain and service the equipment (or to recover it when the employment ends). There will also be requirements for the employee to self-assess their own remote working environment, with guidance from the organization.

There is of course no legal requirement for the organization to provide any equipment to work remotely, but most employers will want to do so if only to retain some control over what is used and how it is used, so there will need to be contractual provision for how this is provided and who is responsible for insuring it – employees will need to check they are not in breach of any of their own insurance or mortgage terms by working with equipment provided by someone else in their own home.

Where employees work in a hybrid way, it should be made explicit how arrangements may differ across the different workspaces used by the employee (if at all).

EXPENSES

As employees work more often from home, they will incur more costs – broadband, utilities and more. The contract needs to specify who is responsible for these, and what kinds of expenses can be claimed and under what circumstances. Some of my clients pay a monthly allowance as a contribution to such costs, although in the UK the Government provides tax relief for household expenses incurred because of working from home (provision of an allowance by the employer would prevent any employee claiming the tax relief).

Where there is travel expected in the hybrid role, it should be clearly set out what travelling costs can be claimed as expenses, and the rules for doing this.

HEALTH AND SAFETY

From a sickness absence perspective, it should be made clear if people are expected to report sickness in a different way. Some of my clients have begun logging sickness in hours rather than days, as they have seen an increase in employees feeling unwell at the start of the day and taking a few hours off before starting later in the day. We will explore the pros and cons of this approach in our next chapter, but the rules need clarifying.

Employees need to be clear that they are responsible for their own health and safety in their remote working environment **and** of those affected by that – as an example, their family members. They should be told what issues need reporting – a good example may be back/neck/wrist pain from working in an inappropriate seating position – and how to report accidents and what will happen if these need on-site (e.g. in the home) investigation.

Policies

While there may well be changes to some contractual terms and conditions, most of the practical and tangible changes employees will experience are likely to come from changes to policies. This isn't a book about policies, and I'm not a people professional who promotes policies as a way to manage people – I prefer common sense and adult-adult conversations – but we have to recognize that most people practice teams will have entire suites of policies already – and they need to work out which policies need to stay, which have been rendered irrelevant by remote and hybrid working, and where changes need to be made as a result. It is something many have struggled to get to grips with.

> Morna Bunce is Chief People Officer at Stowe Family Law LLP, a law firm employing around 225 staff across the UK with a head office in Harrogate. She reports that they have made no changes to contracts but have begun to change their policies. They are trialling an informal principles-led approach in the form of what they are calling a 'Dynamic Working Charter'. This has led to changes to policies such as lone working, clear desks, data protection, confidentiality and more.

In the example above we see that some organizations are slowly beginning to work through the changes that may be needed. We will return to this in more detail in our case study focusing on Clanmil Housing Association who have been changing policies around working time, travel, expenses, insurance and various health and safety policies.

Of course, no two organizations are the same, and nor are their respective sets of people policies. What I'm doing in Table 6.1 below is show a range of typical people policies most organizations will have, whether as standalone policies or combined with others, and raise some issues for you to consider. The names of the policies may differ according to organizational language so I've added a brief description where I think the terminology may differ.

TABLE 6.1 Policies that may require some changes

Name	Description	Issues
Capability	Covering how issues of under-performance will be addressed	This may now need to explain how performance is managed in a remote or hybrid way – perhaps via outputs and a different set of evidence for performance.
		It will also need to explain how issues related to remote communication and/or reading and writing may be apparent and could be addressed, and whether there is a different type of support process for these than there is for technical skill-based issues.
		The formal process and its stages will need review to ensure consistency of experience for those working in-person, remote and hybrid, giving different options to suit.
Code of Conduct	Covering the expectations of behaviour from employees	There may need to be dedicated sections within this to cover expectations of behaviour from remote or hybrid workers – as we have explored in previous chapters, working life is quite different.

(continued)

TABLE 6.1 (Continued)

Name	Description	Issues
Discipline	Covering what is classed as misconduct and how it will be addressed	As we explore in our next chapter, some elements of misconduct have become more apparent and prevalent, and others have almost disappeared. The list of what is considered misconduct or gross misconduct may need updating to reflect the relative severity and impact of various elements.
		The formal process and its stages will need review to ensure consistency of experience for those working in-person, remote and hybrid, giving different options to suit.
Expenses	Covering what kinds of things employees can be reimbursed for and how this will be done	There will be considerable changes needed here, and our case study in this chapter covers some of this. The changes to the work location and the need to obtain specific work equipment, as well as costs incurred from remote or hybrid working, will need clarifying in terms of what can be reimbursed or not.
Flexible Working	Covering different types of working arrangements and how these are accessed and managed	Previously, remote or hybrid working may have been considered a type of flexible working and something that needed an application and approval. That may still be the case but may not be – and the whole concept of flexible working may have changed drastically for individual employees as well as for the organization. The policy will need updating as a result with new definitions and perhaps a more informal approach, noting the inherent flexibility that remote and hybrid working have brought to many.

(continued)

TABLE 6.1 (Continued)

Name	Description	Issues
Grievance	Covering how employees can raise issues about their experience at work and how these will be addressed	As we will explore in our next chapter, bullying and harassment (often the main subject of Grievances) have taken on different perspectives in a remote and hybrid environment and the definitions need expanding, along with more guidance and training on how to spot and address them. The formal process and its stages will need review to ensure consistency of experience for those working in-person, remote and hybrid, giving different options to suit.
Health and Safety	Covering how the safety of employees will be managed by the organization and the expectations the organization has of its employees in terms of safety	There could be potentially double-figures worth of formal procedures related to this, but as a minimum organizations will need to update their risk assessments for those working remotely or in a hybrid way, and consider changes to formal aspects such as display screen equipment assessments, home office safety, stress risk assessments and more. More guidance will be needed about creating a suitable home working environment also.
Job Grading	Covering how jobs are graded and their salary arrived at	Whilst this will not be applicable for many organizations, for those who use any kind of job grading or job evaluation scheme will need to update that to reflect the different demands and requirements of jobs that are remote or hybrid. These may be more, or less, than their in-person equivalents – for example there is a different expectation around communication skills and demands, but perhaps less around other skills and demands. The way jobs are graded may need updating as a result of this.

TABLE 6.1 (Continued)

Name	Description	Issues
Learning and development	Covering how the organization intends to develop its employees	The subject of a later chapter in this book, we need to rely much more on social and collaborative learning, and enhance knowledge management processes, in a remote and hybrid working environment. The associated processes need to cover this as well as explain clearly what remote learning should look and feel like, setting clear expectations on all sides.
Leave and working time	Various aspects including rules around annual and other types of authorized leave, and things like flexitime and time off in lieu where appropriate	As we will see in the case study for this chapter, things like flexitime and time off in lieu take on different forms with remote and hybrid working – often becoming something more informal and trust-based. The policy may need adjusting to reflect this. Annual and other types of authorized leave may similarly need a more informal approach, allowing for more flexibility in the process and the definitions of how such things are accessed and managed.
Parental Matters	Covering maternity, adoption, paternity, and all other related and similar rights, and how the organization provides and manages these	There are likely some significant changes in emphasis here. For example if an employee works remotely or in a hybrid way, their ability and willingness to take these types of leave may change, and their need to disconnect is also likely to be impacted. The formal processes involved will need to be updated as a result.
Recruitment and selection	Covering how the organization handles talent acquisition, onboarding and more	As we explained in our previous chapter the nature of remote and hybrid recruitment and selection is quite different, and any formal documentation that gives guidance to those in the organization managing such processes will need updating to ensure that they can manage these appropriately.

(continued)

TABLE 6.1 (Continued)

Name	Description	Issues
Redundancy	Covering how redundancy processes will be managed and the support available for affected employees	Whilst the legal requirements are unaltered, the way the organization manages this may need some change, particularly around the potential criteria that are used to select people for redundancy – these will need to be examined to avoid bias towards or against those working remotely or in a hybrid way, and to ensure that alternatives to redundancy are able to support those who have worked remotely or in a hybrid way to access suitable alternative positions that may not be remote or hybrid in nature (and vice versa).

The formal process and its stages will need review to ensure consistency of experience for those working in-person, remote and hybrid, giving different options to suit. |
| Sickness Absence | Covering how to report sickness absence and how it will be recorded and managed | As we explore in our next chapter, the nature of sickness absence has changed for remote and hybrid workers. People are still sick, but for different reasons, and for different durations. There are also problems being masked by increased flexibility for remote and hybrid workers, and this has implications for all.

The policies around this will need updating to reflect different working arrangements and expectations around sickness absence, and to note the both positive and negative implications of changing sickness absence reporting and recording for remote and hybrid workers.

The formal process and its stages will need review to ensure consistency of experience for those working in-person, remote and hybrid, giving different options to suit. |

What we see in this table is that there are a number of organizational people policies and procedures that work perfectly well for in-person working, but may need some tweaking or wholesale changes to accommodate remote or hybrid working. In the rush to accommodate remote working in the COVID-19 pandemic, it is understandable that these changes weren't made at the time, but put simply, leaving things unchanged now is not an option.

Pay and Reward

Perhaps the most difficult issue for many organizations to wrestle with is whether to adjust what remote and hybrid workers are rewarded (both from a pay and non-pay perspective). Google were notable among large multinational organizations (Facebook and Twitter were others) who received publicity for planning to cut the pay of staff working remotely, by around 10%. This was echoed by some (unnamed) UK government ministers suggesting that civil servants who do not return to the workplace full time should receive a pay cut also[1]. The strong negative reaction to this, allied to the risks around engagement, discrimination and more, mean that this is a thorny issue for all organizations who consider it.

There are, as I've pointed out in earlier chapters, significant benefits to employer and employees from working remotely, and even in a hybrid way. There should be no need for employers to consider altering pay, but nonetheless remote and hybrid working may expose inequities in pay among employees that foster some resentment. Changing the levels of pay will require full contractual change processes (covered earlier in this chapter) but could create as many discrimination issues as they resolve. Speaking to People Management, Paul Seath, employment lawyer at Bates Wells, explained that it could be argued that remote working is chosen more by women to better suit their caring responsibilities, and therefore different levels of pay for remote workers would have a disproportionate impact on women[2].

Many of my clients have reserved the right to review or adjust pay where there is a change in location, but none have yet acted upon this, and it is likely the risks inherent in doing so that is holding back any changes – plus, the consideration of whether this is actually the right thing to do!

Some forward-thinking clients have begun to give employees more say in how their pay (as part of an overall reward package) is structured, and some others have begun making the process of determining pay much more transparent, so that everyone can see what inputs go into pay decision-making.

One client has begun to move to a skills-based pay model, where the acquisition and deployment of new skills are linked to market rates and will result in a more fluid concept of pay. All of these approaches have attractions, and limitations – however one thing all of these employers have in common is that they realize that pay is but one aspect of a total rewards approach and that remote and hybrid working requires such an approach, and also increasingly needs a very specific and different approach to those working in the office.

My advice is to leave pay alone unless you really need to, but focus on how you can adjust and tweak reward in its widest sense – so let's have a look at some of the things that could be on your radar.

As a start point, you could review the benefits that are **only** available to those who work in the physical workplace. Examples of this could be onsite food and drink, whether subsidized or free, but may stretch to onsite gyms, creches and more. Salary sacrifice schemes such as cycle to work schemes, commuter season ticket loans and subsidized or free car parking are also likely to need reviewing – and all of these are less relevant to remote and hybrid workers, meaning that the money that goes into providing them could be reinvested in providing specific benefits for remote and hybrid workers. Even things like a fantastic physical workspace don't have the same attraction for remote and hybrid workers as they do for those in the office, so positioning this as a benefit is not as easy as some organizations may think in our new world of work.

You could usefully survey your employees, whether anonymously or not, to find out what current benefits they feel they would make more, or less, use of if working remotely or in a hybrid way and what new benefits would be appreciated. Having data to base any decisions on would be helpful and could show different insights, for example the data may show that:

- Working parents have unique stressors in their remote work experience and access to additional childcare (babysitters, virtual tutors, even entertainers) may be well-received.

- Additional funding to create an enhanced home office may be helpful, and that individualizing the set-up of the home office with funding to be used in whatever way the employee deems suitable would increase engagement and empowerment.

- Those with elder care responsibilities in or near their homes may appreciate additional support for this, through provided partnership services.

- That those whose remote location is not as well situated for access to services (banks, shops, and more) as the office may have been, and who may have used their office lunch break or commute to undertake some personal errands, may benefit from concierge service to help them complete the same errands while working remotely and without ready access to the places they would need to visit.

- Employees may appreciate additional flexibility around taking sick leave and annual leave. For sick leave they may like to be able to take this in hours instead of days (explored in our next chapter), and for annual leave they may want the ability to take additional leave if they have produced the agreed output and outcomes for their role by a particular time (something the Virgin Group successfully introduced as far back as 2014 albeit without the link to remote or hybrid working).

- Employees may miss the discounted food and drink and may like access to some subscription food and drink delivery services offered at a discount. They may miss onsite gyms and like access to digital fitness offerings instead.

- Those employees who have taken on pets while working remotely or in a hybrid way may benefit from pet-sitting or dog-walking services or even discounted pet insurance.

- Employees using personal devices for work activities, and vice versa, may benefit from support around identity theft.

There is clearly a lot to consider here. Many organizations already offer a wide range of benefits to go alongside their pay, and consider a total rewards approach, allowing employees to tailor their packages according to lifestyle, preference, and various other characteristics like age.

However, I've always said that one of the best rewards one can give anyone is a great line manager, and while this is something we will touch on in a later chapter also, one of the most important aspects of reward delivered by a great line manager is recognition, and this is something that needs reinforcing in a remote and hybrid working arrangement, lest out of sight becomes out of mind. It is important that managers make the effort to recognize remote workers more – a contact from them may be the only work-related human voice they hear that day.

Recognition

In many Western cultures, there is not a great culture of recognition and praise, compared to some Middle Eastern cultures for example. I always remember holidaying in Turkey a few years ago for the first time and encountering the expectation of monetary tips to anyone providing a service, regardless of how well they performed the service – the tip was simply to reward them for providing it. The absence of such a monetary tip was a slap in the face to some service providers – not providing a tip was akin to making a complaint. The culture in Turkey was one where feedback (in the form of a monetary reward) was both expected and required. It didn't need to be earnt and was a reward for doing a task.

I contrast that with many Western cultures, where recognition seems to be linked to exceptional performance and where it is too easy to ignore decent work done well. This is especially true for remote workers. Employees work hard every day, and may well produce wondrous work, but the daily efforts they make – the little things – should be recognized too, with thanky-ous and well-done comments – appreciation that they are doing a decent job, again something easy to neglect for remote workers.

I once worked in a job for 15 months and in that whole time I counted only one piece of positive feedback received from my line manager. And I did plenty of things well. The one occasion I got positive feedback it looked and felt like the manager felt uncomfortable delivering it, and it was only because I'd done something outstanding that couldn't be ignored that they felt they had to say something. The other stuff I did, the things that I did well but got no feedback for, they were 'just doing my job' and the culture was that I didn't require or need any feedback about those.

Employees shouldn't have to go the extra mile to get positive feedback, and remote workers will need this more than others, which we explore in our next chapter. We all deserve to know our efforts are being recognized and noticed, and this is perhaps the best reward of all.

CASE STUDY

In this case study I'll look at how an organization has tackled the issue of contractual change to enable remote or hybrid working, and what things they have put in place.

Karen Gilmore is the Executive Director of Corporate Services at Clanmil Housing Association, which has just over 300 staff based at numerous locations across Northern Ireland, with a head office in Belfast.

As Clanmil began to emerge from enforced remote working for many of its staff, it was faced with increased demands for hybrid and voluntary remote working and realized its previous approach would no longer work. Gilmore and her team wanted to build something for employees that helped them deliver a great service while allowing them to balance their work and life demands. They were conscious that this approach could help deliver higher quality services and output for customers, but also achieve better work/life balance and uninterrupted focus time for employees. They built a solution that set out the parameters for service delivery and employment to ensure fairness, consistency and equity, while keeping all parties safe. Communication and feedback from all staff and teams was core to how Clanmil moved during this time.

In beginning to build a policy that encompassed remote and hybrid working, Gilmore was conscious that some other organizational policies and contractual terms (things like time off in lieu, flexitime, and city centre allowances) would become almost redundant and were therefore subsumed into this new approach.

From a contractual perspective, no employee was designated as a home or agile (Clanmil's word for hybrid) worker, and therefore the policy to support such arrangements was deemed non-contractual and able to be reviewed and updated regularly as needs changed and lessons were learnt. As a result, individual arrangements were (and are) expected to be kept under regular review between managers and employees, and all parties are aware that there may be circumstances when home or agile working is not possible.

The 'base' work location is still specified in the employment contract and has not changed for anyone who works in a hybrid or remote way, and Clanmil have stressed that all other contractual terms such as compliance with working time regulations, flexitime and more remain in place for those working in a hybrid or remote way.

The ability to access non-contractual remote or hybrid working is dependent upon several criteria being met:

- The ability to deliver the role.
- The organization of work and cover among team colleagues.
- The ability to manage performance including work output, outcomes, and clarity on contribution (with guidance given on how to do this).
- The ability to work safely, healthily and without non-work-related interruptions
- Rotas for essential services & duty.
- The cohesiveness of the team and connection to Clanmil.
- Fairness and equality.
- Individual IT skills.

Clanmil also stress that this arrangement will not be possible for all roles, and for individuals in their probationary period it would be expected that more office-based work would take place – and interestingly there is also an expectation that those working in a remote or hybrid way would vary their own arrangements to support individual inductions for new staff. Other exceptional circumstances where remote or hybrid working may not be available include as sanctions for those with poor disciplinary, performance or attendance records. Clanmil recognize the diversity of their workforce, providing front line care and support and delivering critical in-person services, alongside other jobs that could arguably be done entirely from a remote base.

The Clanmil Home and Agile Working Policy covers several areas we have looked at in this chapter:

- Data protection is given priority and focus, with those working outside of the office reminded of the need for their work area (wherever that may be) to be secure and suitable for the processing of whatever data is necessary, and to avoid paper-based documentation and the use of personal communications methods and devices.

- The need to stay contactable via the company's chosen communication channels and to update availability.

- Employees to set up and maintain adequate broadband connections.

- Employees to complete a Homeworking DSE risk assessment (which may result in changes to equipment provided and/or costs reimbursed).

- Employees to ensure they have completed regular and required health and safety training to ensure a consistent level of knowledge of safe working practices.

- Accidents and near misses in the home environment while working to be reported.

- Confirmation that Clanmil's various insurances cover individual employees working in their own homes, but those individual employees must check their own home/ contents insurance for similar coverage and cover the costs if this is not in place.

It is worth devoting more attention here to some aspects that Clanmil have in place for their home and agile workers.

Reward and related issues

Clanmil stress repeatedly in their policy that as it is a non-contractual policy then no-one's main working location has changed. This means that travel from a home location to the main working location is not reimbursable, and only journeys that exceed this 'commuting' distance will be reimbursed.

Home and agile working is deemed by Clanmil to be a mutual benefit to them and the employee, with a view taken that most additional homeworking expenses are offset by other savings, and therefore Clanmil will not routinely pay for additional costs incurred by employees. However, they will pay a sum of around £300 per annum as a Homeworking Allowance as a contribution towards costs – they already pay a slightly higher value City Centre Allowance to those who need to work in their head office for at least four days a week and are clear that they will not pay both to any individual employee. Those in receipt of essential car user allowances or given fleet vans are not eligible for the Home Working Allowance as they should be mobile based. All these allowances are non-pensionable and non-contractual and would be stopped if an employee was absent for over one month.

Clanmil have asked each employee to ensure that the appropriate tax body is informed of the individual claiming the Home Working Allowance as this would render them ineligible for any government-provided home working tax relief.

In terms of provision of equipment for those working under the home or agile working policy, Clanmil are clear that they would first seek to re-use existing equipment before buying new, and such equipment (whether re-used or new) remains the property of Clanmil and should be returned when the employee leaves. However, when an employee wishes to purchase their own equipment, Clanmil will contribute 50% of the costs up to a value of £200 per piece of equipment, which is paid tax-free.

Working time

Clanmil stress that the time taken for the 'commuting' distance (covered above) will not be counted as working time and only travelling time more than that distance would be counted. Where employees travel directly from home to another location without calling at their main work location, working hours start at the point of arrival or at the point where the normal commuting distance has been exceeded, whichever happens first.

Flexible working hours remain at Clanmil subject to the employee continuing to log their hours on the appropriate system and adhering to the breaks required by the Working Time Regulations.

Case study reflections

As can be seen from the case study, there are a lot of considerations for implementing remote or hybrid working from a contractual, policy and reward perspective, but with careful planning it can be done. Some reflections and key learning from the Clanmil case study:

- Beginning by focusing on the business need is helpful and likely to improve focus for all concerned.

- Avoiding rigid rules but setting parameters within which flexibility and individual preferences can be accommodated while protecting service delivery is likely to be a more sensible and adult-adult approach. Clanmil appear to have elements of both rigidity and flexibility though, and it will be interesting to see how this pans out over time.

- Just introducing a remote/hybrid working policy in isolation is not likely to work – lots of other policies and contractual elements need to change (or be incorporated into it) as a result.

- Specifying a 'base' or normal working location for hybrid workers is likely to be essential in making sense of organizational rules around working time and travel expenses.

- Creating a set of criteria for the establishment of remote or hybrid working, and reviewing arrangements against these criteria, is helpful.

- Setting exceptions under which this provision would be adjusted or even withdrawn is also helpful.

- Keeping such arrangements non-contractual is likely to provide more flexibility to evolve and adapt as circumstances change in the future – for both parties.

- Clarifying the pay, pension, and tax implications of changes to reward (in its widest sense) packages will need careful consideration but is likely, as Clanmil discovered, to have mutual benefits.

The action plan

If you are beginning to consider changes to the ways employees are contracted, managed and rewarded, then there are some questions here that will help shape your thinking:

Contractual terms

- What is the business case for contractual change due to remote and hybrid working in your organization?
- Which of your contractual clauses are worded in ways that could allow for change without going through a formal process?
- With which contractual clauses could you pilot any planned changes with to provide you with useful information on whether the changes would work in the longer-term?
- How clear are you on the way that the contractual place(s) of work need to be worded?
- How will you deal with changes to remote places of work that render them unsuitable (or moves abroad that pose risks)?
- How does your wording of working hours need to change, and why?
- How will you provide the right guidance to managers and staff about taking more responsibility for working time?
- What changes need to be made to the way annual (and other types of authorized) leave is worded?
- How well worded is your confidentiality clause and how much does it cover the specific risks associated with remote and hybrid working?
- What do you need to say about provision and use of company equipment to make such arrangements work for remote and hybrid working?
- How will you make it clear what expenses can be claimed by remote and hybrid workers?
- What aspects of health and safety arrangements need to change to provide the right guidance to and support for remote and hybrid workers?
- What is your best advice to senior leaders on what contractual changes the business needs to make, and needs to avoid, for remote and hybrid workers?

Policies

- How will you explain how under-performance will be managed for remote and hybrid workers?

- What expectations do you have of specific behaviour and conduct by remote and hybrid workers, and how will breaches of this be addressed?

- What can remote and hybrid workers claim in terms of expenses?

- How certain are you that you need a separate flexible working policy for remote and hybrid workers?

- How will you ensure that grievances by remote and hybrid workers are properly identified and dealt with?

- How will you adjust relevant health and safety procedures to ensure the safety of remote workers?

- If you use a job evaluation scheme, how will you update it to properly consider the changed demands and requirements of remote and hybrid working jobs?

- What changes do you need to make to learning and development procedures to make them work for remote and hybrid workers?

- How will policies related to leave be based more on trust and flexibility?

- What do you need to do to ensure that parental types of leave provide the required disconnect for remote and hybrid workers?

- What changes do you need to make to update your recruitment processes to work for remote and hybrid workers?

- What elements of redundancy selection criteria could be biased towards or against remote or hybrid workers?

- How much of sickness absence arrangements need updating to reflect a more flexible approach?

- What is your best approach to helping senior leaders in your organization understand what policy changes are needed to cope with remote and hybrid working arrangements?

Pay and Reward

- What business reasons do you have for reviewing pay for remote and hybrid workers?

- What non-pay benefits do you offer that are biased towards those based in the physical workplace, and how could you adapt these (or replace these) for remote and hybrid workers?

- When you have surveyed employee opinion on rewards, how much have you specifically looked at what remote and hybrid workers need?

- What specific benefits could you bring in for remote and hybrid workers?

- How well do your managers understand the nuances of recognition and praise for remote and hybrid workers?

- What is your best advice to senior leaders in your organization about how to redesign pay and reward for remote and hybrid workers?

Getting the formalities right is important, and there are clearly various options to consider here. The right choices can shape the whole employee experience, but the wrong ones can impact employee relations negatively. In our next chapter we will look at employee relations issues in more detail.

Sketchnote summary

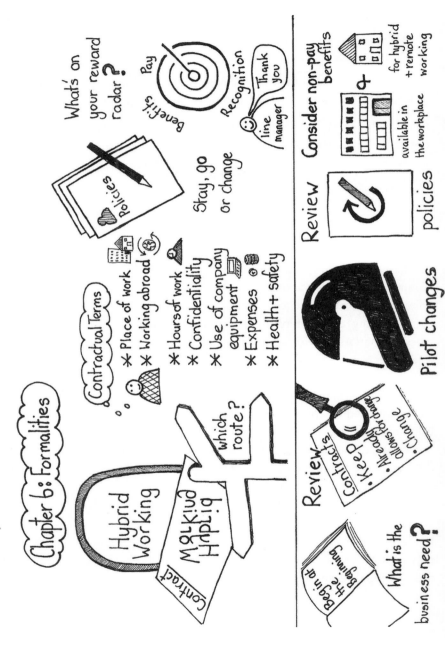

07

Employee relations

The shorter read

The nature of remote and hybrid working can create, or exacerbate, issues around employee relations – including disciplinary and conduct matters, grievances, sickness absence. The role of a remote and hybrid team is different – needing different priorities from its leader, and different ways of working than its face-to-face equivalent.

Remote working has led to different types of conduct issues, made worse by an increased reliance on technology but partially caused by a lack of forethought by many about the rules of the remote workplace. Those who have continued to apply the same rules as the face-to-face workplace have run into problems.

Of course, it would be great if such issues didn't arise at all. Sadly, though, they do. Some remote workers are prone to have not just misconduct issues but problems getting along with their teammates, their manager, or the organization – and therefore also raise grievances, whether formal or informal.

When we consider formal disciplinary and grievance procedures, we must be clear on people's ability to use, or indeed access, technology that levels the playing field for all. Access to information can be problematic for some, and the individual circumstances of each case are likely to mean that unique situations could well need to be considered. Remote proceedings are also likely to have a different emotional impact on the parties, and appropriate support should be given.

From a sickness perspective, this too is perhaps unavoidable, but lots has changed for remote workers in the COVID-19 pandemic about the types of sickness being seen and being reported. We are also seeing remote workers take sickness absence in hours rather than days, and this raises many questions for employers to consider about how they define and record sickness absence.

One of the bigger problems to present itself for remote and hybrid workers is sickness presenteeism – working while ill. This poses some tricky issues to balance from both an employer and employee perspective and only the promotion of healthy working practices, led by senior leaders, is likely to influence culture in a positive way.

Clearly if working relationships are perfect, some of these problems won't occur – but that's highly unlikely. What is likely though is that few in organizations fully understood how remote working changed the nature of a team, and changed the role of its leader, as the COVID-19 pandemic hit. The retention of remote working and its integration into a hybrid model does the same, so we have a good and timely opportunity to look again at all of this.

Leaders need to focus more on giving the right kind of feedback and recognizing the work of people they cannot see alongside those they can. The way performance is managed becomes focused on outcomes, and what it means to work remotely vs in a physical workplace needs consideration in terms of which tasks are done where.

Leaders need to improve their attention on the wellbeing of their remote and hybrid workers (the subject of our next chapter) and have regular conversations with staff about it. The increased reliance on digital forms of communication means that team meetings and one-to-one meetings will take on different formats, and these are easy to get wrong.

Teams themselves are different too. Using the Tuckman model as a structure, we can see how team relationships have been reset during the COVID-19 pandemic and will be reset again when hybrid working commences. This is a golden opportunity to reform the way work is done, the way decisions are made, the way problems are resolved and the way that people communicate with each other.

To make all this work we may need increased and improved data, which our technology (explored in Chapter 4) can provide, but which we need to know how to access and harness to its full potential. Using data about our employees in a style similar to how organizations use customer relationship management (CRM) systems could enable us to unlock greater engagement and make the remote and hybrid working experience an increasingly positive one.

The longer read

When my eldest daughter was three years old, she asked me what I did at work. I don't know if you've ever tried explaining the people profession to an adult, let alone a child, but this was something I struggled with at first. In the end I settled on telling her that my job was to help people feel happy at work. A long time has passed since then, but I haven't managed to better that definition since – if we can get employees feeling happy then they are likely to give their best at work. As a bit of a postscript to that though, my daughter later brought her paints and brushes to me and said that painting was what made her happy – she thought that my job involved getting people to paint at work. Worryingly, well over a decade later she still thinks my job involves painting.

The employee experience is different in a remote or hybrid environment than it is the face-to-face environment that I worked in when my daughter was three, but the aim is still the same – to provide the very best environment for employees to thrive and feel happy.

What is still the same though is that people don't always get on with each other or the organization – they behave in ways that can be deemed misconduct by the organization. They complain or raise grievances against each other or their employer. They don't always turn up for work. They work with people they may not particularly bond or work well with. These things are natural, but in the face-to-face working environment we have processes that can address these things and restore some harmony. In the remote or hybrid environment though, things have proved to be a little different in the way these processes operate, and in the experience they create – and in this chapter we'll look at how and why.

Conduct and disciplinary matters

Remote and hybrid working has had an impact on the types of misconduct that organizations are seeing. Clients of mine have reported issues around conduct on video calls, innocent but significant mistakes such as microphones being left open inadvertently and people overhearing inappropriate conversations, and private chat messages being sent to everyone. In my experience hardly any organization set expectations on such things when the COVID-19 pandemic began, but it was clear that those working remotely were still able to act inappropriately.

This isn't too surprising. As we covered in Chapter 2, lots of people had to quickly change their working practices and were working under considerable pressure which they hadn't experienced before. The rushed and enforced nature of remote working almost everywhere meant that some employers lacked some of the information they needed about employee performance and conduct. Lots of issues quickly came to the fore which are unique to the remote working environment. These included being uncontactable, inappropriate use of company systems, and not working their regular hours (or indeed, at all).

When working in a hybrid manner myself in an organization in the mid-2010s, I would be in the office three days and at home or elsewhere for two. My manager at the time, after I'd handed in my notice to leave the organization, said that she didn't believe I had been working for the company when I wasn't at my office desk on those two days a week, and was at the point of investigating that formally. She felt that I could only possibly be working if she could see me. And that was well before most of the working population began doing remote working full-time, so it is not surprising some of these issues surfaced at that point.

Some of the types of misconduct could be said to be caused by remote working or exacerbated by it. It is possible that those with underlying mental health conditions had them made worse by remote working and that itself may have been a major contributor to some of the misconduct seen from employees working remotely. We have already explored the significant impact of home schooling and childcare responsibilities on employees, and these too could have been a factor in misconduct.

That said, reports from my own clients and from undertaking research for this chapter with numerous organizations all point to formal disciplinary procedures being used far less during the COVID-19 pandemic, and that such matters were dealt with primarily informally. That is potentially something good and bad. It could be good if organizations and employees are adopting more adult-adult relationships and dealing with things informally without recourse to formal procedures. It could be bad if organizations were reticent to use their formal procedures because they were unsure how to do so in a remote or hybrid working environment, as it may mean issues are unresolved. In the next section I'll show how the procedures need to be adjusted to work in a remote or hybrid working environment.

Before we get there though, one of the best pieces of advice about dealing with disciplinary matters is to avoid them arising in the first place. Easier said than done, but if communication is strong enough – if the relationship is strong enough – if enough has been done to create the happiness that I told my three-year-old daughter about – then perhaps not as many issues of misconduct will arise.

From a grievance perspective, while any of the matters listed earlier could and may well lead to grievances being raised, a lot of organizations researched for this chapter report that many staff are unhappy about the intrusions of work (via technology) into their personal and home lives when working remotely. This has led to debates about the right to privacy. For example, if a conversation takes place in a person's home, but is overheard by someone working elsewhere via microphones being left open accidentally on a device, is it a potential breach of individual privacy to act on what was said even if it was inappropriate? The very nature of remote working means a heavy reliance on digital forms of communication, and this can often be open to misinterpretation. Many employees may more easily be triggered into raising grievances, or in feeling like they are struggling with working relationships.

What to consider when carrying out disciplinary and grievance procedures remotely

ACCESS TO TECHNOLOGY

If meetings and hearings are to be held virtually, then you need to ensure that all those involved have access to the right technology – devices and software, as well as stable internet and any other equipment such as headsets that may be required. If you're running the process, then it's likely you will have what you need, but for the employee and any representative, it may not be as easy. If the representative is not an employee of your organization, then their ability to use your company's communication systems may not be as straightforward as you may think – Microsoft Teams, as an example, is not a brilliant experience for people outside of the host organization, and this is further complicated if the external person's organization also uses Microsoft Teams and the person themselves has multiple accounts. Zoom, for example, is blocked by many public sector organizations on security grounds and external people may only be able to access on their own personal, and not work, devices.

All these things can be overcome, but not quickly and certainly not on the day of the meeting itself – so forward planning will be essential to give all the same experience. A test session, whether individually or as a group, would be advisable unless all have successfully used the technology and equipment previously.

Further to this, if there are people with any kind of disability, then specialist equipment and devices may need to be provided.

ACCESS TO INFORMATION AND WITNESSES

Clearly all parties need to be given the right information and evidence to review for the case in front of them, and if any of the parties are going to be reviewing this remotely then the evidence is likely to be electronic. A secure storage area to be accessed with a password for all parties would work well, and any evidence that may only be accessible in the office (including witnesses) would need to be made available remotely also (for example arranging video interviews for witnesses).

Large bundles of evidence may hit issues with file size, and it may be necessary to break the bundle into smaller files and to ask for acknowledgement of receipt. Careful management of who sends it, to whom and when is also needed – some clients told me during the research for this chapter that some trouble in delivering remote disciplinary processes had come from managers inadvertently or deliberately sending files incorrectly.

To help the meeting participants focus, it would be a good idea for the Chair of the hearing to use the Share function on remote meeting technology to give focus on the right document and page. Such privileges can also be given to other participants when they are speaking but will require the Chair to be well versed in the use of the technology.

INDIVIDUAL CIRCUMSTANCES

Some individual circumstances may make virtual meetings difficult, but not impossible. If an employee is working remotely on the day of the meeting, it could be that that is being done to help with childcare responsibilities, and therefore there may be sometimes of the day that are better or worse than others for them. This is not a consideration you'd have to think about for a face-to-face meeting but it is a reality for a virtual meeting, and this may require careful diary management in advance of scheduling meetings and a greater degree of empathy for individual circumstances.

Third parties (people or animals) in the same location as any of the participants could be deemed a breach of confidentiality and security, as well as being an unwelcome and unhelpful distraction. It is worth reiterating this to all concerned.

RECORDING

This is something your procedure is likely to cover anyway for face-to-face meetings, but it is much easier to record virtual meetings, whether using the prescribed technology or not. The meeting can be recorded if all parties agree, and you could use the video recording function to take the place of notetaking. However, if recording has not been agreed by all, then it is worth clarifying to all that any recording that does then happen would be prohibited and without any legal basis.

Even then, there may be issues you want to tackle. If an employee is wearing an earpiece this could be connected to a third party giving them advice, and they may even have someone else in the room (but off camera) giving advice too. You may want to ask all parties not just to confirm that they are alone in their room (and not receiving covert advice) but to evidence this too.

On that note, remote representation may make it more sensible and logical for employees to be accompanied by someone in their remote workplace – and this is likely to be a family member. Does your policy allow for (and would you want to allow for) this?

PRACTICALITIES

It is worth questioning whether the circumstances of the case are right for a virtual meeting and whether, because of the nature of it (sensitive, serious, urgent etc) or because of the individual circumstances, it would be better to deal with it face-to-face? This is difficult to prescribe but it is a question that should be considered.

Some cases may be of a nature where the emotion in the case means that the manager chairing the meeting would find it difficult to deliver the right messages in the right way, and this may again need either a) a face-to-face element or b) more time before, during or after the meeting, or potentially c) both.

If a meeting is being held virtually then you will need to consider screen time and schedule in breaks – let all parties know in advance when they will be.

IMPACT ON THE PARTIES

It is tempting for managers to adopt an out of sight, out of mind mentality and take their time over remote or hybrid disciplinary procedures, but this is not helpful. The same rules should apply, and the need to bring matters to a satisfactory conclusion is perhaps even more important in virtual processes since the impact can be greater.

For example, as we have explored in this book remote working can be accompanied by greater isolation and mental health issues. Disciplinary proceedings are emotionally draining too. Employees subject to them are already under severe stress from a number of angles, so delaying matters, whether deliberately or not, is likely to make things worse. The isolation means more support needs to be provided, and this is likely for all parties – not just the employee but the manager conducting the meeting too.

The other main area we can examine here is sickness absence and how this changes for remote and hybrid workers.

Sickness absence

Human beings get sick and ill, whether they work remotely, in a hybrid way or face-to-face. However the ways in which they will experience absence from work, and the ways in which it can be reported, recorded and managed through formal processes, is likely to be different. In this section we will look at what has changed for the remote and hybrid workforce, and the key things to get right when looking at sickness absence for these groups of employees.

WHAT HAS CHANGED?

In the research for this book, I spoke to multiple organizations, including some of my own clients, to see what types of absence had either increased or decreased for their remote and hybrid working populations.

A lot of organizations reported that they have seen a general reduction in sickness absence being taken by employees who have been working remotely. There is a kind of logic to this – some minor illnesses that would make it awkward to go into the physical workplace and spend time around people are not the same barrier to doing work remotely in one's own home and in relative isolation. That's not to say people should work through such things, but my experience is that many people choose to do so. This is, of course, potentially masking the true level of sickness absence – and encouraging a kind of sickness presenteeism[1].

There has been a general and entirely understandable increase across organizations researched for this book in anxiety and mental health related absences, and in COVID-19 related absences also, but reductions in almost every other category of sickness. However, what stood out in my research was not the changes in causes of absence, but in how it is recorded and reported.

What many of the organizations have also reported is an increase in people taking sickness absence in shorter periods, typically in hours rather than days. This has process implications but for now let's look at the health and wellbeing issues of this phenomenon. If someone is feeling less than 100% at the time they are due to start work, but working remotely enables them to vary their working hours and to start later, many organizations are now seeing employees do just that. Some typical situations are outlined below.

- Joe Bloggs doesn't feel well enough to start his remote work at 9am, so notifies his manager that he is returning to bed for a few hours. After a few hours, Joe wakes and feels a little bit better, so commences work at midday and works for the remainder of the working day.

- Jane Smith is due to work in the office today but doesn't feel well and doesn't want to add the strain of commuting and risk passing on any virus she has to other commuters and those in her workplace, so decides to work remotely today instead. She doesn't do a full day as she is low on energy but does most of it.

Consider the pros and cons of both. On one level, you could consider that an employee doing even 10% of their normal duties is better than doing none, and that a move away from an all-or-nothing perspective is a more adult-adult approach. From a productivity point of view then keeping employees in work – no matter how little they do – may be beneficial. From a health and wellbeing perspective some illnesses may improve if the individual keeps themselves busy and occupied (I have found this with some minor colds). But there are significant potential downsides also – sickness (or e-) presenteeism is a big issue and needs careful management, as stress and other related conditions and illnesses can be made much worse by continuing to work. Research by Collins, Cartwright and Cowlishaw in 2017 showed that if someone worked while ill in the previous three months, their psychological wellbeing suffered[2].

However, it is noticeably harder for managers of those working remotely to ascertain the relative seriousness of any illness – without seeing someone on a video call such illness may go unreported and unrecorded. Nonetheless, the lines between work and home have been blurred and this makes it easy for sickness presenteeism to become prevalent, as we will explore now.

SICKNESS (OR E-) PRESENTEEISM

Presenteeism can take several forms, including:

- Employees working when they are too sick to do so.
- Employees often staying at work longer than they need to, beyond their paid hours.
- Employees regularly responding to communications (emails, messages) outside of working hours (this is referred to as technological presenteeism).
- Employees who turn up to work but are unengaged and unmotivated[3].

Writing for MyHRToolkit in 2021, Camille Brouard cited research showing that e-presenteeism had considerably increased since the start of the COVID-19 pandemic. She found that around one-third of employees had continued to work while sick during lockdowns – some feeling scared of the repercussions, some feeling their illness wasn't serious enough to warrant a spell of sickness absence, and others citing pressure of work[4]. This is not surprising at all – we have looked at some of the difficulties employees have had switching off in remote working arrangements, and this means that many will struggle with knowing not just when to, but how to switch off. The temptation will be to work when others would not. In addition, those just starting a new remote or hybrid role may feel pressure to be present for longer and in a more noticeable way.

There are clearly many cultural issues to be addressed around e-presenteeism, and these centre around ensuring everyone knows what healthy and unhealthy working practices are and why the former are important to everyone. Leading from the top is of the utmost importance in sending signals to the whole workforce. In a previous chapter we talked about ensuring that managers and their teams know about how they need to be taking more responsibility for their working time and avoiding e-presenteeism comes into this responsibility too. As we will look at later in this chapter, the role of leaders is crucial in ensuring that those working remotely are keeping to healthy working practices, checking-in where appropriate and helping people feel included and valued when working remotely.

WHAT NEEDS TO CHANGE?

Some organizations have begun offering 'mental health days' in place of employees taking sickness absence or using annual leave. Men's health charity Movember and global sportswear brand Nike garnered some publicity around this in 2021 by offering their staff – two to five days mental health leave. The more resources an organization has, the easier it would be able to do this, but a simple and straightforward approach would be to make it more acceptable to take sick leave for mental health reasons, even if that is for just a day, or even for a few hours. This will need a redefining of sickness absence in some organizations and a change to how it is reported and recorded.

Some other organizations have been able to extend entitlements to sick leave or have further reclassified some other types of paid leave to cover what they call 'personal emergencies', with little definition of what classes as one. This may be a double-edged sword but again may help some employees to take the required time off and prevent themselves from any worsening conditions. Some organizations researched for this chapter have seen that any illness other than COVID-19 itself can sometimes be derided as trivial and not something to take advantage of the ability to work remotely for.

Clearly though, some people may want to work while recovering from illness and could be allowed to do so – a policy change would be required to ensure that this is done carefully, but in a way that allows for adult-adult conversations to take place between manager and employee to determine and agree what is best for all parties.

Perhaps the most significant policy shift for organizations will be the ability to take sick leave, and record it, in hours instead of days. Failure to report this as sickness absence is masking a problem and not addressing issues around employee wellbeing, but failure to allow it to be taken as sickness absence is perhaps taking flexible working a little too far. Somehow, a middle ground needs to be found here.

Working relationships

So far in this chapter we have explored how the nature of employee conduct and behaviour is changing, and the impact this is having on health. We have looked at how remote and hybrid working change all of these, and how the processes surrounding them need to be adjusted too.

Far better, though, to look than to avoid employee relations issues completely. To create a climate in the team and among its team members, whether working remotely, in a hybrid way or face-to-face, that fosters engagement and commitment. An environment where there is openness and transparency about issues, strong communication and a focus on doing what is right for people's health and wellbeing.

Therefore, in this part we will look at how the role of a leader of remote or hybrid workers is subtly different than that of a leader of face-to-face workers, and how the concept of a remote or hybrid team is also subtly different from its face-to-face equivalent, and offer some advice on how to get these things right.

HOW IS THE ROLE OF A LEADER DIFFERENT IN A REMOTE OR HYBRID TEAM?
A helpful model that I often use with new leaders is Mintzberg's Ten Management Roles[5]. It's a helpful model for new leaders to understand where they need to focus their energies and efforts and divide up their attention. The model has ten roles split into three overarching categories, and these are just as relevant in remote and hybrid teams as they are for those teams that are co-located:

- Interpersonal roles – providing information and ideas – including being a source of inspiration, managing the performance of the team and networking on behalf of the team.

- Informational roles – processing information – including monitoring productivity and wellbeing, communicating information to the team, and transmitting information about the team.

- Decisional roles – using information to make decisions – including solving problems, mediating disputes, allocating resources, and negotiating within and on behalf of the team.

All these roles are still valid in a remote or hybrid team environment, but for many of my clients it has been noticeable that many leaders have not consciously focused on where to put their energies and efforts as a result of the differences that such an environment brings. The roles are the same, but the proportion of time spent doing each can be quite different. Let's explore how.

Interpersonal roles   One of the more critical roles for the leader of a remote or hybrid team to focus on is feedback. Feedback on performance but also on employee's ideas and contributions. This should be encouraged from all team members not just the leader but is more important for remote and hybrid workers as without regular and timely feedback they may feel isolated and be tempted to withdraw.

No-one is above some type of recognition, and this is also critical for leaders of remote and hybrid teams. Whether through digital or other means, recognition must be given to all members of the team to ensure that they know their efforts are being recognized. This isn't just about catching people doing exceptional things, but acknowledging that they are doing their job, doing what is expected of them, and that this is appreciated.

I take part in triathlons. In one race in 2019, I ran out of the lake following the swim and entered the transition area to get ready for the cycle leg. There are strict rules in transition that you must follow and if you break some of them you can be disqualified, but it is a stressful time and easy to forget the rules. Ahead of me was a man who broke the rules, and the nearby marshal shouted at him that if he didn't correct this straight away, he'd be disqualified.

The man was understandably chastened but seeing this unfold in front of me helped me to remember the correct rules and I completed transition flawlessly. The marshal was directly in front of me and noticed – she gave me a double thumbs-up signal and a big cheesy grin before telling me how well I'd done it. Now, I knew she was being patronising. I knew she wasn't saying this for my benefit but for the benefit of the other man who was still visibly chastened at his breach of the rules. Still, though, inside I shouted '**yes!** ' and almost flew out of transition.

That good feeling didn't last long as my bike slipped on some wet leaves and I fell off, but the point here is that I wasn't doing anything special – I was doing exactly what I should be doing – but I felt good because someone in a position of authority noticed. The delivery of the recognition was, of course, patronizing, and I knew that, but still it made me feel good.

Of course, recognition needs to be carefully framed for the individual and tailored to their needs and preferences, and the leader of the team should make efforts to find out these needs.

The manager should also be managing the performance of remote and hybrid workers differently. With online team meetings, the use of cameras should be encouraged to develop relationships and promote engagement, but if there are a lot of people in the meeting then this should be kept as short as possible. Some team members may still not be comfortable though showing their home environments. To help avoid the focus on this, online team meetings should mirror a training session in style and format, with clear objectives, a blended approach and different activities using different functionality.

In terms of organizing the work of the team across its remote and hybrid workers, the manager should be careful to agree which tasks may need a face-to-face element based on co-location. This may help all to agree guidelines on what proportion of each individual's working time is spent remotely and what is spent in the physical workplace.

Informational roles   It is clearly more important to monitor the well-being of remote and hybrid workers since for a good portion of the time they may not be seen face-to-face. Our next chapter explores the management role here in more detail, but leaders have a critical role to play in finding out individual levels of well-being, and encouraging healthy working practices. This may be about encouraging people to switch off or ensuring that the remote workspace is set up in a way that boosts productivity and well-being simultaneously.

At PowerONPlatforms (subject of a case study in Chapter 8), Anna Edmondson (Chief People Officer) introduced Weekly10 check-ins (rather simply, a five-question form for individuals to complete weekly, responded to by their manager, and including wellbeing). This, plus a broader focus on wellbeing (covered in Chapter 8), has helped them clarify a manager's role in having wellbeing conversations with their teams, and move away from purely functional and task-based conversations. The Weekly10 check ins and formal structure of one-to-one meetings shows clear expectations, and makes it easier for managers to understand how to have these conversations. This has led to managers becoming more comfortable with this by sheer repetition.

At the same time, productivity needs to be monitored also. Leaders of remote or hybrid teams need to increase the frequency of their one-to-one meetings and ensure that they focus more on results and outputs, not how long a person is working. Where results are not as expected, conversations in the one-to-one meetings should focus on why this is.

There is, of course, a fine line between asking for too much or not getting enough performance information, and leaders of remote or hybrid teams have often fallen on the wrong side of this line. Working with the team to help them develop their own performance measures and reporting and creating digital methods to report and share this information should be a focus of the team leader.

Remote or hybrid teams will rely a lot on digital means of communication, but no one platform is right for any type of team, and a leader needs to be cognizant of which mediums should be used for situations. Some situations may require video-based communication, some would require audio, and some face-to-face. Technology should be used to support the needs of the situation, and leaders should make careful choices about which is used to disseminate and discuss information.

If a manager is co-located with any worker on any day, they need to ensure they avoid showing favouritism in communicating more with that person just because they are immediately available.

Decisional roles   The leader of a remote or hybrid team needs to ensure that relationships between team members are well established and constructive, recognizing the limitations of digital forms of communication but also clearly having a good grasp of how relationships are operating, both good and bad, and coaching individuals on how to relate better to their teammates. Those working remotely may have particular communication and engagement needs – for example they may not like virtual social events and may need more careful management and business-related engagement events.

There need to be efforts made to agree ways of working, including how flexible working arrangements are, what the expectations between leader and team and between team members are, and in giving everyone the right equipment and support regardless of where they work.

HOW IS A REMOTE OR HYBRID TEAM DIFFERENT?
Many people now have direct experience of this, but at the start of COVID-19 pandemic this was new to almost everyone. Building relationships with team-

mates remotely is not quite the same. If one has never met one's teammates other than virtually, it can be easy to define perceptions of them based on stereotypes or partial truths. Remote and virtual team members need to be fully aware of the potential for bias to creep in and make efforts to get to know each other better and develop a shared sense of identity. But how?

When co-located teams are first put together, they tend to follow several stages – forming, storming, norming and performing. What seemed to escape most teams when the COVID-19 pandemic forced them to move to remote working, is that all teams, no matter what stage of the Tuckman Model they had reached, were reset – everything changed. It was the failure to notice this that led to many relationship issues between team members. The same is true of teams that have been forced to work remotely and are now operating in a hybrid working environment – the model is again reset, and everything needs to be done again. The stages of the Tuckman model are as follows:

- Forming: identifying group and individual responsibilities, being clear on the boundaries of each person in the team, and ensuring each team member clearly understands their role.
- Storming: taking time to build good relationships between team members and with leaders of the team, joint problem solving, sharing issues and new ideas.
- Norming: encouraging the team to self-regulate, share information, and take ownership and accountability of their individual and joint results.
- Performing: establishing effective ways of meeting, communicating, and the rules of working together.

From talking to my clients and from researching for this chapter – very few teams focused on these stages as they moved to remote working. And why would they? The COVID-19 pandemic was upon us – it perhaps wasn't the time to look at such things. However, the move to a hybrid environment as we emerge from that pandemic is a much more planned and conscious event and such focus on team working should now be a priority.

In a co-located working environment, the rules of working together are long and well established. It is part of the culture, custom and practice. There are unwritten rules around meeting etiquette, answering emails, returning calls and so on. But teams moving to remote or hybrid working need to explicitly define these – and if not now, then when? Remote and hybrid teams need to work on defining:

- When and how the team's leader will deal with different situations.
- What the information flow between the team's leader and the team looks like, and how it will be judged as effective, including how all will be kept informed of significant events.
- How the team will keep its customers informed of what is happening.
- How the team will be administered depending on the location of its members.
- Preferred communication methods.
- Meeting management and etiquette.
- Expectations around team behaviour.

Teams need to be given structure to be able to operate effectively remotely, and while the leader of the team can play a big part in establishing this structure, it may fall largely to the team themselves to manage and regulate such structure. Many of my clients have ensured a routine and rhythm to team meetings as well as one-to-one meetings, to maintain structure and continuity for all.

Such meetings should focus as much on social aspects and wellbeing as they do share performance information and other insights. These meetings will, for almost all remote or hybrid workers, replace some of the informal, ad-hoc, conversations that may take place in a co-located workspace, and so the sharing of updates and learning is more critical as a result. Focusing team members on social relationships should be encouraged also. Getting to know people on a personal level and having social conversations can increase rapport and the effectiveness of communication, as well as reducing feelings of isolation, in remote and hybrid workers.

Teams should also be discussing the way they communicate with each other and how effective (or not) this is. As we have covered, digital means of communication can make it difficult to read tone and body language, and to interpret meaning fully. Team members should be encouraged to listen fully to each other and clarify any potential misinterpretations.

We return to PowerONPlatforms here. They have moved their whole company biannual get togethers online. These include a lot of time simply to chat – 20-minute randomized chatting sessions – and the aim is to keep the days fun, build relationships while still checking in with the corporate vision and strategy.

Anna Edmondson also gave advice to managers planning their own mini versions of these team get-togethers, which included:

- Throw out any standard formats for large group meetings... avoid presentation-heavy agendas with only ad-hoc discussions to minimize the risk of losing attention.

- Think about the tools to use for interactive discussions and try to vary and change the format around so questions and answers can be given in different ways.

- Think about scheduling. People need variety, and content in short, sharp sessions. And plenty of breaks.

- Focus on recognition and well-being first and communicating information very much as a secondary goal.

- Consider sending physical items to the team – chocolate, badges, other bits of information and aids for the activities taking place online (e.g. bingo).

- Intersperse serious content with fun. At PowerON, this has involved quizzes, Guess Who played using the new Together view in Teams, and of course PowerON Bingo – typical PowerON buzzwords for people to listen out for during the day, and to shout **bingo** no matter what was going on. They also did an online escape room where teams competed against each other, and people enjoyed that.

USING DATA

In 2015 I attended a talk delivered by someone (whose name escapes me) from United Utilities, and they talked about having data on their employees akin to a Customer Relationship Management (CRM) system. I wrote about this in a blog post following the event[6] but it strikes me that managing a remote or hybrid team could be so much better if we had such Employee Relationship Management (ERM?) systems and data.

If an organization can collect stacks of data about its customers and use this in an interface/system to tailor services and products around what that customer has said, done and tweeted – then the same ought to be possible, and desirable, for employees. Even with a small number of employees it ought to be possible in a more informal way.

For example, most people practice systems store a lot of data about employees but most of this data is relatively static, and although used for statistical purposes I haven't seen many systems, or organizations, who actively use this data to segment employees and map the employee journey in the same way they would a customer group. I haven't seen many people practice systems that have a record of every employee interaction with the organization and that tailor services and the employee experience based on these. Look at how Facebook has tailored adverts based on things you've clicked on. It's like magic sometimes, but the technology is there. Our entire online experience is usually tailored based on past habits.

We could unlock a greater amount of employee engagement by focusing on the employee experience and tailoring that to the individual employee. Personalization at work if you like. Lucinda Carney, whose technology company, and product Actus featured in Chapter 4, explained that Actus can provide greater visibility and data that can be used to manage productivity more effectively, particularly in a hybrid workforce. It can also provide a framework of best management practice that improves consistency across each business. This can only be a good thing for HR and managers as it provides greater information about who, how and what to develop. As Alan Price explained in Chapter 4 the Bright HR software has lots of available data for managers of remote and hybrid teams to use and help personalize the employee experience, but for this to happen managers need to be comfortable using data to gain insights and acting on such insights.

Much of the data will, inevitably, give insight into individual employee wellbeing and inclusion, and so this leads us nicely on to our next chapter talking about both issues. Before then, here is a case study on employee relations issues.

CASE STUDY

In this case study we look at an operational arm of Network Rail, who employ around 43,000 people across the United Kingdom. Kirsty Diamond is an HR Business Partner based in Glasgow and provides operational HR support for around 1,000 of Network Rail's employees based in that region. In our discussion we touched on what she had noticed as different in handling employee relations cases for those working remotely.

Conduct and disciplinary processes

Diamond has noticed a difference in the types of challenges that these present between those working remotely and those working onsite, in that different types of misconduct present themselves in both situations and require tailored approaches to resolve.

In terms of specific instances of misconduct, more traditional categories such as fraud and dishonesty have significantly reduced as workers have been more remote, but misconduct issues caused by poorer interpersonal relationships have significantly increased. The reason for this, Diamond feels, is that it is not as easy for managers and employees to deal with things before they progress to more serious situations – they are robbed of the informal opportunities to resolve issues as communication with remote workers must be more deliberate and consciously planned.

This point is something Diamond feels has impacted those workers onsite too. Many of Network Rail's onsite staff are project and location based, working together in close knit teams, often away from home together. Various iterations of lockdown and a general reduction in socializing with people outside immediate social circles have significantly impacted employees' ability to build relationships and bond as a team, and some minor misconduct can be seen because of this.

In formal disciplinary meetings held virtually, Diamond has noted that the more emotional nature of many misconduct hearings makes dealing with such matters much more difficult, and the people in the meetings have wildly differing levels of skill and experience at using the virtual platforms – things like knowing when to, and how to, turn cameras and microphones on and off and how to share documents, have become noticeably more important for all concerned and the general lack of skill on such things has made some virtual meetings very difficult indeed.

Diamond also commented that virtual meetings often prevent the "'huddle in a corner' discussions that the employee and their representative could have in a face-to-face meeting. Breakout Rooms could be used for such things and so can simply turning cameras and microphones off, but in her experience usually such things are only realized at the end of or after the meeting. It has also become noticeable that other people (for example family members) are often in the virtual meeting but off-camera and providing support to the employee that may or may not be allowable in a face-to-face environment.

Grievances

When it comes to formal grievances, Diamond has noted an increase in the number of these but a distinct change in why they are raised and the types of things they cover. As an example, grievances related to processes and procedures (such as performance management or recruitment) have reduced, but grievances related to individual behaviour and conduct have increased.

When I pressed for examples of types of individual behaviour, Diamond said it was things unique to the remote working experience such as communication difficulties and barriers:

- Camera use on vs off in meetings causing some level of mistrust.

- Some people feeling that others were setting them up to fail in virtual meetings by withholding information or being undermined with things said or unsaid.

- Accusations of managers spying on and micromanaging staff when they were asking for more frequent performance updates – doing this remotely and digitally means that some managers who could 'see' performance without having to ask about it are struggling to cope with not seeing it in the same way.

- The requirement (real or perceived) to be always 'on' and accessible via instant messenger or other virtual platforms causing relationship issues

In summary, Diamond's view of grievances at Network Rail has seen a change in type and a greater level of mistrust bubbling away beneath the surface, meaning that formal grievances only scratch the surface of wider issues – the iceberg effect.

Sickness absence

Over the period of the COVID-19 pandemic, Network Rail saw a net reduction in sickness absence, but a change in types of absence, again largely caused by remote working.

In absence types, clearly COVID-19 as a cause of absence has increased, as has mental health issues, but all other types of absence have decreased. Mental health absence itself has changed in nature – prior to the increase in remote working, mental health absence tended to be almost exclusively a long-term thing – typically lasting many months. In a predominantly remote or hybrid working environment Diamond is finding that mental health absence is a lot shorter in duration, though often just as, if not more, severe (Diamond has dealt with an increase in attempted suicides, as remote and particularly isolated working has deprived some people of their normal coping mechanisms).

Diamond noted that there has been a marked increase in presenteeism, and she suspects this outweighs the decrease in absenteeism. She feels, with some justification, that it is easier for many people to simply 'be there' in a virtual meeting and to contribute less than they would in a face-to-face meeting. It is also seemingly easier to 'work through' some minor ailments such as stomach upsets and headaches when sat at a remote desk in one's own home than it would be to do that in the office. At Network Rail, it has been noted also that people who are feeling slightly unwell will simply vary their working hours – in effect taking a couple of hours' worth of sickness absence instead of what would have been a full day if in the office – starting later or having an extended break during the day. This isn't reported as absence, more as flexible working, but is a sign of a phenomenon covered elsewhere in this chapter – taking sickness absence in hours rather than in days.

On long-term absences, Diamond has noticed that the 'return to work' is often easier with remote workers, particularly those with mental health issues, as there is no physical commitment to return to a place where there are lots of other people. She commented that in these cases though, the barrier is a mental one – finding the will to turn the laptop on. This has meant that the types of support given to those with long-term mental health issues has had to change, and the medium for that support too.

Case study reflections

The Network Rail case study is a helpful one to see some of the issues related to remote and hybrid employee relations processes in action. Some of the reflections I have had while compiling this case study:

- It is entirely possible that the list of things that constitute misconduct and gross misconduct could need reviewing based on experiences of remote and hybrid working.

- There may be benefit in focusing on how remote and hybrid working managers and employees raise and address issues around their relationships in an informal manner – the formal processes may not be the best route for those, and guidance could be helpful here in organizations.

- Team relationships have the potential to suffer greatly when the members are working remotely, and more effort needs to be made to restore and improve this.

- Providing opportunities to use technology and its tools to allow more informal and off the record discussions in formal hearings would be helpful, as would ensuring all parties are confident in its use before a hearing begins.

- Emotions can be heightened in a remote or hybrid environment due to less cues around body language, tone of voice and a general reduction in observable behaviour and performance. Managers (and perhaps employees too) would benefit from guidance on this too and how to avoid over-compensating for it.

- Organizations may need to consider if there is a masking of genuine illness through remote and hybrid workers continuing to work while ill. Decisions may be needed on how and whether to handle and record this.

- The issue of presenteeism is seemingly not just a face-to-face workplace issue and may need specific actions to address it.

- The phenomenon of taking sickness absence in hours instead of days may suit the concept of flexible working but may in itself have consequences for other parts of the employment relationship.

The action plan

If you are planning to make more and longer-term use of remote and hybrid working then you will need to ensure individual and team relationships are set the right way, and that this creates a positive experience for all, minimizing the risk of conduct issues, clashes between employees and ill-health. Here are some things to consider:

- What trends have you seen in employee misconduct and grievances recently, and how much of these can be attributed by the experience of working remotely or in a hybrid way?

- When conducting formal procedures virtually:

  o How can you ensure that all parties have access to and are comfortable with the technology being used?

  o How easily can you provide the right information and evidence to all parties?

  o What individual circumstances would necessitate some adjustment in how/when/where the meeting is conducted?

- What rules will you need to make around recording of the meeting?
- What support would you need to provide to all parties to ensure they can cope with what is happening?

- What trends have you seen with sickness absence types and instances, and how much of these can be attributed to the experience of working remotely or in a hybrid way?

- What issues does it create (or solve) for you if remote/hybrid workers begin logging sickness absence in hours instead of days?

- What steps will you take to determine the level of and deal with sickness presenteeism in your organization?

- How can you help leaders to refocus on their new role in leading remote and hybrid teams?

- What support will teams need to reset their working relationships and establish new rules to manage how they operate in a remote or hybrid environment?

- What data do you have about employees that could offer insight into how they are remote or hybrid working? And what data could you create and collect that would improve this insight?

- What advice will you give to senior leaders in your organization about how to ensure employee relations processes work more effectively for remote and hybrid workers?

Sketchnote summary

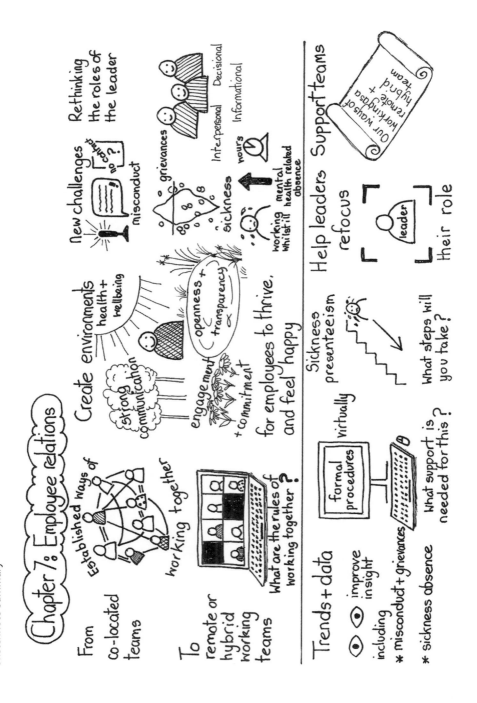

08

Safe spaces – wellbeing

The shorter read

The need for safety, and safe spaces, for remote and hybrid workers, is crucial. This chapter incorporates how we prioritize the health and wellbeing of such workers, as well as all other employees. The following chapter looks at how we ensure that remote and hybrid working addresses barriers to inclusion and doesn't create them, and how we instil a sense of belonging for remote and hybrid workers.

Wellbeing has clearly been a prime focus for many people forced to work remotely during the COVID-19 pandemic. Individual mental health, already more problematic in employment than many realized, became more significant. The effects of isolation, increased reliance on technology and digital means of communication, and other factors made remote working an unpleasant experience for some, and therefore the focus on wellbeing was necessary and important, but one which began to shift away from standalone initiatives delivered by the people team to more of a leadership quality and competency.

One of the main problems though for workers who you cannot 'see' as easily is that mental health and wellbeing issues can go unnoticed or even be belittled. From my own research, not enough organizations take such things seriously and are still under-investing in this area.

Plenty has worked and plenty has not for remote and hybrid workers in relation to their wellbeing. We need to focus on how much can be done by managers and team-mates simply being human, something they have decades of experience and training in. Some of the technological aspects can be tweaked to work much more effectively around someone's mental health issues. However, there are some neglected areas of health that seem to be unique to the experience of remote and hybrid workers.

The longer read

Wellbeing

This is an area that has shot right to the top of people professional's priorities because of the COVID-19 pandemic. In this section we'll explore what has prompted this, and why wellbeing is now something that is embraced and delivered beyond the people function. We will also explore what has worked and what has not for remote and hybrid workers in relation to their wellbeing and look at ideas that can be implemented within your organization to improve wellbeing for everyone. To paraphrase Josh Bersin, who spoke on this subject in 2021 many times – wellbeing is no longer a benefit programme administered by people teams, but a core competency for all leaders in organizations.

According to statistics from the mental health charity Mind in 2017, approximately one in four people will experience a mental health problem each year, and around one in six report experiencing a common mental health problem each week. While these statistics were compiled prior to the COVID-19 pandemic and before the massive increase in remote and hybrid working, they do give some sense of scale to the problem facing employers in general.

WHY WELLBEING HAS TAKEN ON INCREASED SIGNIFICANCE FOR EVERYONE
During my research I spoke to Morna Bunce, Chief People Officer at Stowe Family Law, who is the subject of a case study in this chapter. She is one of many people professionals to grasp that wellbeing is now an issue that is not the preserve of the people function, and to believe that organizational leaders must now take it more seriously. Bunce went as far as to suggest that it could be an item on the risk register for every organization, due to the impact it could have on business continuity and believes that organizations who ignore wellbeing or defer its delivery to just the people team as a 'fluffy' initiative are

merely storing up huge long-term problems for themselves. I'd take this further – as one's own health is one of the major determining factors in one's ability and willingness to perform, it could and should find itself a central part of discussions about individual and organizational performance.

Wellbeing is higher on almost everyone's agenda now though – the COVID-19 pandemic made many leaders focus on their more human qualities and raised awareness around mental health and wellbeing. Rachel Suff, talking on a CIPD podcast in May 2020, rightly pointed out that mental ill-health was a serious issue in workplaces prior to the COVID-19 pandemic, but one made worse by that due to the amount of fear and anxiety and challenge that that pandemic brought[1]. In addition to that, the nature of forced remote (and now hybrid) working means that it can be much more difficult for leaders to notice when a person's wellbeing is suffering. The experience of forced remote working also highlighted an important difference between good and not-so-good managers. The impact that managers have on any worker's mental health is stark, but it became particularly important for managers of remote workers to do more than cursory check-ins, and to find out much more about individual mental health and personal circumstances. It is not just employees working remotely though who suffered, as we see in the example below.

As a result of mental health struggles during remote schooling during the COVID-19 pandemic, my youngest daughter had to move schools. The experiences we had prove we have some way to go before such things are treated with the seriousness they deserve, particularly when assessing the mental health of those working remotely.

What surprised me was the varying range of reactions we received when telling people about our daughter's mental health issues. It may perhaps be a microcosm of society and workplaces in terms of their reactions to anyone sharing mental health issues and from those who are not directly involved.

One teacher paraphrased a line from Star Trek's Doctor McCoy by telling us that they were 'a teacher, not a behavioural therapist' and couldn't help us with our concerns about our daughter. Others told us that our daughter was 'fine when they saw her', suggesting that because they themselves saw no mental health issues when in virtual classrooms with our daughter that such issues must not exist, and took no action as a result.

Even some other parents were less than helpful too. Some ridiculed it and tried to make out that our daughter was being dramatic, and that remote schooling had benefits that made mental health issues less important or noticeable. Some told us to ignore our daughter's issues and that they would go away on their own, which made us feel belittled for raising such issues and for not covering them up.

Just because it isn't easy to see someone's mental health issues or understand the impact they have on the individual, doesn't mean those issues don't exist or can be dismissed out of hand. If a tree falls in the forest and no-one is around to hear it, does it make a sound? If you can't see it, but the other person is telling you it is there for them, listen. Believe them. Support them. Just because it is in their head, doesn't make it any less real – and in many ways it makes it more terrifying for that person.

If our experience with our daughter was anything to go by and can be extrapolated to both wider society and workplaces, we have a long way to go in helping those with mental health issues. Thankfully we were able to help our daughter, who is now much happier. But how many employees – remote or otherwise – suffer in silence and don't speak out because they think their emotions and mental state will be ridiculed, made light of, disbelieved, or dismissed out of hand?

We have a real challenge on our hands to encourage people to speak up, to speak out, and a real challenge to get people to really listen and take such things seriously.

The forced nature of remote working during the COVID-19 pandemic meant that many traditional wellbeing initiatives that had been relatively popular in organizations had to change – things like free fruit, onsite exercise classes, free flu jabs and many more that I have implemented in organizations in the past – had to stop or change format completely. Wellbeing in organizations didn't necessarily suffer because these things stopped or changed, raising some doubt about how much impact they had in the first place. Wellbeing in organizations suffered because of the circumstances that brought forced remote working and was shown to be improved by human connections.

That said, despite the growing acceptance of how important wellbeing is, research by employee benefits provider Benefex in 2021[2] showed that only 43% of organizations have a clearly defined wellbeing strategy, although a further 26% are developing one. Within the same research, 49% of organizations described their approach to providing support around wellbeing as basic (a compliance-led approach focused on health and safety, sick pay and pensions) or foundational (offering static support around things like employee assistance programmes and gym membership). Clearly there is still much work to be done then, and this research reinforced a view I came across in my own research for this chapter that the COVID-19 pandemic exposed how little organizations had been investing in emotional and mental health compared to physical health.

In short, in the lead-up to the COVID-19 pandemic, wellbeing had been about treating the symptoms of poor health and wellbeing, but we now can address some of the causes and create better experiences for all workers. One of the prime causes of poor health and wellbeing for remote and hybrid workers is likely to be poor work-life balance. This could be true for face-to-face workers too, but if these are unable to work remotely or in a hybrid way then organizations will need to provide similar or alternative support to those face-to-face workers. However, the impact of the COVID-19 pandemic is likely to mean that the wellbeing implications many forced remote workers experienced are continued as they move into hybrid work-ing arrangements or back to face-to-face working arrangements.

I've been a hybrid worker for over twenty years. As my family grew in this time, so did my level of seniority at work, and I found myself taking my smartphone on family holidays and, with increasing regularity, looking at emails and listening to voicemails in case there was anything important happening back at work. Again, with increasing regularity, I'd find myself responding to things too. I found it helpful from a work perspective most times, helping me to avoid having too much to do when I returned from holiday, but also on one level reinforcing (in my own head) my importance to the organization – that I had such an important job that I couldn't possibly be out of contact with the organization for a week or so.

One time I noticed glances from my wife as I did it and noticed that I was missing out on quality family time. What was helping me from a work perspective was adding stress I didn't need on a personal level. In short, I was wrong about how important I was – most people's work, and certainly mine, could cope for a long time, maybe forever, without a person being contactable.

> Following this revelation, I haven't replied to any work-related messages while on a family holiday since and found I have enjoyed each holiday more for 'being there'. After each holiday, as people at work would inevitably ask how it had been, I felt an initial guilt in saying that I'd had an enjoyable time but that a major reason for that was the decision to avoid work-related stuff for the duration.

In this example I show how poor work-life integration and balance was affecting my health and wellbeing as a hybrid worker, but I was able to take steps to address this. Similar principles affect other remote and hybrid workers too, but it may not be as easy for them to address it. Having one's home and work in the same location can be tricky and finding that separation and managing it in a way that doesn't detrimentally impact wellbeing is difficult. Let's look at what has worked and what hasn't for remote and hybrid workers in recent years.

WHAT HAS WORKED FOR REMOTE AND HYBRID WORKERS?

It seems clear that organizations must do more, and indeed many have, despite the research by Benefex highlighting that many haven't done enough. Going beyond the basic provision is certainly something that has worked, as we see in this next example.

> In an article in People Management, Laura Ibbotson from Heras outlined some of the things that had worked for her organization, which included (in addition to more traditional aspects like mental health first aid provision and an employee assistance programme):
>
> - Themed wellbeing communications.
> - A digital wellbeing hub containing a range of carefully curated resources.
> - Welfare calls from the people team to employees.
> - Family-friendly virtual competitions and quizzes.
> - An externally provided listening service.
>
> Ibbotson cited the welfare calls as being the most successful of these, appreciated by many employees and of course costing nothing other than staff time[3].

Remote and hybrid workers, beset by a range of issues impacting their wellbeing, have needed more support than previously provided to face-to-face workers. Giving people access to on-demand apps that help with wellbeing can be helpful. The Crown Prosecution Service brought in a wellbeing app, using an external company. This was downloadable to personal devices and asked employees to assess their current level of anxiety, providing them with a rating on a scale for depressive type illnesses. Scores above a certain level triggered a conversation with a qualified psychologist, either face-to-face or by digital means[4].

Using an app, or having externally provided support, has been seen to be very helpful but is no substitute for managers themselves being switched on the individual remote and hybrid worker wellbeing. Many organizations encouraged line managers to incorporate discussions around how people were feeling within regular performance conversations and saw the benefits of line managers going beyond simply asking if people were OK. In addition to this many of my clients have instituted peer support programmes, enabling stronger relationships between colleagues who may find it easier to talk to a peer compared to a manager.

This reinforces how important it is to have those strong personal relationships, regardless of who they are between. Humans need connections with other humans, and technology can help with this when working remotely. Aside from the social-type events that have been a staple of many remote and hybrid working experiences, simply having open virtual rooms throughout the working day where people can drop in and have a chat with whomever else is there have helped too.

Many organizations have made good use of data to find out about remote worker wellbeing, and the Crown Prosecution Service example above is a good case of enabling this, but there are other ways to find out how people feel.

In one organization where I worked, we had a lot of hybrid workers, and those who worked full time in the office were rare. As leaders we sometimes found it difficult to assess individual engagement and wellbeing or to get a feel for how the entire organization was feeling since we could usually only ascertain the views of those we saw that day.

I brought in a daily pulse mechanism, delivered on a straightforward app accessed via internal platforms. It asked just one question – 'How has your day been today?' – to which there were two possible responses – great, and awful.

This was an anonymous question and answer that we encouraged each employee to answer at the end of their day, and the results were then displayed on a graph the following day.

This was good because every employee could access it no matter where they had worked that day, and no matter when their day ended. The anonymity of the responses and the high-level graphs produced were helpful in encouraging people to contribute, and the visibility of the results to everyone helped spark discussions between teams and for managers with their direct reports. I set fellow senior leaders a challenge ahead of each meeting we had to have discussed the previous few days trends with as many people as possible and come ready to share what they had learnt.

The real-time feedback on how people were feeling gave us some interesting observations and we were able to track the impact of happenings in the organization on how people felt, and also see the impact of other factors too – for example on one Thursday there was a huge spike in how those who had been in the office had felt that day, but which didn't appear to have affected those working remotely. It transpired that an ice cream van had shown up in our car park that day and most office-based workers had had an ice cream on a hot day, whereas remote workers hadn't. While there is no hard evidence that it was the ice cream that led to the increased engagement on Thursdays, it was a good way to use the real-time feedback to explore the different experiences of face-to-face and remote workers.

In researching for this section, I spoke to many remote and hybrid workers who had benefitted from creating some artificial divides between their work and personal lives. Some said they put their work stuff in a box at the end of the day and physically put it away, finding that action helpful. Others talked about the value of a fake commute – a quick ten-minute walk – at both ends of the working day. I recognize the latter – I usually do a morning school run and then do a short run or swim before returning home to start work – and find having a routine for how I end the day also helps create the right divides.

WHAT UNEXPECTED ASPECTS OF WELLBEING HAVE SUFFERED FOR REMOTE AND HYBRID WORKERS?

There are several aspects of health and wellbeing where remote and hybrid workers have suffered more than face-to-face equivalents. We have already covered the now-blurred lines between home and work, but there are more.

Many surveys have pointed out how many adults have eaten less healthily since the COVID-19 pandemic began, particularly during lockdowns, which of course tie in with increased remote and hybrid working. People's routines changed completely from a daily commute into a face-to-face office and working at home may make it harder to stop for lunch or make it easier to snack through the day, or more difficult to take regular exercise. As a qualified personal trainer, I appreciate the difference that a quality nutrition and hydration routine can have on performance and productivity, and yet I also suffer from making bad decisions when working remotely. More guidance on this is needed for remote and hybrid workers, from healthy eating campaigns to regular prompts and reminders to take breaks.

Forced remote working during the COVID-19 pandemic has also affected physical health, specifically on musculoskeletal issues. This is something we have touched on in a previous chapter too – workstation and home-office assessments are even more important where the individual remote or hybrid worker is responsible for their own setup. A survey from the Institute of Employment Studies in 2021 showed that more than half of home workers reported new aches and pains, especially in the neck and back, but that only 40% said their employers had done any kind of home office risk assessment. Even things like ensuring remote and hybrid workers are provided with adjustable equipment and sufficient education on good posture will get around most of the issues here, but sadly not enough has been done.

It may also be necessary to help people look after their eyes due to the increased strain caused by longer screen usage for remote and hybrid workers – again there are relevant health and safety regulations on this but more needs to be done to educate all concerned of the risks for remote and hybrid workers. If this isn't addressed, it could lead to more severe impacts on employee health, which could be devastating to the employee and costly to the employer if found negligent.

HOW TO EMBED WELLBEING WITHIN REMOTE AND HYBRID TEAMS

As people professionals, we have multiple roles to play here. We have to provide some basic compliance-led and fundamental wellbeing initiatives but have to ensure these are properly tailored for remote and hybrid workers, and that line managers as well as all within their teams know some of the more important and effective ways to look after their wellbeing. Here are some suggestions:

- We should help managers to prioritise individual check-in meetings and to ensure that these happen.

- We should talk about our own wellbeing issues openly within organizations and to the line managers we support – about what works and what doesn't – and encourage line managers to do the same with their teams.

- We can ensure that teams agree ways of working, communicating and decision-making (covered in the previous chapter) that also cover how boundaries around working times are agreed and communicated, including breaks for lunch, focused time to get individual work done, start and end times to the day and ensuring that people take, and block time out for, holidays and other personal time.

- We can check in with as many people as possible and find out what they are concerned about in and outside work, and how they are looking after their own wellbeing – this can help to normalize such issues and discussions.

- We can be open about taking time during the working day to deal with domestic, family and other non-work issues and commitments, and that it is OK not to be contactable all the time or to spend time working at irregular hours – and if doing the latter, ensure that we convey that there is no expectation of a similarly-timed response.

- We can train managers on what they need to notice when leading remote and hybrid teams – subtle signals around communication, working hours, outputs, and more – and equipping them to have appropriate conversations about wellbeing.

- We can train employees on how to maintain a healthy work-life balance and work successfully in a remote or hybrid way. This may involve giving guidance on working hours and flexibility and juggling personal commitments.

- We could consider a triage type system for those experiencing mental health issues that provides different levels of support depending on how severe their symptoms are – from more regular check-ins and encouraging breaks, to reducing workload and hours, support on resilience and dealing with pressure and more.

We should also remember that remote and hybrid working is still relatively new for many people and organizations, and that mistakes can and will be made by all parties. No-one has all the right answers, and an iterative approach (call it beta testing if you like) is something to impress across the entire organization and ensure all know that it is something that everyone will work out together, as they go. If we do that, we will start to build more inclusion in our culture, which is another aspect of creating safe spaces for employees.

CASE STUDY

In this chapter we will look at two case studies, to underline the importance of wellbeing and safe spaces to the experience of remote and hybrid working.

Case Study One

I first came across much of the content of this case study in Jayne Harrison's wonderful Wellbeing Wednesday blog series, where a version of this was published in May 2021. Portions of that are reproduced with the kind permission of Jayne, and to explore related angles and bring it up to date I contacted the subject directly. The case study shows how very small organizations without access to the resources that larger organizations may have can make significant strides in supporting the wellbeing of remote and hybrid workers.

Anna Edmondson is the Chief People Officer at PowerONPlatforms, an IT services provider of around 40 staff based mostly in York. As a small employer, PowerON had never had anything as explicit as a wellbeing strategy however Edmondson stated that wellbeing is very much a part of their culture as opposed to something distinct, and something they try to do as well as much bigger organizations.

As you may expect from an IT services provider, their employees were capable of and to a degree well versed to working remotely and in a hybrid way before the COVID-19 pandemic hit. They, like many other organizations examined in this book, struggled to manage the additional home-schooling and caring responsibilities that suddenly came with it. As an organization they were incredibly busy supporting some of their clients in health and local government who were also very busy.

In the initial COVID-19 lockdowns, Anna's team sent care packages to employees – wine, chocolate and other small gifts. They also arranged for every child of an employee to receive a handwritten, personalized letter thanking them for the 'loan' of their parents. Neither of these things took much time or effort but both had a massive impact on both parents and children. The Chief Executive Officer of the organization takes a personal interest in every employee, and role models self-care. He ensures that he attends whatever social and wellbeing events are taking place, reinforcing that permission is given to take time out of work for such things.

In October 2020, the organization implemented the Weekly10 platform, prompting weekly check-ins for all employees on:

- Successes – what has worked well, what are you proud of?
- Challenges – what has been difficult, how can we make this better?
- How are you feeling?
- Giving thanks – who do you want to recognize for good work?
- Learning – what have you learnt this week? What future learning do you need?

This system encourages individual reflection and sharing of emotions and feelings. This is often cited in neuroscience research as something that positively impacts wellbeing. However, the system generates data which Edmondson and her team have been able to analyse and respond to. From this Edmondson introduced the 4Cs model:

- Comfort – creating a culture of safety in the workplace, of feeling safe to express ideas and challenge decisions without fear of ridicule.
- Contribution – tapping into the primal desire to feel valued, recognized and acknowledged.
- Connection – to encourage connections between colleagues to build trust and shared purpose.
- Compassion – promoting empathy and tolerance on an individual and team level.

At PowerON, questions and interventions were built around this model, with virtual sessions designed around it with break-out focus group type activities to take the organizational temperature around the key themes in the model.

The Weekly10 system generates a week-by-week snapshot of engagement and sentiment analysis. Individuals can track progress against goals and objectives, understand their unique contribution as they have line of sight to the bigger picture and connect to their line manager beyond standard questions such as 'how are you doing against target'.

Some of the added benefits have been that connections between line managers and their teams have strengthened because the one-to-one meetings are more detailed and positive. Edmondson believes that because the culture was already open and transparent, the system prompts around 'how are you' are welcomed.

Another outcome is that Edmondson and her team are able to get a timely overview of how things are regarding wellbeing so they can create supportive interventions to meet needs, with overwhelming support from the CEO.

Edmondson feels that implementing Weekly10 earlier would have been very beneficial. Using this responsive and interactive virtual platform has had a clear impact on engagement and wellbeing, especially around connections with colleagues. Remote working, in Edmondson's view, shifted wellbeing from being a nice to have to a business essential. Their entire business was built on personal relationships, and remote (and later hybrid) working forced PowerON to focus more on this and be creative about maintaining relationships in order to keep morale high.

PowerON have also introduced mental health first aid provision remotely, and a wellbeing hub accessible to all remote employees, but the culture and general explicit focus on wellbeing means that employees feel more comfortable to talk to the employer when they are struggling and know that the employer has the skills to support them.

We see in this case study how much culture matters, how much wellbeing is less about specific initiatives and interventions for remote and hybrid workers, and how it is much more about mindset and leadership competency, illustrating points made earlier in this chapter. At PowerON, people primarily needed to know that they matter, that their individual challenges and successes were seen, that support was available if they needed it, and that being vulnerable and admitting vulnerability was not something that would lead to a negative reaction.

Case Study Two

In our second case study we look at a larger organization with a different culture, and look at what makes a difference with wellbeing in organizations.

Morna Bunce is Chief People Office at Stowe Family Law, a law firm of around 225 people based mostly in Harrogate but with employees across the UK, and who have gained some publicity around their Wellness Days policy during the COVID-19 pandemic (Figure 8.1).

I asked Bunce what she had learnt about wellbeing in general since the onset of increased remote and hybrid working. She believes that any wellbeing initiative can be undermined by events happening elsewhere in the organization or even other people practices – the standalone initiatives appear to be paying lip service to the idea if they don't reflect the reality of working life. The Wellness Days introduced in

FIGURE 8.1 Wellness leave @ Stowe

Wellness Leave @ STOWE

What is this?

These are dedicated days to look after your mental wellness. We're here to help you find balance and we recognise that sometimes the pressures of work, life and other factors can sometimes be overwhelming. That's where Wellness leave comes in.

We trust you

We're all adults, that's why we trust that you will use this leave when you need to. We believe in honesty, and that's why we trust that employees will use this leave in the spirit it is intended, as standalone days to support your personal wellbeing. Whatever you chose to do during these days is your choice, but we trust that you are taking care of yourselves.

Examples of when you might take it

We're all individual and our reasons for using this leave will be just as individual, but to help guide you here's a few examples of why you may use this leave:

- For a day that has special meaning such as an anniversary of a bereavement, or birthday of a loved one who is no longer with us
- If a beloved pet passes away
- When you're feeling overwhelmed; or things are getting on top of you
- To recharge

Our key principles of Wellness leave

Employees are able to use 2 days per calendar year:

- Days to be taken as whole, standalone days
- Not all Wellness days can be pre-planned; and that's fine, sometimes life takes over and that's what this is intended for
- We will record wellness leave to monitor uptake and engagement to this benefit

Eligibility

All employees who have passed their probationary period are eligible to Wellness leave. Time not taken within the calendar year cannot be accumulated or carried forward.

How much Wellness leave can I take ?

Employees can take up to a maximum of 2 working days of paid leave for personal wellness

Who to contact

We understand that it's important to speak to somebody who you feel comfortable with, as every relationship is different.

Here are a few contact options for you to consider when reporting your wellness leave:

- Get in touch with your manager (direct or indirect)
- Speak to a trained MH champion; or
- a member of the People Team.

2021 were initially very well-received and seemed to be sending a strong message to employees that the organization cared for them and that employee wellbeing was important, reflecting a conscious shift in Stowe's people practices towards a more adult-adult approach.

However, as the initiative started to come to life it became apparent that Bunce's team hadn't joined up all the dots with colleagues in other departments. The best example of this was that the organization hadn't thought about how they reported on lawyer productivity (for anyone not familiar the traditional way output in law firms is measured is in billable units of six minutes). This meant that when a lawyer took a wellness day this wasn't accounted for in Stowe's management information, appearing to reduce their average output measurement which in turn would impact their bonus outcome at the end of the year. Unintentionally, Stowe had placed lawyers under marginally more pressure to achieve their productivity targets which meant they were reluctant to take wellness days.

This example perfectly illustrates how wellbeing initiatives are better positioned as part of an overall cultural shift and not as standalone activities. Bunce's feedback mechanisms were quick to pick up on this, and they have begun addressing it – there is now a conscious effort to challenge, across the longer-term, the ways that productivity and performance are judged, away from a traditional way of measuring output and towards a more sustainable alternative. This is something I feel many organizations, now beginning to judge remote and hybrid workers on output and outcomes, will need to address in future also.

To do this effectively, Bunce feels (and I agree) that people professionals need to listen to, and understand, what is happening on the front line of their organizations – and to understand what support people need to be effective in their roles. Bunce points out that in remote or hybrid environments this is more critical as many managers won't necessarily have 'eyes on' their teams all the time to pick up on the right signals.

Bunce's experience at Stowe reinforces that wellbeing is no longer the preserve of people professionals and is something everyone needs to take some level of responsibility for. For example, Stowe are transitioning to a more team-based way of working. It means employees can take annual leave and know that their clients and cases are being managed by someone else who knows just as much about the case as them and has a relationship with the client. It means that junior lawyers aren't shouldering the burden of their caseload alone. In the legal profession, burnout is a very real problem for junior lawyers, and Stowe lost a disproportionate number of junior lawyers during 2020-2021. While Bunce feels there were some external factors at play, it also highlighted that, at Stowe at least, they simply did not have the right support mechanisms in place for the employees to thrive in a remote working environment.

To make this work, Stowe and Bunce are working on several things. As the previous paragraph shows, teamworking is a huge part of this. They have also tightened up on induction processes so that they have a programme which works much better in a hybrid workplace and involves line managers in a much more hands-on role instead of it being delivered via the People team.

Stowe has also been working to create organic opportunities for development – for things they feel cannot be replaced by a virtual meeting. Their approach to hybrid working is their Dynamic Working Charter which relies on a series of principles, one of which is that some activities are better undertaken face-to-face. Managers and their teams are encouraged to work together to adopt a working pattern which facilitates overlap in the office to meet the needs of the whole team.

In response to the feedback to wellness days, reward is another key area being looked at. Stowe are now asking themselves if they are driving behaviours such as leavism and presenteeism by glamourising and rewarding unsustainable levels of over performance? They are now transitioning to a reward mechanism which is more values-based.

Bunce commented that to get wellbeing right for remote and hybrid workers, Stowe needed to look at every aspect of the employee lifecycle with a critical eye and ask if there is another, better, way. In her view, wellbeing interventions such as Stowe's wellness days have their place, but she feels organizations run the risk of virtue signalling in this space without really tackling the underlying systemic issues. At Stowe, they've come a long way from free fruit (although that was always popular for those in face-to-face roles). Bunce observes that her team of people professionals have to resist the urge to default to adopting the role of caregiver.

At Stowe, the role of line managers is now critical, reinforcing discussions elsewhere in this chapter. Says Bunce: 'Managers have to understand what support mechanisms are in place where they work so they can ensure their team can access them when required. They have to role model. It's sometimes the only way to give people permission, regardless of what a policy says. If a line manager is demonstrating behaviours such as leaveism then that is the culture that pervades.'

As a result, Bunce is now focusing on how people are prepared for managerial positions. As you'll no doubt have experienced, too often people are promoted into managerial positions on the strength of their technical – and not their leadership – ability. Bunce recognized that Stowe had been guilty of this in the past and has now invested significantly to build leadership capability among line managers. They have been more explicit with managers exactly what is expected from them in face-to-face, remote and hybrid working environments, and have put in place an ongoing rolling programme of masterclasses to learn new skills, refresh on processes and learn from other managers. Added to that Stowe are also looking at how to better prepare people for promotion and people management responsibilities. This is in part via formal development programmes but also through creating opportunities for people to be exposed to mentoring and supervising others early on in their careers.

As we have explored in this and other chapters in this book, the role of a line manager in remote and hybrid teams is even more critical – and different – than that of a face-to-face line manager. The boundaries between life and work are blurred. Bunce commented that 'while the benefits of increased flexibility are undeniable, work increasingly bleeds into home life and that price is too high. While we wish to encourage flexibility with choice, empowering our colleagues to choose when and where they work to better suit them that doesn't mean we can completely throw out the rule book which is why we have developed our Dynamic Working Charter to guide managers and their teams. We support our managers to employ relatively simple strategies to try and reinstate those boundaries.'

Some things that Stowe have included in this rulebook to enable remote and hybrid teams to focus on their wellbeing reinforce things covered in earlier chapters around (re)setting team rules around communication, ways of working and more.

Case study reflections

In the first case study the following things stand out as key learning points for us to consider:

- Improving wellbeing is not something that need take up lots of resources, and can be done on a small scale through changes to organizational culture.

- Small gestures and showing humanity and empathy (and humour) can make a big difference to people.

- Leadership from the very top of the organization around wellbeing is an important signal for everyone else.

- Simple, regular check-ins work well for all concerned and improve focus on wellbeing.

- Data helps to generate improvements if used in the right ways.

In the second case study the following things stand out as key learning points for us to consider:

- Standalone wellbeing initiatives can often fail simply because they are standalone, and not integrated into the organization.

- Organizations need to consider whether their wellbeing initiatives are verging on virtue signalling or are genuine attempts to help and provide support.

- If the provision of wellbeing can impact how productivity and performance is measured, it can be counter-productive.

- Building team-based working can be helpful on several levels, but from a wellbeing perspective it can help address isolation and feelings of being the only person who can do certain duties.

- Addressing wellbeing for remote and hybrid workers is likely to need other parts of the employee lifecycle to be similarly addressed and aligned

- The role of line managers is once again shown to be critical, and the right support and guidance needs to be given to them.

The action plan

If you need the remote and hybrid working environment to be a safe space for your workers and their wellbeing, here are some questions to get you thinking how to do this:

- What does your existing data tell you about the proportion of your remote and hybrid workers who are experiencing, or have experienced, poor mental health recently?

- How central to your organizational strategy is the wellbeing of your employees? How well do senior leaders understand the links between wellbeing and productivity/performance?

- What proportion of your overall approach to wellbeing treats the symptoms of poor health, and what proportion treats the causes? How can you shift this more towards the latter?

- What guidance do you need to give to remote and hybrid workers about managing the divide between their personal and professional lives?

- How could you replicate the intent and effect of welfare calls (that some organizations did for remote workers during COVID-19 lockdowns) for your remote and hybrid workers?

- How could you better measure the mental health of your remote and hybrid workers?

- What do you need managers to be able and willing to do in creating the right environment in their remote and hybrid teams to support wellbeing? How will you equip them to do that?

- How can you equip your people professionals to curate and provide guidance on things like hydration, nutrition, musculoskeletal and vision issues?

- What cultural signals need to be sent to give remote and hybrid workers confidence and reassurance that it can be OK to deal with personal issues during working time, or to adjust working time accordingly to enable better division between their personal and working lives?

- If you implemented a triage style system of support for those suffering from poor health and wellbeing, what would be in the different tiers?

- What is your approach going to be to senior leaders in your organization to get them more engaged with the things they need to do to ensure the wellbeing of remote and hybrid workers?

Sketchnote summary

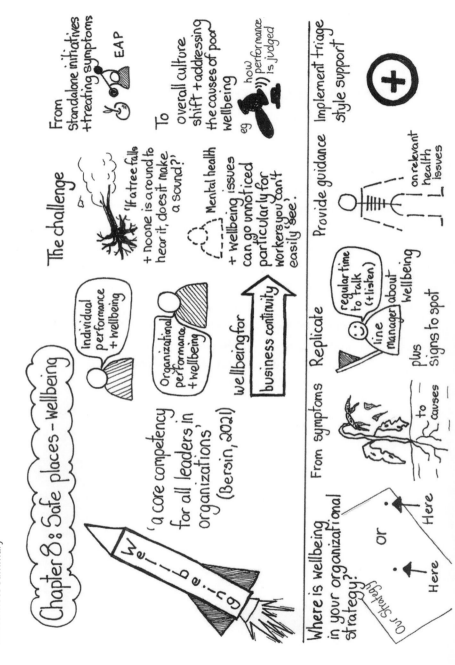

09

Safe spaces – inclusion and belonging

The shorter read

In the last chapter we looked at how we prioritize the health and wellbeing of such workers, as well as all other employees, but in this one, we look at how we ensure that remote and hybrid working addresses barriers to inclusion and doesn't create them, and how we instil a sense of belonging for people, no matter what their working routine or environment.

A key aspect of creating a safe space for remote and hybrid workers is the creation and nurturing of a diverse and inclusive culture. While remote and hybrid working can remove some barriers for employees, they can (directly and indirectly) create them as well. A poor focus on inclusion can impact specific groups. Having the correct things in place can help these same, and other, groups to feel more included in the workplace. Things like using data, providing more structure and involvement opportunities, demonstrating empathy and sensitivity, and more, will all help remote and hybrid workers feel included.

But will this be enough to make them feel safe? Hopefully, but the need for safety is affected by other things besides what we have mentioned already. People need to not just feel well, and feel included, but feel like they belong. Belonging matters as it is fundamental to our ability as human beings to thrive and survive. There are often common denominators that shape someone's feeling of belonging and the creation of a psychologically safe space, and while these things are not unique to the remote and hybrid working environment, they can become more pronounced and necessary for such workers.

Creating the sense of belonging but also making someone feel unique and special both have roles to play in creating safe spaces for remote and hybrid workers. This can be achieved through developing line managers' ability and willingness to be human.

The longer read

Inclusion

Key to providing a safe space for all employees is the ability to create and nurture a diverse and inclusive culture. Many organizations did this successfully before the COVID-19 pandemic and others struggled with it, as some media stories have shown. However, what may not be fully appreciated is the impact that remote and hybrid working has on diversity and inclusion in organizations. It improves it in some respects and makes it potentially worse in others. In this section we will look at both and consider what people professionals need to do as a result.

I will start by sharing my view that having a diverse and inclusive culture goes hand in hand with having a truly amazing workplace where employees are highly engaged. If you focus the right way on engagement, you'll get a diverse and inclusive culture, and vice versa. Therefore, many of the things we cover in this book are all likely to help diversity and inclusion, without specifically focusing on it. There are times, though, when specifically focusing on it is necessary. It is a truism that you reap what you sow at work, in every sense. If organizations are willing to put the effort and energy to make the workplace amazing and inclusive, they'll achieve it. If they are not, they won't, and it won't be a safe space either.

WHERE REMOTE AND HYBRID WORKING HELPS DIVERSITY AND INCLUSION

The ability to work remotely, whether full time or in a hybrid way, is likely to help inclusion for several groups of people. Requiring a job to be done in the office is likely to disadvantage these groups.

While there are potential negative impacts on women, with the majority of those with primary family care responsibilities being women, removing the requirement for a daily commute is likely to have a positive impact on those responsibilities. It isn't just women who could benefit either. Anyone with any kind of caring responsibilities who can do more of that, or do what they always have but better, is more likely to be more engaged with their employer, and more productive as a result. Working asynchronously can be beneficial for those with caring responsibilities too.

> For me, as a father of four, hybrid working has made many things possible for me that a constant daily commute would prevent. It allows me to manage at least half of the school runs each week as well as allowing me to attend some school activities that parents are invited to that always seem to take place during the working day.
>
> I started one new role and could no longer undertake hybrid working (and sometimes including a stay overnight to get to offices in far flung places) – my health suffered, my marriage suffered, and my performance suffered. Suddenly, my wife had to take on the full burden of caring responsibilities, and she and her work suffered too. As soon as I could I left that organization and restored what balance we had.

There can also be positive impacts on those with disabilities, for whom commuting may prove a major challenge, and may also find the physical set-up of offices difficult. Jane Blade, Compliance Manager at the Gambling Commission, told me that her physical disability made remote working preferable and the trend for many jobs to now be advertised as remote first has to a degree levelled the playing field for those with disabilities. Annette Lewis, Learning Partner at AstraZeneca agreed – stating that remote and hybrid working was better for those with neurodivergent characteristics, and for those with hidden disabilities too. Jon Robinson, Operational HR Manager within the NHS felt that remote working allows those with mental health issues or sensory overload to manage such things. Many of these barriers can start to be overcome by having more control over their home workspace and schedule.

Remote working particularly, if done fully, can bring with it greater cultural diversity by allowing employees to be recruited from a variety of geographically dispersed locations. The ability to contribute asynchronously and in many cases without being physically seen can also help to minimize the risk of bias in how such contributions (and by extension the employees) are perceived.

Meetings that are entirely virtual, regardless of whether its participants are in the office or remote, will normally be more equal a platform for employees, as it is harder for the louder (or closer to the leader) voices to dominate, and can provide more equal representation. Using digital means of communication (especially without cameras) can equalize employee voice and ensure everyone is heard. Again, it minimizes the risk of unconscious bias changing perceptions of employee contributions. Virtual meetings may also be easier for larger (and more diverse) groups of people to attend than face-to-face meetings could be – geographical proximity to (or ability to attend) the office no longer being a barrier. This also opens up improved chances to see and hear from senior leaders in organizations.

These are all potential positives, but not necessarily definite positives – careful management of the remote and hybrid working arrangements in place is needed, and people professionals should ensure that they are able to assess whether these potential positives are being realized. Otherwise, some of the downsides of remote and hybrid working from an inclusion perspective could be realized instead.

WHERE REMOTE AND HYBRID WORKING CAN HINDER DIVERSITY AND INCLUSION

While there are some groups that can benefit from remote and hybrid working, this is of course a doubled-edged sword and those who do more – or exclusive – remote and hybrid working could be less visible to organizational leaders, less involved in decision-making and less active in organizational life. This needs careful management too and ensuring that the playing field is level when employees work face-to-face in the office, in a hybrid way or fully remote. This means giving them the same access to opportunities and equipment, and ensuring they feel as if they are valued and can contribute to the organization regardless of where they are based.

One piece of research strongly suggested that the COVID-19 pandemic and associated home-schooling had a greater detrimental impact on women than it did men, as women tended to take up more domestic duties than their male partners[1], and this may make it much harder to include those who balance domestic with professional responsibilities. That it may, but it does not make it impossible.

Those with disabilities may need additional support to work effectively remotely – speech to text software, specialist phones, or even interpreters may be required. While this may be no different than what is necessary in the face-to-face working environment, it could easily be assumed (wrongly) that an individuals' home workspace is already set up for such things, leading to further exclusion.

Digital divides have also become apparent during the COVID-19 pandemic, for people of almost any characteristic whether protected or not. Not everyone has an environment suitable for remote working and may have to share space and equipment with others. Not everyone has reliable and stable internet connections, or their own devices to properly access their work. Many people may feel embarrassed at their lack of access to suitable spaces and equipment, and perhaps even their lack of skill and knowledge of how to work remotely. Organizations need to take their responsibilities for ensuring an effective remote working environment carefully.

HOW DO PEOPLE PROFESSIONALS ENHANCE DIVERSITY AND INCLUSION FOR REMOTE AND HYBRID WORKERS?

I have worked in an organization that has fully embraced and made diversity and inclusion work and many of the lessons I learnt there apply now to remote and hybrid working environments too.

- Using data. This goes beyond compliance but using data to drive service improvement and engagement. In my organization we used data to target and evidence improvement, rather than as a stick to beat ourselves with. For example, many people professionals will have access to data showing who has taken special leave, who has left, who had been furloughed, who had been promoted, recognized and rewarded (Dale, 2021), and this data may tell a story about how remote and hybrid working is affecting particular groups.

- Provide development. This may be for line managers on unconscious bias and addressing stigma, or for all employees using innovative methods (I have seen drama-based training work particularly well here).

- Give line managers some structure. Help them to maintain informal records of how frequently they are engaging with their team members, and review this with them when appropriate. This data can build over time to be as useful in assignment of responsibilities and assessing how rewards are being distributed, to show whether remote or hybrid workers are being consciously or subconsciously excluded.

- Involvement in decision-making. In my organization I set up various listening and involvement groups for staff with different characteristics. These allowed them to voice any concerns they had and for the organization to act upon these, as well as celebrate any successes. Using such groups to focus on the remote and hybrid experience for those with shared characteristics could identify whether there is equitable access for all, as well as building some of the social connections necessary to combat feelings of isolation, loneliness, and exclusion.

- Be sensitive. If face-to-face events and meetings are to take place, help managers to schedule them at times that are less likely to impact individual caring responsibilities, and at inclusive locations also.

- Being inclusive. Educate line managers to avoid prioritizing employees who are face-to-face with them, and to keep group events virtual. Provide them with technological solutions that allow team members to work asynchronously when appropriate and aid collaboration by standardizing the way teams work across remote and hybrid environments.

Helping remote and hybrid workers feel safe

As we have explored in this chapter, and to a degree in others earlier in the book, the experience for remote and hybrid workers can be a different one to those working face-to-face, and such workers can be exposed to loneliness, anxiety and a greater feeling of stress than their face-to-face equivalents. The impact that remote and hybrid working can have on organizational approaches to improving diversity and inclusion is equally considerable, and both, if done well, help an employee to feel safe at work.

The need for safety is an important human desire. The need to belong within a group is a strong motivator too, and the two when met can create significant engagement. As organizations grapple with remote and hybrid working, they need to consciously create an environment and organizational culture where all can flourish, not just a select few. In this section we will explore some of the important aspects of safety and belonging in the remote and hybrid world of work.

My own approach to looking after my mental health now often involves physical exercise. It is my way of processing the emotions I need to when I'm working remotely and is even more important when I'm away from home – my work takes me to all kinds of places and one of the first things I work out when I know where I'm heading is whether there's somewhere I can exercise. I know I'll be without my usual support network (i.e. my family) when I'm there so physical exercise takes on increased importance.

However, when I was in an employed position and working in a hybrid manner, one of the most important things to me there was close friendships at work, and with one person who lived close to me and with whom I car shared each day to and from work. He, too, was a hybrid worker, and we managed to work our schedules so that our office days coincided.

Everyone, no matter what their role, needs someone to whom they can talk and have a bit of a rant or moan to now and again, someone who will keep these discussions private and who will both support and challenge. Both my car sharer friend and I were senior leaders at our organization, and we car shared for over ten years. Spending two hours a day together in a confined space, three days a week for ten years – you become close, you end up telling each other almost everything and you come to rely very much on that person as a source of support and guidance.

Most journeys home from work were each of us telling the other what we'd done that day and, on the occasions where we'd interacted in the workplace, discussing how those things had gone – discussing our views on other people's behaviour, our own behaviours, our view of the organization and its direction, and almost everything to do with what was causing us to feel emotion at work. We coached each other, challenged each other, argued occasionally but always felt much better at the end of the journey. This helped me to download my emotion and get home able to focus on what was important there, without having to bore people at home with it all or being distracted.

I needed that, and so did he. As hybrid workers it helped us both to arrive at the physical workplace in a better state, and to arrive home likewise feeling better. On days when we both worked remotely, we would often spend time on the phone doing the same kind of interactions. And when we both left the organization and couldn't car share any more, both our levels of mental health suffered a little.

What I'm reinforcing in this example above is how simply the wellbeing and feeling of safety and belonging for remote and hybrid workers could be provided. It is about connection – about feeling safe enough to open up to other people. I achieved it via car sharing on my non-remote days and building a friendship, but we need to ensure all remote and hybrid workers can do something that does similar for them. Work is done best when we have close friendships with those we work with. For remote and hybrid workers this may be about creating opportunities to socialize and develop friendships more outside of formal work events.

WHY BELONGING MATTERS

The concept of belonging is fundamental to our ability as human beings to thrive and survive. If created, it can help to prevent many of the issues felt by remote and hybrid workers such as anxiety and loneliness. An article written by Jeremy Snape, interviewing leading performance coach Owen Eastwood, summed it up well – our ability to survive across millennia has been determined by how well humans can work together and take care of each other, and the need to belong is an express of that reality – not feeling a sense of belonging can see one's health suffer[2]. I would suggest that we are pushing at the open door that is an employee's desire to fit in and contribute to a group, to unlock motivation.

I have seen belonging manifest itself in different ways. In a speech I gave to the CIPD Northern Area Partnership Conference in 2016, I talked about someone wanting to fit in being influenced by the attitudes of the people around them, in that the feeling of belonging can be enhanced by things that other people do. I've belonged to various teams in the workplace and the sporting world and have often felt complete belonging and the opposite – complete isolation. In both extremes it has been the attitude of my teammates that has had the greatest impact on my feelings.

Based on my own experiences, I feel there are certain things that help employees to feel as if they belong in the workplace:

- Mutual respect with their manager.
- Having opportunities to socialize with colleagues (and being encouraged to do so, whether they end up doing so or not).
- Feeling like the organization wants them there, need them to do something and that their skills are respected.

These things aren't unique to the face-to-face environment and can be replicated for remote and hybrid workers, and indeed reinforce many things already discussed in this book. Key, then, to installing the sense of belonging are the things that managers and team-mates do to create it (or not). Individuals who don't get these things will be susceptible to anxiety and can't be themselves or thrive in that environment. This isn't about being friends with everyone all the time or straight away – in my car-sharing example it took many months to get to that point, and the car sharing didn't start until we'd known each other for about a year. But as new people come into our organization, and particularly if these are remote or hybrid workers, we need to ensure they are welcomed and brought into the team straight away.

In a remote or hybrid environment this requires a degree of proactivity and humanity from all concerned. This means that to create – and foster – the sense of belonging we need to focus on establishing and maintaining relationships on a social level and prompting contact between people even when there are no work issues to discuss.

In a previous organization, as a new starter and hybrid worker (and senior leader), I tried building relationships with my new senior colleagues by using my time in the office to simply catch up with them individually over a coffee. The reaction of three colleagues stood out to me.

- One was thrilled, reacting in the way I'd hoped and the way I'd have reacted – we quickly bonded and became good friends outside work too.

- Another was surprised and a little suspicious at first but grew into the arrangement and found it beneficial for his mental health.

- The third flat out refused to do it as soon as they realized that there would be no agenda or work-related aim for the meeting and stated that they were not at work to have meetings that did not provide them with any tangible output. Suffice to say, we didn't get on after that!

STANDING OUT FROM THE CROWD

As a counterpoint, there are views that standing out from the crowd and actively going against prevailing views can build confidence, aid perception of competence and, if one can express oneself authentically, increase engagement and commitment to organizations. There is something in that – the desire to fit in is strong, but we don't want to encourage conformity or groupthink, so managers need to put extra effort into encouraging nonconformity and recognizing diverse views and opinions, making it OK for people to be themselves and be different, to help people identify the unique ways they can contribute to the group, and bring their own diverse strengths to that group.

Therefore, the feeling of being safe can be dependent both on an employee's sense of belonging and their sense of feeling special and unique. If that makes sense to you, you'll also be thinking that it makes things more complicated, and you'd be right. There is a real challenge for managers of remote and hybrid workers to ensure that they connect socially with the whole team and feel like they are a valuable part of that team, but somehow also encourage that person to bring their unique strengths to their work.

A hybrid-working Director I once worked with really stood out as being quite different to anyone else in the organization. He was creative, innovative, thought constantly about the future, but consequently not about the present. He was awesome at initiating new things and bringing new ideas into the organization, a real blue-sky thinker, but unfortunately not at seeing them through to fruition or (often) thinking about the practicalities of implementing his ideas. He was the only such person in the organization and yet, irrespective of his position of authority, he was perceived as having a higher status and being more competent than others in the organization, including other people at the same level as him. He also was very vocal about his ideas and enjoyed being isolated and having to argue his position – he gained confidence from this and always came across as supremely confident. And because the organization gave him time, space and freedom to develop his ideas and express them in very public ways, backing him, he became very committed to the organization and its causes, a true organizational champion and defender.

In the example above I am drawing a distinction between feeling special, and being recognized as having different strengths and characteristics, and I would suggest that the latter is the more powerful motivator and something for managers of remote and hybrid workers to focus on – to lead teams in a way that encourages that diversity.

This need to recognize difference is also key to creating safe spaces for employees, and for remote and hybrid workers this can manifest itself in lots of different ways – for example we may be setting up a face-to-face event for a team but need to recognize that some people will feel very uncomfortable with face-to-face events or be unable to attend it because of some other personal circumstances. These people may not feel comfortable speaking up about such things, and we want them to – so the need for safe spaces where people feel both healthy and included is paramount.

SAFETY

Writing for the Harvard Business Review, Amy Edmondson established that the concept of psychological safety as a critical driver of high-quality decision-making, healthy group dynamics and interpersonal relationships, greater innovation, and more effective organizations[3]. She also acknowledged how difficult this was to create, and it could easily be said that remote and hybrid working make this even more difficult. The line between work and life is, as we have explored in this book, blurred, and managers of teams need to factor both into their decision-making, creating additional layers of complexity.

At the end of the previous section, I mentioned how individual circumstances may dictate working arrangements. They certainly used to for me when I began hybrid working – the days I chose to work remotely were days when my then-two children were staying with me, and days when I worked in the physical office were days that they were with my ex-wife. Changing these arrangements was possible, but only with enough notice and only if my ex-wife's circumstances allowed for the change. I worked in one organization where everyone knew that and it was easy for me to talk openly about such things, but in another organization if I voiced any concerns about changing plans at short notice, I was told to be quiet and stop moaning. My experience of hybrid working was therefore different in different places, as was the concept of psychological safety – but the point is that these types of individual circumstances apply to almost all remote and hybrid workers, and managers need to factor them into their own decision-making and communication. If they do not, then the employee is likely to feel disengaged, as indeed I did.

I would recommend that we, as people professionals, encourage managers to have open discussions about the challenges that come with remote and hybrid working from all sides – this involves transparency and honesty from managers and as people professionals we need to support and develop managers to be able to do this. This may involve managers taking risks and sharing their own vulnerabilities and circumstances, so that others feel the same and reciprocate. It will build trust.

We also need to ensure that all concerned see initial working arrangements as a constantly evolving picture, and that individuals may not initially feel comfortable sharing their own vulnerabilities. Going back to my car sharing example from earlier in this section – it took a long time for both of us to open up to each other, but we knew it didn't have to happen straight away and didn't force it either – so when either of us did share something, we both knew that that needed to be welcomed so that more sharing would follow.

It is also important that if people do share their vulnerabilities that they are not shot down. My experience in one workplace was to be shot down for asking for more remote working on a temporary basis because I was dealing with a pregnant (and sick) wife and a mum undergoing chemotherapy. I didn't share anything ever again in that organization and left soon after.

Finally, we need to ensure that the language used within the organization when implementing hybrid working is helpful and not harmful. Certain phrases (such as 'we could really use you in the office for this meeting') could put psychological pressure on employees to accept, and to create feelings of resentment. Additional guidance for managers and coaching on their language – both subtle and overt – could really help.

Put simply, we need to create safe spaces for all employees, but remote and hybrid working makes that more complicated. In the following case study, we will look at some lessons learnt particularly around wellbeing and the cultural aspects that are important.

CASE STUDY

In this case study I've spoken to an ex-colleague and diversity and inclusion expert, Cam Kinsella. She is now a Director of the Aster Foundation, a charitable department of the Aster Group (currently working towards charity registration to become an independent entity) which has over 1,000 employees, located in the south of the UK. Kinsella's focus through her whole career being around inclusion and overcoming barriers for people, whether that be employees, service users or stakeholders.

Prior to the COVID-19 pandemic, the entire Aster Group already offered a flexible approach to work which meant different things for different roles. Kinsella explained that the pandemic had accelerated the pace at which the organization moved towards its 'virtual first' model. This meaning that where possible – virtual will be the way at which meetings will be conducted unless there is a need not to. This approach also being experimented with in non-stereotypical roles such as engineers or lettings colleagues which previously were wholly face-to-face. The Group have instead been trialling technology to diagnose repairs/ view homes – which means such roles can be opened up to a wider array of talent, particularly among those who could not have applied previously due to their physical limitations. Kinsella rightly views this as a big positive in inclusion terms.

Kinsella feels that socioeconomic inequalities have been noticeable with remote and hybrid working. Some of colleagues lack a designated space to work due to their accommodation type, meaning that they didn't have the helpful 'change of scenery' to allow them some kind of separation between their home and working lives. This was further exacerbated by having children at home at the same time. In response, Aster really pushed the flexible working approach – encouraging employees working remotely or in a hybrid way to set their own working hours and patterns, within reason. This resulted in a better connected workforce with employees able to see that the organization genuinely cares about their needs with recent colleague survey results showing that employees do believe the organization cares about their mental wellbeing.

One unexpected positive socioeconomic change as a result of remote and hybrid working was the reduced reliance on needing one's own transport to get to and undertake work. Not only is this great for the decarbonization agenda, it's also helpful for people with certain disabilities who are unable to drive and/or those in financial hardship to be able to work on an equal footing with others, and Kinsella feels Aster's roles will only be more inclusive as a result.

Kinsella stated that remote and hybrid working gives many working mothers with young children the flexibility to progress in the workplace while balancing caring responsibilities, and as a working (step) mother herself feels that Aster's virtual first approach – in essence, allowing employees to work from any place at any time to suit their personal and professional needs – has brought benefits to her own work/ life balance. She believes that for working mothers, the opportunity to stay working and flourish in their careers during the years in which they are also raising children has the potential to be truly transformative in increasing female representation in leadership roles and closing the gender pay gap. Within Aster, two-thirds of executive positions are held by women, all of whom are open about being mothers/ carers and are extremely positive role models.

Finally, Kinsella feels that at Aster, remote and hybrid working has removed some location bias. For example, roles that cover particular geographic locations no longer need someone to be based in that location – Kinsella has recruited colleagues from the North of the UK to cover locations in the South of the UK, something that would never previously have happened. Says Kinsella: 'Different geographies, different social circles, different voices – (remote and hybrid working) opens up a world of different conversations and access to diversity of thought which we may not have tapped into as easily before,'

Case study reflections

The Aster case study is an interesting one looking at some of the positives and negatives around inclusion and belonging in organizations. Some key points stand out:

- Moving to remote and hybrid working **will** impact diversity and inclusion. Knowing your employee base – now, and how you would like it to be in the future – is helpful to ascertain the level of impact.

- As some jobs, or parts of jobs, become more remotely delivered, those with disabilities may find some barriers reduced or eliminated. This may mean that jobs could be carved up to enable their delivery by those whose needs mean that they are fully remote. Therefore, it may require a different approach to job crafting, in that job duties are what are considered for remote and hybrid working rather than jobs.

- Remote and hybrid working will expose, but also help to address, socio-economic issues in the workplace.

- I feel it may be difficult to see the impact of this in the short-term, but may be possible to see the longer-term impact of remote and hybrid working on inclusion and diversity through tracking representation and pay data in the workplace.

The action plan

If you need the remote and hybrid working environment to be a safe space for your workers, here are some questions to get you thinking how to do this:

Inclusion

- What aspects of inclusion are impacted where you have jobs that can only be done in the office, or done remotely? How do you know?

- What guidance can you give to managers on how to manage virtual meetings and events so that all feel included?

- What support can you give remote or hybrid workers with caring responsibilities so that they do not feel excluded from any aspect of working life?

- What support can you give to those with disabilities that ensures that the remote and hybrid working experience benefits and does not hinder them?

- How can you become more aware of digital divides and exclusion in your employee population, and what can you do to address it?

- What data do you need to collect about the inclusion impact of remote and hybrid working, and how will you collect it?

- How could you create a situation where parts or aspects of jobs are able to be done remotely instead of whole jobs?

- What commitments to improving the lives of all employees can remote and hybrid working support in your organization?

- What is your best approach to convincing senior leaders of the benefits of remote and hybrid working on inclusion?

Belonging

- How do you encourage friendship in employees, particularly those working in a remote or hybrid way? How can you create situations and structures where friendship can naturally occur?

- What steps does your organization need to take to identify, recognize and promote the unique talents that individuals have? How can you do that for remote and hybrid workers in a way that doesn't disadvantage them?

- How psychologically safe is your remote and hybrid working experience? How do you know?

- What is your best advice to senior leaders on how to ensure that remote and hybrid workers feel as if they belong in the organization?

Sketchnote summary

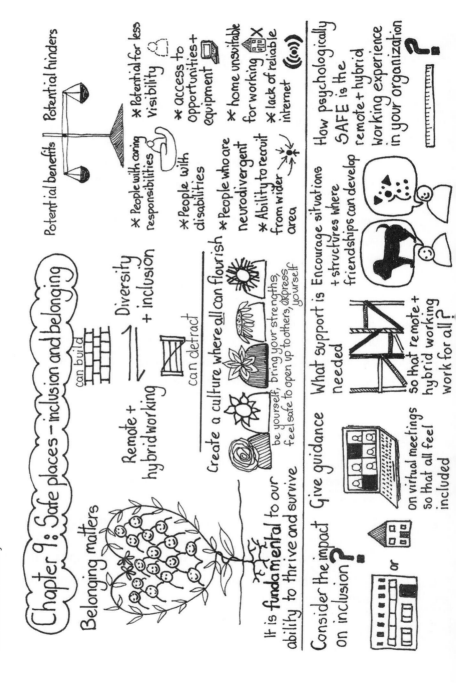

Chapter 9: Safe places – inclusion and belonging

Belonging matters

It is **fundamental** to our ability to thrive and survive

Remote + hybrid working

can build → Diversity + inclusion

can detract

Create a culture where all can flourish
be yourself, bring your strengths, express yourself
feel safe to open up to others, express yourself

Potential benefits | **Potential hinders**

Potential benefits:
* People with caring responsibilities
* People with disabilities
* People who are neurodivergent
* Ability to recruit from wider area

Potential hinders:
* Potential for less visibility
* access to opportunities + equipment
* home unsuitable for working
* lack of reliable internet

Consider the impact on inclusion?

or

Give guidance on virtual meetings so that all feel included

What support is needed

Encourage situations + structures where friendships can develop

So that remote + hybrid working work for all?

How psychologically SAFE is the remote + hybrid working experience in your organization?

10

Learning and development

The shorter read

The move to greater remote, and now hybrid, working has had a transformational effect on learning and development (L&D), but not always a smooth and straightforward one, with many organizations feeling it was a rushed and not immediately effective change – there were many significant challenges.

With a more conscious transition towards a hybrid working environment, we can consider why remote learning, whether in a live virtual setting or asynchronous on or offline experiences, is necessary for the organization of the future. It certainly isn't new for individuals, who are used to learning in this way in their personal lives.

Where live virtual sessions are part of the organizational L&D offering there is a need to review the skillset and mindset of those designing and delivering such sessions, as there are distinct differences that make the learner experience unique – and simply replicating the face-to-face learning environment is a mistake.

There are some good practice tips which will help you design and deliver live virtual sessions more effectively – blending the approach, investing more time in the design stage, creating engagement from the initial marketing of the session, and maintaining this as people join it, keeping sessions short and including lots of meaningful interactions, and using a wide variety of tools and functionality included in the web conferencing software or third-party apps.

Some organizations will be actively considering what we will call a hybrid approach to learning, where learners are participating in synchronous activities while based in different locations, or where the facilitator may have learners present in the physical training space as well as online. These types of events carry some risk – careful thought needs to be given to how to minimize the risk of attention bias, as well as how to ensure the equipment in each location and the tool use levels the playing field and provides similar experiences for all learners.

All this pales into insignificance compared to the cultural shift required to reposition and repurpose the process of learning for a modern hybrid working environment. We need to ensure that senior leaders are more active participants in asynchronous and synchronous learning, and that we change the focus of L&D professionals to act more as performance consultants, diagnosing performance issues at the source, and facilitating solutions that address those issues in real time and at the point of need.

To do that we need accurate and usable data and technology (though not always the most complex) to help us. It requires us to think of L&D more as a process than an event. It needs us to help connect people, encouraging them to share their tacit and explicit knowledge, as well as providing L&D solutions that blend a variety of different media in shorter, more accessible formats. These are good things to do anyway, not just in remote or hybrid environments.

Given the amount of change to the way we are and will be working, learning is needed more than ever now. For remote and hybrid workers the most common form of learning won't be the live session, whether that is virtual or not. We must recognize this and shift the culture accordingly.

The longer read

One of the areas that saw a bigger shift during the COVID-19 pandemic and experienced forced and quite rapid transformation was learning and development (L&D). While many organizations had been progressing along the journey towards virtual learning, this had been slow progress. It took the enforced lockdowns to accelerate this change and bring about new ways of working.

However, this wasn't necessarily a smooth transition. The rushed nature of the transformation meant that many lessons were learnt about how to design and deliver virtual content, and these highlighted many cultural issues which also need addressing if we are to ensure that learning for remote and hybrid workers is to be effective. In this chapter we will summarize many of the lessons learnt and clarify some of these cultural challenges.

Many reports hint at the scale of the challenges. Industry analyst company Fosway examined the impact of the COVID-19 pandemic on L&D and highlighted that 59% of organizations felt their adoption of virtual learning was immature and rushed, and that 42% found the transition difficult as a result. Despite this, 82% felt the demand for this type of learning had increased in their organizations[1]. Online learning expert Cindy Huggett, in her State of Virtual Training report for 2020, noted that the top challenges faced by organizations had been:

- Technological challenges.
- Unengaged participants.
- Lack of buy-in/not enough resources.
- Unskilled facilitators.
- Lack of sufficient bandwidth[2].

As with many organizational changes though, it is important to start with 'why?'. We know why virtual L&D took off in 2020, but if it is something that is going to become a default option for our remote and hybrid workers then we need to answer the 'why?' question again. Many organizations may adopt a virtual-first approach for their entire workforce not just those who are already working remotely or in a hybrid way. To do that effectively, they need to consider why the learning is needed in the first place, why the organization wants to do this in a virtual method and why those coming to the virtual sessions would do so – what's in it for them?

There is, of course, a place for all forms of learning activity, as the CIPD point out in their report on the impact of the COVID-19 pandemic on the L&D profession[3] – they make the point that a blended approach (a hybrid, perhaps?) is going to provide more of what individual learners need – high-quality in-person interventions with lots of social interaction, with well-designed and delivered virtual learning and a range of online and offline self-guided materials.

And this isn't new for individuals in the way we have experienced it as new for organizations. Many have been learning this way in our personal lives for a lot longer than we have been doing it this way in our professional lives – we are tapping into a population that already embraces this approach to learning, and is comfortable with doing it remotely, we must get it right.

Design and delivery of virtual live sessions

The need to do more when designing and delivering virtual learning – to do it differently than face-to-face learning, is something that seemingly took many by surprise when they were forced to do it. I class myself as an experienced virtual facilitator and had been designing and delivering live virtual sessions – and upskilling others to do so – for many years before it suddenly became something everyone needed to do. After a few months of everyone doing it in mid-2020, I started noticing bits of feedback I would get after delivering my sessions. Clients pointed out that they'd enjoyed them because of the opportunities to interact and take part in the sessions, because the sessions included lots of use of different functionality, because the visuals were different and didn't seem like they'd been simply lifted and shifted from face-to-face content, and because I seemed human and not robotic in my delivery.

This made me realize that the delivery of live virtual sessions, to people working remotely or based in the office, was a distinctly different skillset – than that I'd started out with in L&D over two decades previously – and the evolution of my own skillset had happened almost unnoticed by me – but clearly many now designing and delivering virtual sessions were falling into some common traps, and not creating the most engaging or effective of live sessions.

Put simply, some people were trying to do what they'd always done face-to-face (and which admittedly for most had worked well) without realizing remote L&D is very different. The Learning and Performance Institute's (LPI) Certified Online Learning Facilitator (COLF) and the CIPD's Designing and Delivering Great Virtual Classrooms accredited programmes both go into a lot of detail about the specific design and delivery skills and mindsets that one needs to effectively work in this space.

It must be said that delivering virtual learning opportunities is not for everyone – many experienced L&D professionals are brilliant at designing and delivering face-to-face learning and may not want to operate in the virtual space, delivering learning remotely. To succeed in this remote world, those designing and delivering need not just to know how to do it remotely, but to actively enjoy doing that. Perhaps those delivering virtual sessions need to think of themselves like radio presenters – a slightly more outlandish and outspoken version of themselves (while still being authentic). Someone with whom learners are likely to find themselves interacting with almost unconsciously. I confess that analogy helped me in my early days of delivering virtual sessions and is something I bear in mind and try to adopt even now – but I'm aware, from attending other sessions, that not everyone has this approach.

This type of learning isn't going away though. Almost every research report I have come across in putting together this chapter and in my professional activities day to day show that, despite many teething troubles, remote or virtual learning is here to stay and likely to grow. It is not just because we were in the middle of a global pandemic, or because it can be more cost-effective. It has been shown to be at least as effective for learners as face-to-face delivery – if done in the right way[4].

So, what is the right way? So much here depends on the context – why the virtual learning is taking place and what it is intended to achieve. However, simply replicating the face-to-face experience using technology for those working remotely is not giving anyone the best experience – it also isn't using the skills facilitators need to use or paying due respect to what the technology itself could bring us.

However, there are some common principles that could be easily followed for those designing and delivering virtual sessions to those learning remotely:

- Adopt a blended approach. In this I always consider live virtual sessions as a piece of a part-completed jigsaw puzzle. There will be asynchronous learning taking place before the live virtual session, and asynchronous learning taking place after the live virtual session. Quite what shape and form these take will depend on the context of course – but the live virtual session is not a standalone activity. Those designing and delivering it need to be able to fit the live virtual session into the existing jigsaw pieces, and to signpost to where and when further pieces will be found. In essence, the facilitator is showing the learners the picture on the front of the jigsaw box – giving them the big picture as well as a piece of the detail.

- Spend proportionately longer designing live virtual sessions compared to their face-to-face equivalents. Design for this type of remote learning needs to be a more conscious, deliberate approach – the use of the tools, the choice of the activities, the way you want to interact with learners all needs planning much more in advance than face-to-face. In contrast, the delivery may not take as long as the face-to-face equivalent, largely because learners can complete activities simultaneously using some tools compared to having to take turns in a face-to-face classroom. Many operating in this space have grown up with school environments and an implicit understanding of the physical learning environment. Learning how the remote and virtual learning environment is different is a real challenge for many, as few have the reserves of knowledge to draw upon to help them with this.

- Ensure that the set-up and initial promotion-/-marketing of the session gives sufficient information to convince remote workers to attend the live virtual session and begins the process of engagement, which should be carried on through asynchronous remote learning ahead of the live session.

- Ensuring people are engaged from the moment they arrive – using the initial period to welcome and settle those for whom remote learning can be an isolating or awkward experience. The first five minutes, and how people feel in that time, can often dictate whether the remote session will be effective or not.

- Keeping live virtual sessions shorter than face-to-face sessions – Cindy Huggett's research suggests that 60 minutes is the most common length[5] – to keep engagement high and to avoid digital fatigue. If sessions need to be longer, then factor in sufficient screen breaks to make the content more manageable.

- Building in meaningful interactions that include and involve remote learners frequently throughout the live session. Meaningful means avoiding closed questions and things like token use of polls.

- Avoid insisting on webcam use – it is replicating the face-to-face learning experience and can end up being the only way you check people's presence in the live session. Instead use it, like other functions in the web conferencing platform, as a tool to be used when it adds value. This is rarely through the whole session, where it becomes the focal point for the session and hinders learning from other interactions as well as providing distractions for those in the session

- Use the available tools to create the right type of engagement – this may be breakout rooms, chat functionality, whiteboards, polls, or third-party apps, along with appropriate camera and open microphone use and many more. A great remote session often comes down to how the facilitator treats people.

It is also important for organizations to understand the features of the web conferencing platform they are choosing to use – not all platforms are created equal, and they were all designed for uses that may not match what you want to use it for. Sometimes, the platform itself may be a barrier. Some platforms were designed for video-based communication but aren't brilliant at delivering live learning events and may need supplementing with third-party apps for remote workers. Some platforms were designed for live learning events but aren't great at video-based communication. When looking for a suitable platform, there will be many interested parties in your organization and no doubt compromises may need to be made, but you need to ensure that you have a platform that you know how to use, know how it differs from other platforms and the advantages and disadvantages it brings, and how to access third party apps to bridge any gaps there may be.

From a very simple perspective – the things those who design and deliver great face-to-face learning do are necessary and helpful in the remote and hybrid learning environment, but additional skills, different mindsets and new approaches are needed on top of these things.

Hybrid approaches

I've mentioned the jigsaw puzzle analogy in the previous section. In that I talked about some asynchronous learning taking place before or after a live virtual session, but the same could happen either side of a face-to-face session, and it could help sessions that have a more hybrid approach.

But what does hybrid mean from a learning perspective? So far in this book we've talked about hybrid meaning different places where someone would work, and so far in this chapter we've looked at hybrid learning being different places – face-to-face and online – where people could learn. Of course, learning isn't necessarily such a binary choice and can happen in lots of different ways and in different places. But many organizations are beginning to consider how to deliver what they are terming hybrid learning events – where there are learners in the office and learners who are remote, and where the facilitator could be in either. There are lots of ways in which this can be done, and, in this section, I'll explore some things to consider if that is an option for you.

There are several options here. The facilitator is either located in the physical training space, or is located remotely, and the learners, likewise, as shown in Table 10.1. Let's explore some of these in further detail.

DIFFERENT SCENARIOS FOR HYBRID APPROACHES

TABLE 10.1 A four-box model for hybrid learning sessions

Facilitator is in physical training room Learners are in the physical training room	Facilitator is remote Learners are in the physical training room and / or remote
Facilitator is in physical training room Learners are in the physical training room and / or remote	Facilitator is remote Learners are remote

When the facilitator is based in the physical training space, there is likely to be a mix of learners based in that same location and remotely. There is a big risk therefore of bias in the facilitator's behaviour and actions towards those in the same location, and the experience for those accessing remotely would be affected. To combat this, the physical space itself needs to have high-quality audio and video capabilities to connect those accessing remotely with the facilitator who may be moving around the physical training space – the facilitator may need to wear a microphone attached to them and the room may need directional cameras to follow the facilitator. The facilitator may also need explicit guidance on how to avoid delivering solely to those in the room.

In this situation, careful thought needs to be given the tool use. Physical flipcharts would only be accessible to those in the physical training space, and unless each of the in-person learners has a suitable device, virtual whiteboards and chat functionality may be inaccessible to them. If cameras are used to connect the remote learners into the physical training space, there needs to be space – somewhere – for those in the physical training space to see those cameras, and this may take up space needed for visual aids perhaps. So when visual aids are not needed, the facilitator may need to stop sharing their materials to allow more space on the screen for those remote learners cameras.

Breakout rooms, if used, would pose a further challenge that can be overcome either by subdividing the in-person learners and the remote learners into separate breakout rooms, allowing for slightly different tool use in each and a different style of feedback, or by mixing groups up and encouraging them to use virtual spaces for the breakouts to level the playing field.

When the facilitator is based remotely, and if there are learners also based remotely as well as some in the physical training space, there is a risk that the facilitator may show bias towards those who are also remote, simply because it may be easier to engage or 'see' them. The experience will be different for each group of learners and there may be no way around this unless each learner in the physical training space is given a device to replicate the remote experience. Assuming that isn't the case, it may be sensible to sub-divide the learners based on their location and create slightly different activities for each group. However, aim to create more inclusive experiences by turning cameras off for the remote learners if not all of the learners in the physical training space can be seen by the remote facilitator, or asking the learners in the physical training space to use chat functionality to connect better with those remotely. With that though, again the physical training space needs to have good audio and video set-up, and device access, to enable such levelling to take place.

These considerations may seem inordinately complicated, but they don't need to be. Just as getting used to facilitating live virtual sessions was a leap for many but done successfully after a period of adjustment, so will facilitating a live hybrid session. With the correct planning and preparation, it can be done – but what this may also show is that it may be much more straightforward to keep things virtual by default, and to ask any learners who would normally be in the physical training space to access remotely for any live session. For many organizations without access to the technology needed to level the playing field for hybrid learning events, this may be the path of least resistance.

Sara Duxbury is Global Senior L&D Manager at the UK clothing retail organization All Saints. During the COVID-19 lockdowns, while the retail teams that make up most of All Saints workforce were furloughed, the remainder were working remotely. After a period of adjustment, Duxbury's team began delivering live virtual sessions to these employees, who enthusiastically embraced them because, in Duxbury's view, it gave them an opportunity to talk to and connect with other people, which was something they needed to break up remote working isolation. This is something she noticed is different about live virtual sessions compared to face-to-face delivery – there is often a greater human connection, with people opening up and talking about wellbeing issues much more – and she now considers this a major part of any L&D offering to any business.

Duxbury's team realized quickly that the content for live virtual sessions **had** to be really very good to generate and maintain engagement. They actively partnered with subject matter experts elsewhere in the business to make sure this was the case, taking a view on quality of design and delivery accordingly before any session went ahead. They also built a loose structure using internal social media to wrap around any live session, and found that all learners, whether remote or in-person, used this to discuss learning, share and curate their own content without any active intervention from the L&D team.

As All Saints have returned to mostly in-person working, remote learning has stayed in place. There is now a real appetite for learning which wasn't there when all the learning was in-person, says Duxbury. However, to help those who work in-store to access the remote learning and live virtual sessions, they are given blocks of time – usually full-days as this is easier to manage from an operational perspective and creates more focused time for the learners – to spend on their own development, and access the learning either from an in-store device or from their own remote working locations.

All Saints' live virtual sessions will often last for a full day, broken down by regular breaks, a huge variety of different tool use to avoid spending too long on any one activity, and use of walking and talking conversations to encourage screen breaks. Duxbury feels this approach is still a work in progress, but one that will only accelerate from here.

A cultural shift

Much of what we have covered in this chapter so far has focused on some very tangible changes. Get the technology right, get the skills of those using it right, manage the environment right, and all is well – right?

Perhaps not. As with any organizational change, the biggest challenge is usually cultural. In this section we will explore how organizations need to change their culture around learning, how learning itself may need to take on different forms, and the implications this has for those delivering traditional L&D.

Lots of research points to how big remote learning is getting. The CIPD's Digital learning in a post-COVID-19 economy[6] pointed out that the top areas of growth in organizational digital learning content have been: video; mobile; blended learning; user-generated content; microlearning; and curated content. These are all things that lend themselves to, and are probably driven by the growth in, remote and hybrid working. They also provide cost-effective approaches to L&D that can be delivered more easily in the flow of work and at the point of need. Both the CIPD and Fosway research (cited earlier in this chapter) show how remote learning delivered via digital means has grown significantly since 2020, and is expected to grow further still in future years, despite some of the barriers that we have discussed already in this chapter.

Simply investing in more live virtual sessions would, no matter how well designed, not necessarily shift the culture in the way we need to. Using the aforementioned digital learning content would allow for a more effective blend of different delivery methods and may also create a different perception of and appetite for learning, one that all workers could benefit from no matter where or when they work. There are several things we need to consider from a cultural perspective to ensure this happens though.

One is the role of the senior leaders in the organization, who, from anecdotal research for this chapter, seem to be more willing and able to get involved in remote learning than they ever were for face-to-face learning. This is critical – it goes beyond mere sponsorship and other learners will see the active participation of senior leaders and take their cue from that. Switching the senior team on to remote learning is a good start, but we also need to change how we operate as L&D professionals to be able to do that.

PERFORMANCE CONSULTANCY

L&D professionals need to and should be doing far more than just designing and delivering material, and be getting far more involved in the business, not simply so that we can become better L&D professionals, but so the business itself becomes better for our interventions.

As L&D professionals, if we are to do our work properly, we need to know about the strategy and operations of the business, and how it judges performance at various levels. We need to be able to bring people together (virtually or in person) and help them to collaborate to solve performance issues, and to curate resources that will help them do this even better. We need to see organizations as systems and understand their processes.

As we are no longer the sage on the stage, the font of all knowledge or the single source of the truth, we must be able to arrange learning in real time for people at the point of need. This involves creating video content, audio guides, encouraging coaching conversations, using VR and AR, and facilitating social learning. We must be comfortable with people learning wherever and whenever they may be, and not just when they are in a session with us.

By doing those things we will start to behave like performance consultants and less like trainers – diagnosing performance issues at the source and facilitating solutions that address those issues, again at the source in real time.

The concept of performance consultancy is well established. The principles underlying it appear in the Learning and Development area of Specialist Knowledge and the Commercial Drive area of Core Behaviours in the CIPD Profession Map, becoming more critical the higher up the levels one goes. It is also present in the LPI's Capability Map where there is a specialist area for it. If the drivers for this shift in L&D focus are represented in the frameworks from two professional bodies, so is the guidance from those bodies to get to that point. And in a remote and hybrid working environment, where L&D professionals are far less likely to see their learners on a regular basis, this is even more critical.

Many learning experience platforms (LXPs) can provide data about what people do when learning, how they learn and apply it. It is entirely possible that this data, along with other organizational data about what people do and how they operate, can be used to predict what learning people will need and deliver it remotely to them. In our chapter on technology, and at parts of other chapters, we have talked about how technology can give us insight into people's needs, and here is where it can help us to identify their learning needs. However, the LPI report that 63% of learning leaders say that they have no reliable way to measure people performance, and 72% believed that the L&D function was not equipped to meet the needs of the business, with the biggest barrier cited being the time needed to access learning[7]. These statistics point to L&D needing to frame its role more as aiding performance. So, we need to engage people working remotely and in a hybrid way so that learning isn't seen as an interruption, and something incorporated into their regular work routines.

LEARNING IN THE FLOW OF WORK

When we talk about delivering performance interventions, as opposed to L&D, it reminds me more about coaching and supporting performance in a sporting sense. But it is a recurring theme in the annual Mind Tools for Business (previously Emerald Works and Towards Maturity) benchmarking reports on the L&D profession, regularly stating that L&D need to develop ways to support performance at the point of need, and that this is a growing requirement, going up by 47% year on year.

This, to me, positions L&D interventions as a process rather than an event (something that I also said about inductions in an earlier chapter too). L&D practitioners should be delivering just-in-time support in the flow of work. The challenges here are to integrate new and developing technology to help us do that, and perhaps to incorporate lessons from the sporting world too.

Technology helps with the provision of information – the rise of wearable technology and artificial intelligence tools really assist knowledge workers to access information and data to do their job at the point of need, and this is often done remotely and away from other people in the physical workplace. But what about softer skills, and how could such technology help with that? Knowledge workers can increasingly rely on technology to deliver just in time information rather than storing it in their own heads – if your employees can Google the answer to a question what does that mean for the role of L&D professionals?

Consider a manager having a difficult conversation. As L&D professionals now, we could deliver a live virtual or face-to-face workshop on how to prepare for that, and through roleplay and practical activities we could witness the skills being used and give real-time feedback. And continuous feedback is cited by CIPD as the most common way L&D professionals add value despite only a minority identifying performance issues before suggesting solutions[8].

But can we be there when remote workers need us? If this were sport, and we say the football manager or cricket captain is the L&D professional, then they can **see** and **hear** what's going on and can deliver in the moment feedback to the individual that allows them to adjust their performance. I'm also a qualified personal trainer, and a key aspect of that is observing individuals when they are performing, give them feedback and help them improve their performance there and then. To do this effectively in the remote and hybrid work environment, we need to use technology to bring the L&D professional closer to the individual at the point of need.

This is where augmented reality or wearable technology could really come into its own. This would allow the L&D professional, or an AI version of the L&D professional, to be able to see or hear what's going on and give the manager (in the example above) instant feedback and ideas. In an instant this changes the role of the L&D professional to becoming more like a coach, more like a cricket captain or a football manager, coaching from the technical area or on the pitch. This is where we can use technology to deliver performance interventions at the point of need – or perhaps can enable managers and employees to do this.

It also reprioritizes the skills an L&D professional needs and means we need to be faster, more technologically enabled and be comfortable in providing support on real-life, real-time issues. The changes to not just L&D but all people professionals skillsets are discussed in our final chapter in more detail.

That said, we should be conscious of going at the right pace with technology, and not asking too much of any learner. The path of least resistance – in this case the simplest tools available – may be the most appropriate option. The NHS Do OD (Organizational Development) guides[9] make similar points – look for light-touch systems that people may have ready access to, for example on mobile phones, and which they will already be familiar with and can more readily use.

MOVING FORWARD

This is a big shift – as Michelle Parry-Slater says in her book *The Learning and Development Handbook*[10] – a real move forward to modern learning principles and methods, and away from the injection education of the classroom. One that is focused on learners needs, offering multiple touchpoints to help people understand what they are doing and learn from it. One that connects learning to things they already know and do. It is, however, increasingly what remote and hybrid workers need.

For this to work, we need clarity on the overall learning philosophy, ensuring everyone in the organization knows what technology can and will be used to support learning for remote and hybrid workers. The wider environment is something that needs to be aligned correctly too – we have established in this book already how relationships and connections matter to remote and hybrid workers, and we need to ensure, in our L&D offerings, that we provide can enhance these relationships and connections, getting people to share tacit and explicit knowledge and using data to gain insights into and support performance across the organization.

Responding to a request I made when researching this chapter, David Perks shared some thoughts via Twitter on how these connections can and have been made when he has provided L&D services to organizations. He said that the biggest change he had seen was the ability to record, replay and re-use learning content within organizations, something that has only really taken off since the COVID-19 pandemic. The live virtual sessions he has delivered have gone well and been interactive, but what has made the biggest difference culturally is the ability to repackage the recording of the live virtual session into micro-learning and embedding the learning via key points being shared on internal social media. Up until recently, he had not noticed this kind of learning agility being common practice, and he shared a screenshot of this happening for one of his clients:

FIGURE 10.1

SOURCE Reproduced with permission from David Perks via Twitter @FeedbackDave
NOTE Showing how learning is happening organically in the organization (Perks, 2021)

Perks' example is a good one and reinforces many of the ways in which we can repurpose learning for a remote and hybrid world of work. This is a form of social listening – we should be scanning internal social media channels to look for people asking questions and use that to make the right intervention. From an L&D perspective we need to recognize the points when learning is needed – and it isn't going to be mostly in a live virtual session, but outside that. There are numerous touchpoints where we can predict learning is needed – when an employee joins the organization or changes roles, or if something changes in their role or in the organization. We should be able to create structures and opportunities to connect with other people, access resources and share ideas both remotely and in-person. We may need to be more proactive about helping those who work remotely to find and take advantage of those opportunities, as we know this could help with other aspects of remote working also.

We need to help leaders in teams to create opportunities for all workers, regardless of location, to benefit from learning opportunities on the job and from working with others, and to guide them to spread such opportunities around the widest possible groupings. We can use these leaders to cover some of the necessary pre- and post- live virtual session work with learners to ensure it is embedded into the flow of work and engage them more in delivering the value that all stakeholders want the learning to deliver. We can create internal content in different media – audio, video and more – that can be accessed asynchronously and at the point of need – and encourage user-generated content to be created by all workers based on where they recognize performance can be impacted the most.

CASE STUDY

Once again in this chapter we will have two case studies, contrasting the experience of two quite different organizations and the ways in which they repurposed their people practices for remote and hybrid working.

Case Study One

Kathryn Palmer-Skillings is the Volunteering Learning and Development Lead at Macmillan Cancer Support, with around 1,850 staff based around the UK and a larger number of volunteers. The case study below is adapted from Macmillan's successful Learning Awards entry where they were the winners of the Digital Learning Transformation Award in 2020, and I have worked with Palmer-Skillings to expand upon and bring the content up to date.

Like many, Macmillan had to pause its face-to-face L&D when the COVID-19 pandemic hit – L&D for volunteers had, up until that point, been entirely face-to-face, with a view held that volunteers would not engage with remote learning – however the L&D team was now faced with developing a way of training 1,500 volunteers using digital means within a matter of weeks, with the added criteria of utilizing platforms already in use by the organization and which were accessible to the greatest number of volunteers. This led to the decision to utilize Skype, but to repurpose some other internally available platforms, all with the aim of providing consistency of experience as well as increasing confidence levels.

The team developed step-by-step guides for both Skype and the online learning platforms, plus individual sessions for those who were nervous, and with accessible versions of the training for those who found technology a barrier. Different learning requirements were catered for with four learning pathways being developed to reflect different levels of experience for the learners. There was a mix of self-guided and live sessions that linked together to blend the overall approach.

Time was of the essence, with only a week to create the first piece of content, requiring a cross-organizational team to identify easily repurposed existing content, but which could be updated as learners worked through it.

This approach ensured that some 928 volunteers were able to access the programme across the summer of 2020, accessing 2,950 self-guided learning hours and 1,397 live virtual sessions between them, and with the Volunteering Department reporting a real shift in the assumptions around remote learning, increased interest, and support for digital learning solutions. The team were able to engage with a more diverse range of volunteers, including those who were more geographically as well as medically and socially isolated, and who were previously unable to access face-to-face learning or take up emotional support volunteering roles for Macmillan.

The cross-organizational team approach helped enormously, engaging people outside the L&D team in content-creation and knowledge management, and helping shift the culture towards one where L&D content can operate on a 'progression not perfection' basis, with quick, agile development supported by strong and robust feedback mechanisms.

This overall transformation was delivered by a team of two, including Palmer-Skillings. Both of the team were already confident with remote and virtual learning but had to design and deliver some train the trainer style sessions for front-line managers for them to support live sessions. Since this time, the team has shifted to full virtual learning, and achieved greater organizational buy-in due to the success of this initial programme.

Case Study Two

Jo Brimacombe was the Project Manager – People Experience at the CIPD, an organization of 375 employees with a headquarters in Southwest London, but which has increasingly adopted hybrid working in the last year. A team comprising Brimacombe, Chris Baldwin (L&D Manager) and Deepa Raval (Learning and

Organizational Development Lead), led the CIPD's remote and hybrid learning transformation. The CIPD had a strong face-to-face L&D programme prior to the COVID-19 pandemic, and like Macmillan had to repurpose this when the entire organization had to work remotely.

One of the initial challenges faced by the team was how to address skillset and mindset issues around remote and hybrid learning. They had used mostly external specialists to deliver L&D, and found that among these, there was a mixed approach to whether the provider was willing and able to repurpose their solutions for a remote world of work – with some very slow to do so.

The team became very aware that the nature of virtual learning sessions meant that those facilitating them required skills to flourish in this setting – things like creative design, strong online facilitation and presentation skills and coaching skills became more important. Design was highlighted as an area that providers needed to get right – there was real competition for learners' attention, so the design of live sessions needed to be fun, engaging and very visual. The competent use of tools such as dynamic interactive presentation software, online whiteboards, videoconferencing and more became a critical part of the providers' skillset, and those who could engage with these tools flourished in the CIPD's new world, enabling better interaction between participants, and with the facilitator too.

They also realized that learners had not just other things to think about but a relatively limited attention span when learning online, compared to in-person learning, and that full day workshops were no longer appropriate. In response, the CIPD moved to delivering shorter, bite-sized, sessions spread out over days or even weeks. They selected providers and facilitators who possessed not just the skillset to do all the above, but the mindset to adapt their existing solutions and/or develop new ones that delivered what learners needed.

I asked Brimacombe, Raval and Baldwin what else had changed as part of this shift. They reported that there was a huge move towards technical learning, developing new ways of working and supporting wellbeing. As a result, a bespoke, online programme of development was developed. They felt that they had to be ahead of the game, anticipating what their employees (and learners) would need at specific points in time – for example when they may need technical training and when they would need wellbeing support. This was a complicated thing to work out – it had to be timely and address the points of pain people were experiencing as they adjusted to remote working. This meant using data and insight from a new fortnightly engagement tool to identify what employees needed to do their jobs well, and what was on their minds.

Conscious that people's attitude to learning was changing, each available session was made short – a maximum of 90 minutes and recorded for those unable to make the live session. They were also supported by follow-up learning via a variety of mediums to meet people's preferences to learn on demand – including further reading, something to listen to and something to watch, using content the CIPD had available on an external platform.

From a cultural perspective, CIPD employees were used to attending face-to-face L&D sessions, and even though all employees had access to virtual learning opportunities prior to the COVID-19 pandemic, they were very much seen as a lesser option. As the pandemic gathered pace, the CIPD's employees were thrust into a steep period of required learning as skills in new technologies were no longer optional but required – and the requirement for these skills was so strong, say Brimacombe, Raval and Baldwin, that it drove people to attend the new bite-sized virtual live sessions. The short duration and accessible nature meant that people could fit the learning into their work easier and didn't need to take long periods out of the business to attend.

The team noticed that people valued the opportunity to connect with others as much as, if not more than, the learning content itself. Through encouraging use of chat (and other) functionality and creating an opportunity to learn and share with peers, these sessions became and continue to be highly desirable within the CIPD. Not only have they proven to be a flexible type of learning, but they are also now very much seen as the preferred way for people to access learning – so much so that a move to hybrid working or even close to fully in-person working is not seen as likely to change this.

That said, Brimacombe, Raval and Baldwin feel that there is still a desire for and value to be had from face-to-face learning and are intending to mix up courses with a blend of live online, on demand and face-to-face sessions. The CIPD have adopted a virtual-first approach to learning – there would need to be a clear business case to run a face-to-face learning session and a clear explanation why it could not be delivered virtually. They also feel that, moving forward, there is a need to promote more asynchronous learning and communication to reduce time spent in meetings and increase the chance for socializing and networking for remote and hybrid workers. Things like collaborative chats, and voice notes instead of meetings and more. They have also been designing learning to support people with working in a hybrid organization and creating the desire in people to direct their own learning more.

To conclude the case study from the CIPD, Brimacombe, Raval and Baldwin state that, in a remote and hybrid working environment, they have learnt that learning does not have to be as detailed as we may previously have thought. Learning can, and indeed should be, shorter and more task-focused – delivered, as we have noted in this chapter, in the flow of work.

Case study reflections

In the first case study, Macmillan Cancer Support, the following points stand out as interesting:

- It is possible to create a full virtual L&D offering from an almost standing start if the right cultural and organizational elements are in place.
- Utilizing familiar platforms and creating accessible materials can help to increase confidence and engagement – don't introduce shiny new platforms if you don't have to! If you are making a big change like asking people to go online for learning sessions, then don't ask them to do it on a new, unfamiliar platform.
- Having several different pathways to cater for different skillsets and requirements avoided a one size fits all 'sheep dip' type approach and helped build engagement also.
- Remote and hybrid learning programmes can increase take-up and inclusion if done right.
- A small L&D team is not a barrier to achieving large-scale impact, but they will require support from cross-organizational teams particularly around content-creation but also delivery.
- Embedding content-creation and delivery across the organization is a good way to leverage cultural change around remote and hybrid learning.

In the second case study, the CIPD, the following points stand out:

- Being clear with external learning providers about your requirements is likely to have a mixed response, but one that will identify the providers with the best fit for your organization's needs.
- Clarifying the skills that are needed from those designing and delivering virtual learning sessions is important for helping such sessions be engaging and effective.
- Building shorter, bite-sized, sessions that fit into people's working day, supported by on-demand learning content, is likely to have a greater impact.
- Linking L&D solutions to available data from other people practices is helpful and impactful also.

- Learning sessions, whether face-to-face or remote, need to have a significant element within them that encourages collaboration, connection, and networking.

- Adopting a virtual-first mindset and asking for exceptions to this to be evidenced is an effective way to embed virtual learning in the culture of the organization.

The action plan

If you are considering how to repurpose and reposition L&D within your organization to make it more effective for remote and hybrid workers, then the following questions could help you to plan your approach:

- Why do you want, or need, to run live virtual sessions? What problem will this solve for your organization?

- How skilled are the people who will be designing and delivering live virtual sessions? How can you raise their skill level – focusing on what is different and unique about this type of learning?

- How will you position live virtual sessions within a wider L&D offering? What can you blend with and around them?

- How can you create and maintain engagement ahead of and at the start of live virtual sessions?

- How will you make your live virtual sessions a distinct and different, but primarily useful, experience than a face-to-face one?

- What are the advantages and disadvantages of your chosen web conferencing platform for delivering live virtual sessions? What workarounds, or third-party apps, could help you with this?

- What is your current preference for delivering hybrid learning events? What are the benefits and limitations of this approach?

- How well equipped are your physical training spaces to deliver hybrid events where some learners won't be in that space?

- How will you ensure your facilitators of hybrid learning events minimise the risk of attention bias, and create learning experiences that provide a level playing field for all learners?
- How will you engage your senior leaders to take an active part in remote and hybrid learning?
- What do your L&D professionals need to do to become more like performance consultants?
- What data do you have, or can you get, about people and their performance needs? How can you use this to create learning solutions?
- What technology do you have, or could you use, that would give you real time information about where remote and hybrid workers need support? How can you leverage this to best effect?
- What are the likely touchpoints in your organization where remote and hybrid workers are likely to need more focused support? What learning solutions can you create to provide more support here?
- What is your best advice to senior leaders in your organization on the role that L&D needs to play for remote and hybrid workers?

Sketchnote summary

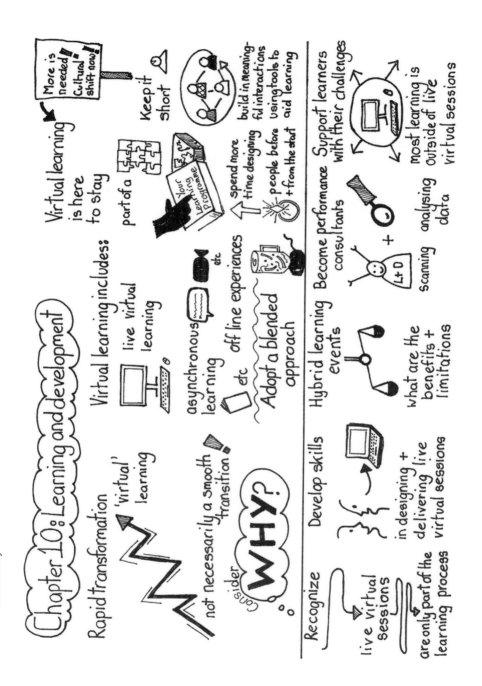

PART THREE

The world we are headed to

11

Spaces and places

The shorter read

We have looked at how people practice needs to change, but that's not all that needs to change. Our organizations – culturally and physically – do too. To make remote and hybrid working work on a more permanent basis for all involved, we need to avoid thinking about it as a binary choice, and work on a much more granular level.

Even the term hybrid working, though featuring heavily in this book of course, is perhaps misleading as it suggests simply combining the remote and face-to-face worlds. It isn't as simple as that. It is something more conscious and deliberate, needing a different approach. We must change what work is, as well as where it takes place.

It is important to maintain as individual an approach as possible – everyone's circumstances, environments, needs and preferences are different, and have led to different experiences so far. This means that hybrid working won't be, and could never be, a one size fits all approach.

What we use our places and spaces for will change. To do that effectively we need to consider what type of work is done in the organization, whether remotely or in the office, and determine how it is best done. Doing this properly will not be achievable on a job-by-job basis, and it may be necessary to look at individual job tasks and activities instead. This will help determine the most effective and critically necessary, adaptable, workspace. Think of this as a beta-test and being adaptable will enable you to course correct quickly if you don't get pieces of it right first time.

The longer read

Now that we have explored how each element of people practice can and should change, we will look at what this means for our organizations and our teams of people professionals. In this chapter we will look at some of the aspects that people professionals need to consider in helping our organizations to adapt to the future world of work. There are many things to work through before we can fully embrace remote or hybrid working, from how we help our businesses to plan for best- and worst-case scenarios, how we help them to transform physically and culturally, and how we ensure that the changes are sustained and embedded.

I think a good place to start is to note that many businesses simply do not have a choice around remote or hybrid working, and that means many individuals do not either. There will always be work that needs to be carried out face-to-face, and there will always be individual preferences around ways of working. But it is not necessarily a binary choice – there are lots of different options to consider and an individualized approach, even down to individual tasks and a job crafting system, may prove a more workable solution for many.

One of the main lessons learnt during the COVID-19 pandemic was that the switch to remote working was not as simple as replicating what happened in the office but virtually. We can, therefore, safely say that hybrid working is not about trying to somehow merge the remote and face-to-face worlds of work, despite what the label may suggest. It is about something different, more conscious, and deliberate, something that changes both remote and face-to-face experiences of work into something greater than the sum of its parts, something better than either are individually.

In years gone by, remote working was about quiet time, focused time, time to get stuff done without interruption, without meetings. For remote work to be effective this is what it needs to largely return to. This, then, changes what the physical office needs to be – it can no longer be about doing individual work sat at one location and often not interacting with others. The physical workplace becomes a place for collaboration, for communication, for those oft-mentioned watercooler moments of inspiration.

Marc Weedon, Senior International HR Director at Zuora, runs a network called the International HR Forum. The group met during 2021 to discuss progress towards implementing hybrid working, and Weedon was able to summarise the following points from the discussions:

- Individual experiences have differed during the COVID-19 pandemic, and therefore individual attitudes will likewise differ. Flexibility is therefore important and mandating a particular way of working is unlikely to succeed.

- There appears a cultural dissonance between those at the top of organizations who seem to be focusing on bringing back entirely face-to-face working, and their employees who want the opposite. It is important that organizations listen to both.

- Both the benefits of working in a physical office and working remotely can be accommodated and managed side by side, if employees are sufficiently empowered, and if the physical workplace can be sufficiently reconfigured.

- Rethinking people practices will be necessary when not everyone will be in the same place at the same time.

- Given how quickly the COVID-19 pandemic came upon the world, it is sensible to build business continuity plans that provide for a worst-case scenario as well as a best-case scenario regarding remote and hybrid working. (Weedon, 2021)

The International HR Forum have succinctly captured many of the things we need to now consider, and strike what I feel is the right tone for organizations to adopt moving forward. Let's now look at some of the more important aspects.

Spaces and places

Speaking at the CIPD Conference in November 2021, Lynda Gratton shared her view that remote working – usually done in a person's home – needs to be a source of energy, a space to work, with minimal interruptions and the benefit of no commuting. This is how remote working was for many, including me, up until the COVID-19 pandemic. It enables quiet and focused work to take place. Gratton contrasted this with the office being a place of collaboration, coaching and mentoring, face-to-face interactions and serendipitous moments. This, though, will need some careful design and implementation, and there is a role for people professionals to ensure this is done effectively.

This comes with challenges. Gemma Dale suggests is that a fixed mindset of what a workplace is (be that remote or physical) is not a good thing, and that all workplaces and spaces need to be capable of providing for a wide range of different types of work[1]. This means ensuring that those places and spaces are equipped to do that and allow people to do their best work.

Gratton, in her conference speech, made some similar points. She asserted that work is not just definable by where it takes place but by the type of work being done. This could be synchronous, alongside other people in real time, or asynchronous, working alone and at a time when others may not be. I'll represent this visually here with a four-box model to help you see where this is leading:

FIGURE 11.1   A four-box model of hybrid working environments

	What type of work is taking place?	
Where the work is taking place?	Synchronous work, in the physical workplace	Asynchronous work, in the physical workplace
	Synchronous work, remote and online	Asynchronous work, remote and online

As you can deduce, each type of work needs to be enabled to be achievable in each type of place or space. For example, the same type of technology needs to be accessible in each place or space to allow for the different types of work that may be done there.

Lynda Gratton expanded on her research and thinking in an article for Harvard Business Review in May 2021. She set out four examples of roles, or four example types of work, each enabled and delivered by a different axis – place and time – which are like the four-box model above (Gratton, 2021). This helps us better understand the drivers behind work and what it needs to be considered effective. Where Gratton goes further than my four-box model though is in overlaying individual employee circumstances onto it, showing how specific environments at home may make types of work unsuitable, and how specific lengths of service at an organization may make locations and types of work more suitable.

To make this happen, we may need to consider job crafting in more detail and break down roles into semi-distinct responsibilities, working out which of these can be done synchronously or asynchronously, and which are best done face-to-face or remote. Looking at jobs in this level of granular detail may be time consuming, so using an approach like Tailored Thinking's Job Canvas may help and provide a more visual and insightful way of doing this. Regardless, the outcome will be a different way of looking at hybrid working – it isn't necessarily something that can be solved by looking just at individuals, or by looking just at jobs, but by looking at duties and activities individually. Seeing a bigger picture version of this may enable you and your organization to see what percentage of duties fit into each of the four boxes in the table above. This may lead to more informed decisions about real estate and technology – and the employee experience. Overlaying individual circumstances can then be done more effectively, along the lines Gratton suggests.

TYPES OF SPACES

The physical workplace thus needs to be quite different. It can no longer be purely about banks of individual desks, cubicles, and the odd meeting room – the balance of these things needs to change to allow for different types of working. Types of spaces that will be needed include:

- Touchdown spaces for people to work for short bursts of time before moving on to another space. An organization I worked for in the early 2010s did this very well, with the ability to dock laptops and other devices or connect to Wi-Fi accordingly. These spaces were often located close to shared areas and meeting spaces, to allow for people to move easily between them.

- Flexible spaces with easily moveable chairs, tables and other furnishings and equipment to enable those using the space to tailor it to their needs, with plug and play technology that enables quick access to whatever people need to work together. A conference venue called the Successfactory in Cheshire stood out to me in the mid-2000s as doing this well – it was ahead of its time, and now physical workspaces are catching up.

- Areas that replicate the atmosphere one may find in a library – quiet, focused and largely interruption free spaces that enable people to work individually on asynchronous work. The offices at Reward Gateway in London have had such areas – that look like Victorian-era reading rooms – for a long time, and they are well-utilised.

- Hot-desking facilities, bookable in advance and enabling people to work with others who have booked such spaces for their entire working day, perhaps building new relationships, or working on existing ones.

- The more traditional fixed settings we may be more used to for those duties that may always need to be performed synchronously, in the office, by co-located people.

Writing about his experiences at the CIPD, then-People Director Brad Taylor pointed out how conscious choices need to be made, and the delivery of such spaces and places is much more than simply asking people to work partly in the office and partly at home. He also rightly stated that this requires close collaboration between the People teams, and those responsible for IT, and workplace/facilities[2].

All of this shows that the way we approach spaces and places needs to be ultra-flexible. They need to be tailorable to the needs of the individual – not just the way they need to work, but what duties they are undertaking at that time. This will mean that hybrid working is not, and could never be, the same for everyone.

The Sovini Group, based in Merseyside, UK, won the Best Flexible Working Initiative at the People Management Awards in 2021. This was based on how they approached redesigning work and the employee experience during the COVID-19 pandemic. They noted that their unique organizational culture was not a product of their physical location, it was the product of the people within it.

There was a concerted effort within Sovini to ensure performance was put at the heart of how the organization was transforming. This is something Lynda Gratton reinforced at the CIPD Conference later in 2021, noting that hybrid working will be viewed to have failed if it does not improve productivity and performance. Sovini took the same view.

The actions taken by Sovini focused on improving communication to enhance performance, noting that remote and hybrid working had potential detrimental impacts on both if not carefully managed. This was achieved through training sessions for leaders on how to manage communication and performance in a remote and hybrid world, a bespoke support and best practice sharing page on the in-house employee app to improve connections and reviewing managers on their engagement of their teams.

Employees were encouraged to work in an agile way and to work out, with their managers, the best way for them to deliver the outputs they needed to (People Management, 2021).

While Sovini's approach won awards, there is something very straightforward and logical about it – and eminently adaptable to your organization. Talking to employees about their working day, their outputs and how these things can best be delivered, must be a good thing and likely will lead to real improvements in engagement, performance and productivity if the right arrangements are put in place.

However, we should note that not every duty or task can be looked at in this way and for some there is zero flexibility. Speaking on the CIPD Podcast in January 2021[3], Neil Morrison, HR Director at Severn Trent Water, suggested that as much as 60% of the working population may be in jobs that can only be done in co-located physical environments. He may well be right, though changing the way people do their jobs, and the duties they do may enable some of that to be changed – which are also points Morrison went on to make.

We need to rethink our use of places and spaces, and soon. A poll by People Management magazine in May 2021[4] reported that only 15% of organizations were planning to enforce a full return to the office, with most likely to adopt a hybrid approach, but worryingly 42% of organizations were not planning on making changes to the physical office space. This despite around half of the workforce confessing to being worried about spending more time in the office, and 95% recommending changes to the physical office space. As many have said, this is a once in a lifetime opportunity to build back better – but one that we people professionals need to ensure our organizations grasp fully.

We focused on Clanmil Housing and its Executive Director of Corporate Services Karen Gilmore in chapter six. In the research for this chapter, I asked how Clanmil had been getting on with hybrid working, specifically around some of the themes explored in this chapter.

Gilmore reported that they had engaged an architect to redesign the office space to allow for different zones dependent on the type of work being done. At the time I spoke to her in November 2021 the organization had recommended its employees spend one day a week in the office, but Gilmore had noticed that organically, and with no encouragement, more and more employees were booking more time in the office and that overall usage of their main office was slowly increasing. A few weeks later, when the Northern Ireland Government told employees that they should work from home if they could, Gilmore noted some resistance from some, citing the increased pressure on mental health of enforced remote working.

From a recruitment perspective Clanmil had begun advertising some jobs, mostly at senior level, as fully remote. For example, an Executive Director post had attracted a majority of candidates from mainland UK (Clanmil is located in Northern Ireland), opening the organization up to whole new recruitment markets.

The Clanmil example is an interesting one because it shows how, with no guidance, employees and their managers may slowly drift back towards old ways of working. Left unchecked, this could mean the hybrid experiment fails. The example of how recruitment has changed for Clanmil is a good indication of new ways of working. However, the benefits of this could be lost if the organization reverts to recruiting for office-based roles. That said, continuing to recruit for fully remote-based roles may prevent the organization slipping back into old ways of working. In the next section we will look at what we can do to avoid this.

How do we avoid slipping back into old ways of working?

As I mentioned in chapter one, hybrid working isn't new, and it is something I've done for over 20 years. It has enabled me to be who I needed to be, personally and professionally, through that time. I often feel that the traditional way of working – 9am to 5pm, Monday to Friday, in one physical office space, is predicated on whomever does that having someone at home to do the cooking, cleaning, washing and any child or elder care needed. It is an outdated concept therefore and no longer compatible with modern life. There was one year in my life when, just because of the ages my four children were each at, they went to four different schools/nurseries/colleges for that one year. The school run, twice a day, was a nightmare, and only manageable because of hybrid working.

Hybrid working meant that when I met my wife, who lived 100 miles away, I could work from her location and keep our relationship going in its early stages. It also meant I could flex my work to fit things in my personal life better (like nativity plays, sports days and parents' 'evenings' that started at 3.30pm in the afternoon), and work at times that suited me on my largely asynchronous work and devote my office days to synchronous work. There was no way that I could have worked all my time in one fixed location, and no danger that I would gradually slip into such ways of working overtime.

Indeed, when I moved to a job where exactly that happened, my performance and health suffered, and I quickly moved to start my own company.

This personal story illustrates how hybrid working was integrally linked to my own wellbeing, my performance and my commitment to an organization. I think I am typical of millions of others and being forced into an office at fixed times for the sake of being physically present backfired in my example. In what has been dubbed 'The Great Resignation', we hear of employees being perfectly willing to change their employer if the way it makes them work no longer suits their personal circumstances. While the concept of 'The Great Resignation' is seen by some to be exaggerated in scale, it is certainly not a new phenomenon and in my view is indeed likely to have been increased in scale by the COVID-19 pandemic and people's experience of remote working. Our role as people professionals is to advise and partner with our organizations to adapt to people's personal circumstances rather than the other way around and use the influence and visibility that the COVID-19 pandemic gave the people profession to ensure that our organizations do the right thing and don't tell people what they must do or cannot do.

This may mean that people practices are not set in stone. That we don't have the answers straight away and need to view organizational working practices as a beta-testing version of what is to come. It may also mean that individual experiences differ – policies for the many, instead of policies against the few, to quote Lars Schmidt, speaking at the CIPD Festival of Work in June 2021.

WHAT ARE WE FIGHTING AGAINST?

We are, ultimately, fighting now against many of the reasons why that move to remote and hybrid working was glacial in its progress before March 2020. Some of these are succinctly expressed by Gemma Dale in her blog:

- Views that knowledge can only effectively be shared by people who are co-located.
- Views that people cannot use technology effectively.
- Views that the serendipitous moments of connection can't happen remotely.
- Views that those who wish to work remotely or in a hybrid way aren't as committed to the organization as those who work face-to-face (Dale, 2021).

While we have explored in previous chapters of this book how many of these can be overcome, treating everything as a pilot, a beta-testing version of what is to come, could be used across the board. If something isn't working, change that aspect, rather than deeming the whole experiment a failure. Dale[5] goes as far as to suggest simply declaring roles as hybrid, removing the need to request this.

Marissa Goldberg, in a thread on Twitter in February 2021[6], offered some interesting solutions to many of these barriers. She rightly pointed out that the so-called serendipitous moments happened not by chance but because of structure, and therefore structure could also create such things for remote and hybrid workers. She gave suggestions such as randomised coffee breaks, and open virtual meeting rooms, as examples of how informal conversations can be facilitated and may lead to serendipitous moments of their own. Crucial to this was not just permission, but encouragement, from leaders of the organization to talk about non-work things and have fun – essentially, being human, something remote work can often take away from people, as we have explored. Goldberg's thread is in the references for this chapter and contains more of her views on how to make hybrid working work for individuals.

WHAT CAN WE DO TO ENSURE THE CHANGE STICKS?

To answer this, I have returned to five of our case study organizations from previous chapters, looking at how they have been implementing elements of hybrid working – I asked each person what had worked, what had not, what changes they were making and how they were ensuring that people and the organization weren't slipping back into the old ways of working.

Views from Annette Hill, Hospiscare (seen in Chapter 3)

What has worked?   Being very flexible yet clear about which roles can be done from home and which can't, as our workforce includes clinical, retail and warehouse staff as well as office-based – treating people fairly and transparently albeit not equally.

Recognizing that remote working isn't for everyone and enabling staff to decide if they would prefer working in the office all or some of the time for their wellbeing.

Allowing teams to self-organize their hybrid working patterns, so that each goes into the office once or twice a week on different days.

What has not?   Meetings where some people are in the room and others attend virtually. Those in the room have benefitted from social interaction and informal time with colleagues, which has been hard to replicate virtually. Those attending virtually can benefit from the chat function with others attending virtually. Some have found quite off putting that they are 'present' on a big screen, especially if they are the only one.

What changes need to be made?   Reviewing policy and risk assessments so that the approach is now permanent and not a temporary response to the pandemic.

We carried over our old ways of working, such as lots of email, into the remote world without fully exploring or exploiting what different technology could give us, and now feel we could do more here.

How are you ensuring people and the organization don't slip back into old ways of working?   This hasn't been an issue for us yet as we are still acting as though all Covid-19 restrictions are in place.

Views from Gail Hatfield, Energy Systems Catapult (seen in Chapters 2 and 5)

What has worked?   Productivity being linked to remote working as a way of justifying its continuation.

Encouraging hybrid working and a return to the office instead of mandating it.

Giving people the choice to return to the office if their personal circumstances were not suitable for remote working and seeing some groups of people make clear choices to do that.

Getting people to see the offices as a tool like phones or software are – and to decide how and when to use them.

Treating hybrid working as an experiment and being open with people about making mistakes, learning from what works and being adaptable and agile in making changes.

What has not?   Hardly anyone has used the office, even for team meetings, despite it being made available. Managers seem reluctant to ask people to attend the office and average occupancy each day is less than 10%.
Despite the link being made to productivity, remote working does not seem to have impacted it either way, and we are, generally, not satisfied with the way of working now in place.

What changes need to be made?   Events that are created in the office to bring people together need more careful marketing as there is currently reluctance to attend them. Types of events that may work include project launch meetings, awaydays, celebrations, show and tells, 'Town Hall' style meetings – these will be done with lots of advance notice and clear reasons for the event taking place face to face.

Promoting the technology to support hybrid working and different types of work being done in the office.

Consideration may be given to producing rotas for people to work in the office.

How are you ensuring people and the organization don't slip back into old ways of working?   ESC is facing almost the opposite. With over 100 people starting with the company since the COVID-19 pandemic, they have never known any other way besides full remote working, and we are struggling to change this.

Views from Michelle Reid, the Institute of Occupational Medicine (seen in Chapters 2 and 5)

What has worked?   Giving people the choice about how to work and letting them work together to produce hybrid solutions for their teams.

Working with caution as if the Covid-19 pandemic were at its height and encouraging people to work from home where possible.

What has not? Initially we gave no guidance on hybrid working, and found many people struggled and even bickered amongst themselves. The lack of guidance was a real problem.

What changes need to be made? We will be introducing 'personas' that people can refer to or use as examples to help guide their decision-making and conversations with colleagues and managers. We hope this may remove the need for many basic questions about what is allowed or not and empower people to think for themselves.

How are you ensuring people and the organization don't slip back into old ways of working? We have reviewed our strategy, culture and values and produced a refined behaviour framework and coaching culture. We are also sharing hybrid success stories and coaching those who are exhibiting signs of reverting to old behaviour.

Views from Anna Edmondson, PowerONPlatforms (seen in Chapters 7 and 8)

What has worked? Giving teams the freedom to work out their own working pattern – this has worked out quite harmoniously with all team members happy/willing to be in the office on the agreed days and enjoying the balance of work and home. It has also meant that team members have been able to retain a lot of the flexibility for caring responsibilities which came with lockdowns and remote working, e.g., team members are generally able to do the school run before starting work without having to make formal flexible working requests.

Virtual training – we have always used this as our default approach, and this served us well in the Covid-19 pandemic and will continue to work well in the future.

What has not? We had hoped to avoid having to have a formal keyholder rota for the office but realized that uncertainty about being able to get in was a barrier to people accessing the office when needed.

There are also roles where individuals do need to be in the office for certain tasks. A lack of forward planning led to wasted time through people driving in, but this has improved as people learn from experience.

In inductions we have recognized a hybrid new starter – previously people would have a homeworking kit provided, or a desk in the office. Now almost everyone needs a homeworking kit AND a space in the office. Recognizing this requirement has solved the root cause of various day one issues.

What changes need to be made? We need to create a hybrid working policy in the future but feel there is no urgency as individuals have settled well into the informal approach.

How are you ensuring people and the organization don't slip back into old ways of working? Primarily through messaging from line managers – we have a monthly management meeting (one of the few events we have restored to face to face) and use that as a discussion forum to ensure that leaders are taking a unified approach and adopting consistent requirements.

We do still place a high value on getting together in person, when it adds something, and are finding that people respond well / enjoy being face to face when the opportunity arises as they can see what they get out of it.

Views from Eleanor Gooding, Boost Drinks
(seen in Chapters 2 and 5)

What has worked? We launched what we call 'smart working', as opposed to hybrid working, hoping to send the signal that this was in search of a smarter way of working. This is a mixture of fixed location days in the office and flex location days where people can choose where they work from. On fixed days (Monday and Thursday) anyone who is contracted to work from the office, works their normal office hours from the office. On the flex days people can work from anywhere if they are available, contactable, and able to do their work. This smart model allows for flexibility, but also certainty, which helps around booking meetings and the like.

We found that treating people individually worked and recognizing that a perfect solution may not exist for everyone. However, we have been able to achieve greater flexibility in some form for each employee.

A different kind of communal spirit existed when we worked largely remotely, and this created some desire from all to recreate some of the face-to-face communal spirit.

What has not?   Trying to create a permanent flexible working model that also took COVID-19 into account. It was easier to forget about COVID-19 when designing the smart working model, with COVID-19 as a second step to design and implementation.

Anyone with health issues, anxiety etc got the chance to create their own return to work plan with a lot of flexibility. However, in the excitement most of these plans were neglected, and the return was too much for some people.

What changes need to be made?   Ensuring everyone takes up the offer of personalized working plans.

Adapting the guiding principles of smart working, which had already had 'looking after our people' as one principle, to make some sub-principles explicit: 1) facilitating physical and mental wellbeing, 2) accommodating personal choices where possible, and 3) trialling new ways of working.

How are you ensuring people and the organization don't slip back into old ways of working?   The rationale and overall process has been very transparent with good levels of individual involvement, meaning people have some stake in making it work.

Giving thorough guidance about the types of things that people should come into the office for, such as creative sessions and critical people conversations.

What we see here are five organizations at different stages of their journey, all finding some things working well – particularly empowering individuals and teams to determine their own ways of working. All are finding lessons to learn along the way and adapting as they go, which is an important principle also. The changes being made are for different reasons but all valid in the specific context of the organization, but no one organization here has managed to get things perfectly right from their or any other perspective. That's a key point to remember – there isn't a badge at the end of your journey towards hybrid working that says you've achieved it. It may always continue to evolve.

In our case study though we look at the innovative ways that one organization, admittedly ahead of the game, have been enabling remote and hybrid working.

CASE STUDY

Robert Hicks is the Group HR Director at Reward Gateway (RG), an employee benefits provider with over 120 staff based in their London headquarters, but more working in other countries. RG are an innovative, forward-thinking organization who embraced remote and hybrid working many years before others were forced to during the COVID-19 pandemic, with every new starter since the COVID-19 pandemic began being given a desk, chair and laptop accessories for their home to ensure they could work effectively remotely or face-to-face during that pandemic. I spoke to Robert several times in the research for this chapter, focusing on what they had done up to and during the COVID-19 pandemic, and their plans for moving hybrid working forward after it.

In 2016, RG introduced Work Modes – an activity-based model of where to work based on the type of work an employee was undertaking. This has striking similarities to job crafting as discussed elsewhere in this chapter, as it breaks down over 75 different work activities and groups them into eight different themes, known as Work Modes. All RG's physical offices globally were redesigned to support different types of working also, and this was working successfully up to the COVID-19 pandemic beginning.

Full remote working was, according to Hicks, challenging and disruptive for some, but an opportunity to thrive for others, and it was clear that hybrid working would, post-pandemic, become the norm.

The organization has only two types of employment contract – remote workers (a very small number of roles fit into this category and their main place of work is their home, with only rare face-to-face contact); and hybrid workers (most of the organization). All roles come with flexibility by default, based on individuals sharing what they need to achieve in their working week and discussing with their manager how best to achieve that with flexible working patterns. RG's golden rule on flexible working is that individuals should never miss an important life or work event.

RG manages performance through its Employee Feedback system – employees are asked to complete a weekly check-in to let their manager know how their week has been, how they are feeling, what they have accomplished, and what they'll be working on next week. They are encouraged to spend 15 minutes every Friday completing this, and to expect regular one to one time with their manager via face-to-face and virtual methods, according to preferred communication styles.

The Work Modes inform ways of working and protocols about where to work and when, mapped to a variety of different workspaces to support the tasks undertaken in each Work Mode. In 2021 the existing Work Modes were updated to cover how these activities could be done at a home or face-to-face location, and the tables below show how RG define and explain the different Work Modes to employees.

TABLE 11.1   RG Work Modes, reproduced with kind permission from Reward Gateway

	Recommended Home Modes		
	Retreat	Plugged In	1-to-1
I feel	Recharged	Accomplished	Supported
I can	De-stress, reflect, refocus, decompress, relax, balance, meditate, reset, wellbeing session, read,	Produce, flow, focus, concentrate, accomplish, work on complicated task, LTTV Virtual Sessions, virtual volunteering	Hold client demos, meet and strengthen relationships, mentoring, make decisions, address concerns, provide feedback
This supports our value	We are human	We work hard	We speak up
These workspace elements support my success	Quiet and private space, ability to step away being empowered to take time	Headphones, music, no distractions, desk, wifi, charger, monitor, clean desk	WFH Desk Bundle, well lit, privacy encouraged, headphones, video conferencing

	Recommended Office Modes				
	Meeting Little	Meeting Large	Buzzin'	Briefing	#rgfun
I feel	Connected with my team	Connecting with Clients	Collaborative and Productive	Aligned	Happy

(continued)

TABLE 11.1 (Continued)

	Recommended Office Modes				
	Meeting Little	Meeting Large	Buzzin'	Briefing	#rgfun
I can	Brainstorm, connect with teams and clients, hold demos, plan, learn, focus, huddle, bond, share, set goals	Align with my team, collaborate, inspire, share, problem solve, learn, communicate, celebrate, boom!Fest	Do lively work, mindmap, create ideas, show I am available, talk on the phone and video calls, shadow and mentor, have impromptu meetings, work side-by-side	Learn, onboard, training, mentoring, network, align, celebrate, interact, inspire, EP!C events	Socialize, play, drink, gather, celebrate, learn, team wellbeing, EP!C events, de-stress
This supports our value	We push the boundaries	We think global	We own it	We delight our customer	We love our job
These workspace elements support my success	Bookable spaces that allow social distancing or video conferencing, privacy encouraged	Bookable large spaces that allow social distancing, seamless connectivity, high energy, bright and airy, transparency	Comfortable noise, movable chairs, teamwork, collaboration with team mates	Seamless connectivity to global teams, large spaces, digital displays, whiteboard, sticky notes, notepads & pens	Games, food, activities, events, dogs, downtime, well, Experience Manager support, non-disruptive space

To support the office-based Work Modes, the physical set-up of Reward Gateway has been transformed accordingly:

- The Annex has 18 workstations for individual focused work – a relatively quiet area, to provide that option for people who need to really focus on a task. Hicks says that if people sit there, it is a signal that they need to focus without having to shut themselves away from the rest of the office.

- The Patio is for more lively individual work. Some people work alone, some work in pairs. Hicks says that if people sit in this area, they are signalling they are open for interruptions and quick chats with colleagues. There are spaces to take conversations elsewhere if needed too.

- The Kitchen is the centre of RG's office. They use food to bring people together, promote wellness, and keep people energized and happy. There is always a buzz of noise, and Hicks says it is a nice place for casual meetings, socializing, relaxing a little, and catching up with teammates.

- The Dens are for quick meetings or working sessions. They are less formal for both internal and some client-facing meetings. Conducting business in a semi-open environment sends a strong message about RG's commitment to transparency.

- The Living Room and Lounge can be used as two medium-sized rooms or combined for large meetings, typically for presentations and training events.

- The Conservatory is the meeting room for active thinking, standing meetings, and brainstorming sessions. An entire wall is a whiteboard for visualizing ideas.

- The Snug and the Dining Room are two small meeting areas. These are for private conversations, one-on-ones, and smaller meetings. These rooms are bookable and provide much needed privacy for more personal conversations.

- The Garden is a beautiful place to step away from the traditional office environment. RG use it as a quiet alternative to desk space in the Annex, and as a social space.

- The Attic is a place to retreat and take a break from work or make a quick call. It can be used for power naps or practicing mindfulness for a little bit.

- The Library gives people a chance to get away from everything, with a range of resources available to ensure that people are always growing.

RG have also provided guidance for people to work effectively with collaborating and communicating with others:

- Share good news via video conferencing and bad news in person.

- Have meetings that are entirely virtual for everyone, or entirely face-to-face for everyone – and be consistent.

- One-on-ones should happen in spaces that ensure privacy – and working from home is perfect for this.

- Presentations are effective on video conferences, and working from home whether delivering or attending the presentation should make this more effective.

- Avoiding on the spot meetings, and forward planning the need to meet formally.

- Make a conscious effort to ensure a balance of voices and be inclusive in the way this is done, whether face-to-face or remotely.

- Ensure appropriate breaks in between meetings, which can be achieved by ending them five or ten minutes before the hour or half-hour – and this applies to face-to-face as well as virtual meetings.

- Use web conferencing software tools to create better virtual meeting experiences – such as using the Raise Hand function rather than opening microphones to enable better reading of body language and a more inclusive approach to contributions.

I spoke again with Hicks some six months after all of this was put into place, and he reported no changes to how this was working but felt that with the pandemic in full flow that there was a little reluctance for some employees to come into the office. He felt it would be another full year before the effectiveness of the principles explained here would be seen. However, RG's approach remains very innovative, and they have applied the principles of job crafting and analysing the types of work being done, along with changing their spaces and places to suit.

Case study reflections

The Reward Gateway case study is a good one to consider how we may need to redefine what work is and how it is done to make hybrid working a reality. The following points stand out:

- Taking a granular approach to identifying types of work activities and how these are best performed is a good start point for working out what the physical environment needs to look and be like, and how hybrid working can work.

- Designating everyone as either remote or hybrid workers lends a feel of inclusivity to the approach, as does the flexible by default approach. Of course, individual circumstances and arrangements will differ though.

- Expecting weekly check-ins and updates but not being too prescriptive about how these happen may allow for better communication between manager and staff according to preferences and enhance the way each works.

- Grouping the different work activities (in RG's case, 75 of them) into categories like RG's Work Modes gives greater clarity to all concerned about what the type of work may look and feel like and may enable more informed decisions to be made.

- Tailoring the physical workspace to enable different types of working is likely to tap into each individual's sense of flow and purpose and generate greater engagement as a result.

- Giving guidance about how other less frequent types of work events and activities need to look and feel like adds a more rounded view of the employee experience.

The action plan

If you are now considering moving forward with hybrid working more permanently than before, and planning how to make it work, the following questions may help:

- How will you avoid mandating a particular type of working arrangement? What consultation are you doing (or will you do) to factor in individual circumstances, environments, and preferences?

- What kind of business continuity planning do you need to do to work out both a best- and worst-case scenario for hybrid working? What does this change for your organization?

- Using the four-box model shown in this chapter, what aspects of organizational work activities will fit into each category, and how will you sense-check this with others to ensure it is accurate?

- If you distilled each job and its individual activities and tasks into the four-box model, what type of job crafting and (re)design might then be necessary and how would you enact this?

- How reworkable is your physical workspace (particularly the office but to a lesser degree at home too) to allow redesign for the types of spaces and places that types of work might need?

- How do you recognise and accommodate your remote workers who do not have a designated workspace at home, or who need to share this with other people?

- What effect would it have if your organization declared all jobs as hybrid and flexible by default?

- What do you need to do to ensure that people, and the organization, don't slowly drift back into old ways of working?

- What approaches will you take to best advise and coach your senior leaders that will help your beta-testing be successful?

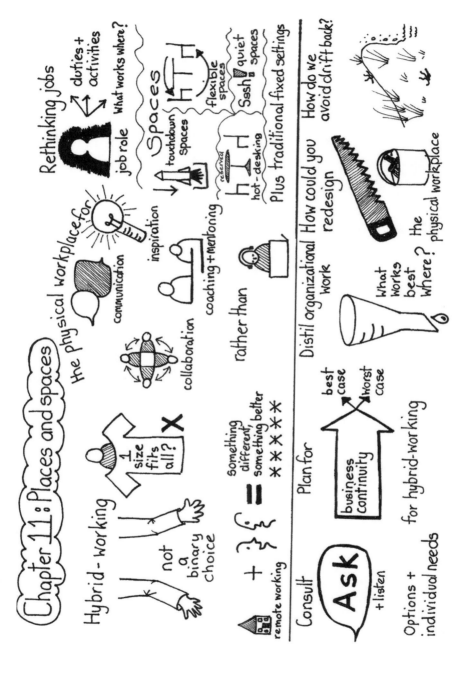

12

People professionals in the future

The shorter read

This final chapter pulls together many themes explored so far in the book and considers the implications for people professionals in more depth. The areas of focus for people professionals have become obvious through the COVID-19 pandemic – change, organization design, digital transformation, the employee experience and more. Some were in play prior to the pandemic, and most have been accelerated by it.

We have mentioned several times in this book how the individualized employee experience is not just likely but necessary for remote and hybrid working to work effectively. We must follow through on this, and this means our remit has changed, along with the skillset we need as people professionals.

We need greater digital skills. We need more business partnering skills. We need more knowledge about mental health. We need more organization design and development skills. We need a range of different types of skills useful in L&D in a remote and hybrid world. And we need more analytical skills to be able to use data and technology better.

This changes some of the job roles we are likely to need in the people profession too. More people whose focus is data analysis. More whose focus is wellness, and the employee experience, and more whose focus is performance coaching. In some organizations this may not be achievable with small teams, and it is likely one or two people may become ultimate generalists. This would be achievable if technology can automate many routine tasks – and it can. That may also mean that the structure of the team changes.

Our work with individuals, leaders, teams, and the organization must take on different forms, different functions. We need to work with them to understand their pain points, to deliver more tailored solutions, and be closer to what really matters in organizations. To do that we need to focus on organizational culture, on providing the right intelligence to the organization, on building psychological safety and wellness, and on building something that is flexible enough to change in the future, but is nonetheless bigger, better and more fit for our future.

The longer read

In our final chapter I will pull together many of the themes explored so far in the book and relate them to what this means for us as people professionals. We have looked at people practices – redesigning them for a remote and hybrid world of work – and as we have gone along, we have noted the implications for us as people professionals, whether that be a necessary change in our focus, an update to our skillsets or ways of working, and perhaps all of these. In this chapter I'll look at what this all means for us.

The CIPD's forward look at what 2030 might bring for the people profession, published in November 2020[1], summarized the focus for people professionals as being:

- Internal change – evolving organizational models, structures, and processes.
- Digital and technological transformation.
- Changing demographics and diversity and inclusion strategy.
- Diversifying employment relationships.
- Sustainability, purpose, and responsible business.

It is possible to see how many of these trends were part of wider changes in the profession and/or business before the onset of widespread remote working in the COVID-19 pandemic, and before hybrid working became a major focus for many organizations. However, it is also possible to see how some of these priorities have been shaped by that experience.

For example, in our previous chapter we talked about changing the way work is done to cope with hybrid working, and that fits neatly into the first of CIPD's areas above. However, it requires a great deal of agility within the organization, and a demand for more organizational design and development skills within the people profession.

The organizations who could foresee and predict the onset of remote and hybrid working, covered in our first two chapters, were already good at horizon-scanning and anticipating how external events would shape the world of work. The events since March 2020 have probably enhanced that need in other organizations.

Digital and technological transformation and remote and hybrid working clearly go hand in hand, and we have talked in chapters four through ten about how we must use technology to deliver our people practices and how we must use data better.

In our ninth chapter we covered how inclusion and belonging take on slightly different forms and aspects in remote and hybrid working environments. We explored how different characteristics are impacted positively or negatively by those types of working and how we need to give more guidance to those leading and working within teams to foster a sense of belonging.

We talked in many chapters about how individual circumstances and environments need to be considered, and how hybrid working is not a one size fits all approach but a likely highly individualized employment experience for most. We have also covered how supporting employee's mental health and wellbeing is perhaps now a major organizational challenge. Rather than a solely people practice initiative, we must ensure organizations follow through on building a culture supportive of wellbeing.

Collectively, this means that our remit has changed – some things are now more important than they were before, and as people professionals we have seen that we are involved in more than we ever were. This means that we must adapt and grow alongside that and has implications for our skill levels too.

The CIPD commented on this in their 2021 People Profession Survey[2], noting that most respondents felt that the people profession had increased its standing in organizations, but that around two-thirds of people professionals had had to up their skills (or reskill completely) because of this.

What has changed in our skillsets?

It is easy to see how certain types of skills have become more important for the people profession now. Let's take a look at some of these:

- Digital skills, if not already towards the top of the list of required skills, are now critical.

- Given the amount of organizational change and (re)design our organizations have gone and will go through, business-partnering type skills are also likely to be more important – ensuring that people professionals can talk the language of the business and contribute as equals within it.

- Awareness of the factors that influence and impact mental health, and how to leverage these in a positive way, is also a critical skillset for people professionals because of the impact of remote and hybrid working.

- Greater levels of organizational design and development skills to navigate organizations through the challenges of the future are more important. Thinking of organizations as the systems they undoubtedly are, and approaching our work in that way, given that we will be working more asynchronously and away from other people, is a growing area for people professionals.

- From an L&D perspective, the move to online learning and particularly live online classrooms has illustrated the importance of production skills, hosting skills, online facilitation skills, and knowledge of instructional design and learning technology. These could well be specialist roles but maybe we need to emphasize their use in face-to-face environments as well as remote and hybrid ones, given how critical they have been.

- Use of data and analytics, leveraging what technology can provide us particularly in relation to employees who we may not be co-located with and more effectively linking performance data to other aspects of people practices, will be challenging for some people professionals. The ability to analyse and interrogate this data, though – and help others to do it too – is also critical. We must be able to know what data we have, where it is, what state it is in and how each interaction between employee and organization creates information that we can use to improve the employee experience. We must get better at that – the technology is already there, but our skills may lag. We must deliver the right intelligence to the right people, teams, and organizations so that all of these can perform better. A useful parallel was drawn by Gianpaulo Barozzi, from Cisco, writing for HRD Connect[3], when he said that we need to consider how the wearable technology industry delivers intelligence to individuals at the point of need, for the users to decide about and do something with. Can we do the same in the people profession?

EMERGING ROLES

I listened to Margaret Heffernan talk as far back as the 2016 CIPD Conference, where she said that people professionals need to fuse technology, innovation and people. How prescient a talk that was for our remote and hybrid world of work. The events of 2020-2021 illustrated the importance of Heffernan's points perfectly. To me, this means we have four main people professional roles emerging as more critical in this world:

- Data analysts. We need people professionals who can select and use the right data. Who can throw data sets together, correlate them, analyse them, and predict trends. Currently, not enough can.

- Wellness advocates. Not just in an individual sense, but also in an organizational sense. We need people professionals who can be the guardians of organizational wellness, looking at systems of engagement and motivation and performance and how these all link together and complement each other.

- Experience champions. Plenty of large firms like Netflix, and Virgin Group, are already ditching bureaucracy and encouraging their people teams to let go of policy and focus on the individual. We will need more of that, of social engagement in the workplace and looking at how people are treated and how they feel about work.

- Performance coach. An old role but a growing one. Helping people to identify what performance actually is, and the best conditions under which to produce it. Clive Woodward also spoke at the 2016 CIPD Conference on this, and how he got players/employees to visualize being under pressure and practice performing under such conditions. He used the available technology to capture performance data and made sure players had the skills to analyse, share and discuss it. A better understanding of psychology, of how people interact, think and behave goes hand in hand with this, and would enable us to make performance management more focused on the individual, and address issues at a deeper level.

I spoke with Perry Timms, from PTHR, when researching this chapter and he made some similar points, particularly around wellness and experience being linked heavily to organizational culture as focal points for our skillsets and duties. Does this mean we need dedicated people professional roles for these things? Maybe in large organizations, but in smaller organizations this will be part of the general duties of the people team, perhaps distilled into one person in some organizations.

Many people professionals in smaller organizations are becoming the ultimate generalist, able to turn their hand and skills to almost anything the organization needs, and that has certainly been the case across 2020–2021. I see the people professional role, in its entirety, being a bit like the decathlon event in the Summer Olympics. We may not enjoy all the different disciplines, or be able to perform at the same level in each either, but we recognize that only by doing all of them (whether individually or as part of a wider team) can we reach the levels of performance and contribution we need to.

We also need to consider that many of the more routine, transactional people practice functions that we may have done ourselves in years gone by are now much more likely to be automated and delivered directly from a system (with or without artificial intelligence) to the employee, cutting out the middle persons – us. Delivery of most of these types of functions is likely to be a digital by default approach. That may enable us to reposition our skillsets accordingly, and move away from a focus the delivery of knowledge since systems and technology will do that for us. This will enable us to focus on the aspects mentioned above, individualizing the employee experience.

In these examples I spoke to subjects of previous chapters' case studies to find out what implications they felt remote and hybrid working had for their people teams, the skillsets they need, and functions they undertake.

Robert Hicks, from Reward Gateway (Chapter 11), has been helping his team to work in different ways according to the functions they undertake. The recruitment team at Reward Gateway are going to be regularly working in the office as this enables them to build strong relationships with hiring managers as they generally support in only one or two geographies – in essence they are matching the style of work of their main stakeholders. In contrast, the L&D team at Reward Gateway are remaining working mostly remote in the country they live in, as they support all geographies that Reward Gateway operates in. The success of online learning in reaching larger, more dispersed audiences and being delivered in more manageable chunks means that this is more suited to more frequent remote working in the Reward Gateway hybrid model.

Coaching and mentoring is also remaining as a predominantly remote activity for similar reasons. The way that these and other people practices are now delivered has heightened the need for the people team at Reward Gateway to centralize administration and move to a shared service type of function, and highlighted the need to have (ideally) one end-to-end system to handle all of the different aspects of service delivery. If Hicks can achieve this, then he acknowledges this will change the nature of many transactional services and, as a result, some roles in the people team for the better also.

Annette Hill, from Hospiscare (Chapter 3), has a small team which she felt already had a very flexible mindset and could cope with a wide range of ways to support individuals and personalize the employee experience. Hill's team have made a long-awaited and needed move away from paper-based and manually driven systems which has created considerable efficiencies and changed how the team's people professionals can focus their time. The ability to use digital forms of communication has increased the ability to get together quickly on different issues without having to worry about everyone being in the same place before an issue could be discussed.

Anna Edmondson, from PowerON Platforms (Chapter 8), feels that the move to remote and hybrid working has sharpened her team's thinking, as they have been forced to question how every aspect of their people practices are delivered – from how jobs are designed, to how candidates are attracted and recruited, how they determine where and when work is done, to what value being co-located (or not) may have. She also notes the increased focus on wellbeing, and her team are needing to recognize and deal with the increased emotional transparency that remote and hybrid working has brought for many, and support those with strains on their mental health. The need to have more conversations about mental health and encourage employees to bring their whole selves to work – and to encourage the people team to do the same – is an increased focus for Edmondson's team.

Changing our focus

All of this means that the entire nature of the people profession has changed. In conversation with Perry Timms while researching this chapter, we spoke about how remote and hybrid working has made us all think about where we need to be – not just physically, but metaphorically-speaking too. He believes that we need to be more comfortable as a profession not having close physical proximity to our stakeholders but being more connected with them in different ways. He gave examples of recording audio and video messages instead of holding out for video and face-to-face meetings, allowing asynchronous work to take place more effectively, and getting better at sharing knowledge and curating resources that support such ways of working.

This sounds like a big step, but it may not be – there are many people professionals already doing it, and some who had globally dispersed teams and organizations working across different time-zones may have relevant experience that could be shared with others. It may also be that some in our profession make a conscious choice not to work in such ways, and to find organizations that cannot or do not want to embrace remote and hybrid working. We may find new people entering the profession though as a result, and I asked Timms how he would explain the new people profession to those who may be thinking about entering it. He said he would explain the transactional nature of work – individuals exchanging their skills for reward – but add that work should be something individuals enjoy and should be done in an organization that values them and treats them well. He felt he would then explain that the people profession is about helping individuals to navigate their way to achieving those things – designing work based on good principles, whether that work be remote, hybrid or face-to-face. I think this is a good explanation and reminds me of how I once explained my work to my then-three-year-old daughter, a story shared in Chapter 7. A nice update to that would be for us to measure the effectiveness of our work by how we make other people feel – and clearly good work for all is a big part of that.

Timms felt that the base unit with which people professionals should now start to work towards achieving good work for all is the team – feeling that these are the nodes within the organizational system, and that we can change organizations one team at a time. I'd go further and suggest that we need to focus more on the leaders of those teams. Much of this book has focused on the key role that leaders of teams play in creating the right employee experience, and how this has changed in nature in a remote and hybrid world of work. This is something stressed in the CIPD's *People Profession 2030 report*[4], where they comment on the need for managers to manage hybrid workers more effectively and fairly, positively influence employment relationships, maintain organizational culture and values, and navigate development opportunities for and with their teams. While the events of the COVID-19 pandemic have accelerated this change in focus for many in the profession, they didn't create it.

VIEWS FROM PROFESSIONALS

Working more closely with leaders in this remote and hybrid world will help in many ways. We will be closer to and more aware of the pain points of our internal customers, allowing us as people professionals to deliver tailored and targeted solutions. We are also more likely to see the data that those leaders rely upon to make decisions about remote and hybrid working, and better placed to leverage this – as opposed to only using data held in our people systems and only sharing that when we feel there is a need to. It will also help us be closer to the stuff that now really matters in organizations – how people are treated at work.

It also reinforces that making remote and hybrid working work is not about the technology – it is about the people and the culture. Ed Monk, CEO of the LPI, comments well on this in a Go1 podcast recorded in February 2021[5] – speaking obviously from an L&D perspective he cited the number one challenge for Chief Learning Officers as being creating a learning culture, ahead of digital transformation. This backs up a lot of what this book has been saying – that people matter more than the technology. That culturally, organizations need to be able to cope with remote and hybrid working, not just have the right technology in place. There needs to be true psychological safety, a sense of inclusion and belonging, a focus on wellbeing and treating people well, for remote and hybrid working to work. And that's our focus as people professionals.

Steve Browne, Chief People Officer at LaRosas, echoed views shared in this book about people professionals having to be more intentional in connecting and communicating with people because those people are no longer just 'down the hall'. Browne viewed this as a long overdue shift but feels the challenge for people professionals in the future is to sustain this connection in the absence of a crisis. Like me, Browne believes the workplace has changed forever. He rightly feels that people professionals took the lead in this change, and should now build on this.

I spoke again to Michelle Reid, from the Institute of Occupational Medicine who featured in our case study in Chapter 2, about how she sees the future of the people profession. She felt that it hadn't necessarily changed much but had highlighted the value that people practices bring to organizations. She felt that the challenge was to hold on to and capitalize on that value – being vocal, visible, and supportive of people and leaders, enabling the organization to be at its best, not just in a crisis, but every day.

Reid's views are echoed by the CIPD's Responsible Business Through Crisis report, published in November 2021[6], making the point that the coming years represent opportunities to do things differently, rebuild on a new footing, and undertake a long-term transition to something new. The report makes the point that the initial experiences in the COVID-19 pandemic were not necessarily helpful, though a lot of learning came from that, and that we now have a better opportunity to be more conscious and deliberate about the way we want our organizations to work. The report calls this 'the great rethink'.

Indeed, in ways explored in this book, it is. It is an opportunity to do things that are not just a blend of remote and face-to-face work but somehow access the best elements of both and do something greater than the sum of its parts. To do that we need people professionals who are flexible – not driven by policies and procedures but guided by principles and frameworks. It means an organizational focus on wellbeing of employees as this is affected greatly by remote and hybrid workers, and a renewed focus on leaders being human and authentic at what they do.

It is the role of people professionals to ensure that this happens, and that it works when it does.

In each of the chapters of this book I have shared my thoughts, my research, and examples of good practice about each of the people practice aspects I feel are necessary to make remote and hybrid working effective. I'll summarize some of the key points made here:

- People practices need to have flexibility built into them and join up well with each other.
- People professionals need to have sufficient visibility and credibility within the organization so that they are sought out by senior leaders when making decisions.
- The people team needs to develop close working relationships with other functions that shape the employee experience, doing joint planning and working together to promote a better employee experience.
- Jobs in the organization need to be flexible enough to be recrafted, potentially at speed.
- People technology needs to be fit for purpose and should allow for just the most important people processes to be automated and improved. It should also help employees manage their working time.
- We need to be certain of the touchpoints in the organization where remote and hybrid workers need more focused support and create said support.

- We need to guide both managers and remote workers on the implications this style of working has for intra-team communication, developing strong relationships, handling informal conflict and more. Further, we should help leaders refocus on their role and what things are different for them with remote and hybrid teams and help the team itself establish its new rules of engagement.

- People professionals need to be proficient in handling and using data, but we also need to find out what data we have or could get about people and their performance needs, and about what support remote and hybrid workers need and how they are working.

- Wellbeing of employees needs to be central to organizational strategy, and people professionals need to help senior leaders understand the links between wellbeing and performance.

- People professionals involved in L&D need to be skilled at designing and delivering live virtual sessions, and if there are hybrid events, to be able to minimize the risk of attention bias.

- People professionals involved in L&D could act more as performance consultants to provide more just in time learning at the point of need.

In researching this chapter, although I spoke with many leading thinkers and accessed a lot of relevant research about the changing role of the people profession, and the skillsets and mindsets that need to change, I could not uncover one organization that had successfully done it. Perhaps I am asking too early for this, and perhaps a better case study will emerge if this book gets a second edition in a couple of years' time.

What may be the case though, is that having read this book and particularly this chapter, you may be ready to embark on making these changes yourself in your organization.

Maybe you are the case study, and therefore the case study reflections also. Make it count.

The aim has been that, after reading this book, you are more aware of how some other organizations have been tackling many of these issues and have got lots of ideas of how you might do this in your organization. If nothing else, you are armed with the right questions to ask.

I do hope you have enjoyed the book and my thoughts, and if you need any help moving forward with redefining your people practices for a remote and hybrid world of work – I'm more than happy to talk to you – I'm not hard to find.

This could be the start of something bigger. Something better. It is in your hands.

Good luck.

The action plan

If you are looking to change people professionals' roles, including skillsets, mindsets and actual duties undertaken, the following questions could help you prepare:

- What can you do to improve the level of organization design and development skills in your people professionals?
- What will you do to increase the confidence your people professionals have around mental health and wellbeing issues?
- How useful is the current data and analytics you have access to, and how well versed are your people professionals in using it?
- How can you increase the focus that your people professionals have on the employee experience?
- What can you do to improve the level of performance coaching in your people function?
- What new roles do you think you will need to design in your people function, and what roles will no longer be needed?
- What cultural changes need to be made to ensure remote and hybrid working is effective in your organization?
- What is your best advice for senior leaders at your organization about the role people professionals need to play in shaping the future?

Sketchnote summary

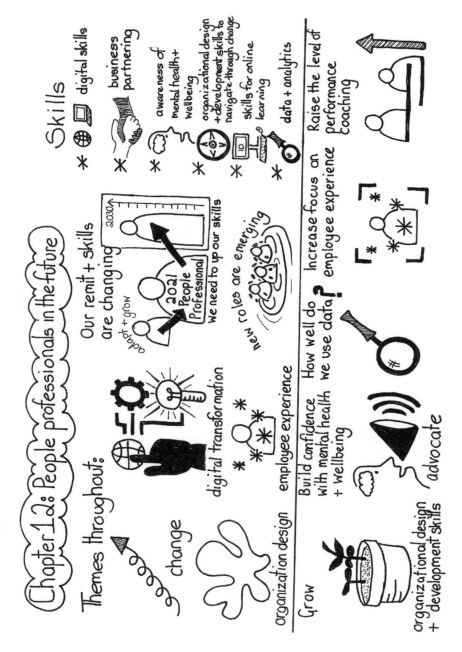

Chapter 12: People professionals in the future

Themes throughout:

change

organization design

digital transformation

employee experience

Our remit + skills are changing

adapt + grow

2021 People Professional → 2030

We need to up our skills

new roles are emerging

Grow

organizational design + development skills

Build confidence with mental health + wellbeing

How well do we use data?

advocate

Increase focus on employee experience

Raise the level of performance coaching

Skills

* digital skills

* business partnering

* awareness of mental health + wellbeing

* organizational design + development skills to navigate through change

* skills for online learning

* data + analytics

REFERENCES

Foreword

1 Milner, M (2011) *A Life of One's Own*. Routledge.
2 Crawford, I, and Heathcote, E. (2014) *A frame for life*. Rizzoli.

Part one

Chapter one

1, 2 Ec.europa.eu (2021) https://ec.europa.eu/jrc/sites/jrcsh/files/jrc120945_policy_brief_-_covid_and_telework_final.pdf (archived at https://perma.cc/9MMZ-U3YS)
3, 4, 5, 6 Beauregard, T, Basile, K and Canonico, E (2013) *Home is where the work is*. Research Gate. www.researchgate.net/publication/259053477_Home_is_where_the_work_is_A_new_study_of_homeworking_in_Acas_-_and_beyond (archived at https://perma.cc/AU84-5T8R)
7 People Management (2017) 'The easiest place to hide is in the office' https://pminsight.cipd.co.uk/the-easiest-place-to-hide-is-in-the-office (archived at https://perma.cc/4FS4-QSHB)

FURTHER READING

Acas.org.uk (2021) *Flexibility in the workplace: implications of flexible work arrangements for individuals, teams and organisations* www.acas.org.uk/flexibility-in-the-workplace-implications-of-flexible-work-arrangements-for-individuals-teams-and (archived at https://perma.cc/J5FH-YGDZ)
Cipd.co.uk (2016) www.cipd.co.uk/Images/employee-outlook-focus-on-commuting-and-flexible-working_tcm18-10886.pdf (archived at https://perma.cc/Q9EG-3LR6)
Felstead, A and Reuschke, D (2020) *Homeworking in the UK: before and during the 2020 lockdown*, WISERD Report, Cardiff: Wales Institute of Social and Economic Research. https://wiserd.ac.uk/publications/homeworking-ukand-during-2020-lockdown (archived at https://perma.cc/J5FH-YGDZ)

Pyöriä, P (2011) Managing telework: risks, fears and rules. *Management Research Review*, 34(4), pp. 386–399

Chapter two

1, 2, 7, 8, 11, 12 CIPD (2020a) *Business Survival in the Age of COVID-19 | Podcast | CIPD*. www.cipd.co.uk/podcasts/business-survival-coronavirus (archived at https://perma.cc/J5CJ-AG5W)

3 People Management (2020a) *Third of businesses have no plan for if an employee tests positive for coronavirus*. www.peoplemanagement.co.uk/news/articles/third-of-businesses-have-no-plan-for-if-an-employee-tests-positive-for-coronavirus (archived at https://perma.cc/EFY5-WXH9)

4 People Management (2020b) *Coronavirus: how can employers avoid redundancies?* www.peoplemanagement.co.uk/news/articles/coronavirus-employers-avoid-redundancies (archived at https://perma.cc/P8HQ-8W8K)

5, 6 Felstead, A and Reuschke, D (2020) *Homeworking in the UK: before and during the 2020 lockdown*, WISERD Report, Cardiff: Wales Institute of Social and Economic Research. at: wiserd.ac.uk/publications/homeworking-ukand-during-2020-lockdown

9 CIPD (2020b) *CIPD responds to Coronavirus threat | CIPD*. Available at: www.cipd.co.uk/about/media/press/covid19-030320 (archived at https://perma.cc/NR4W-DUSJ)

10 CIPD (2020c) *Employers must expect disruption and support working parents through school closures | CIPD*. www.cipd.co.uk/about/media/press/working-parents-school-closures (archived at https://perma.cc/FD92-MFA5)

Chapter three

1 Buffer.com (2021) *2021 State of Remote Work*. buffer.com/2021-state-of-remote-work (archived at https://perma.cc/SFC3-XWYB)

2 Blanco-Suarez, E (2017) *The Neuroscience of Loneliness*. Psychology Today. www.psychologytoday.com/us/blog/brain-chemistry/201712/the-neuroscience-loneliness (archived at https://perma.cc/C6EF-6AJ7)

3 CIPD (2020) *Flexible working – lessons from the pandemic CIPD*. https://www.cipd.co.uk/knowledge/fundamentals/relations/flexible-working/flexible-working-lessons-pandemic (archived at https://perma.cc/UA96-VU39)

4, 5, 12, 13, 15 CIPD (2021) *Building back better post-pandemic Podcast CIPD.* www.cipd.co.uk/podcasts/building-back-better-post-pandemic (archived at https://perma.cc/D2WD-XL5B)

6, 10 Herd, C (2021) https://twitter.com/chris_herd/status/1402621502902738944 (archived at https://perma.cc/JN2W-CGGG)

7 Understandingsociety.ac.uk (2021) *Covid-19 | Understanding Society.* www.understandingsociety.ac.uk/topic/covid-19 (archived at https://perma.cc/F3GS-9XYQ)

8 Sharma, M (2021) *UK office workers would agree to pay-cut for remote working.* [online] HRreview. www.hrreview.co.uk/hr-news/uk-office-workers-would-agree-to-pay-cut-for-remote-working/130367 (archived at https://perma.cc/Y7X3-4UHF)

9 Cohen, E (2009) *Rowers' high: behavioural synchrony is correlated with elevated pain thresholds | Biology Letters.* royalsocietypublishing.org/doi/abs/10.1098/rsbl.2009.0670 (archived at https://perma.cc/9482-YD6V)

9 Launay, J (2015) *Choir singing improves health, happiness – and is the perfect icebreaker | University of Oxford.* www.ox.ac.uk/research/choir-singing-improves-health-happiness-%E2%80%93-and-perfect-icebreaker (archived at https://perma.cc/7DYX-8D2H)

11 Atkin, N (2017) *HR Magazine - Halton Housing Trust: Our default position is trust.* [online] HR Magazine. https://www.hrmagazine.co.uk/content/features/halton-housing-trust-our-default-position-is-trust (archived at https://perma.cc/7DFB-G6KU)

12 Forbes (2021) *Microsoft's Hybrid Return-To-Work Plan For The 'Biggest Shift To How We Work In Our Generation'.* www-forbes-com.cdn.ampproject.org/c/s/www.forbes.com/sites/jackkelly/2021/05/23/microsofts-hybrid-return-to-work-plan-for-the-biggest-shift-to-how-we-work-in-our-generation/amp/ (archived at https://perma.cc/XLS4-PU2C)

14 Owen, J (2020) *5 Challenges of Managing a Remote Team (and How to Overcome Them).* Kogan Page. www.koganpage.com/article/5-challenges-of-managing-a-remote-team (archived at https://perma.cc/4QFW-AQZR)

FURTHER READING

(2021) https://twitter.com/eatsleepwkrpt/status/1361325992963420166?s=21 (archived at https://perma.cc/T6BT-TFN3)

Blogs.bmj.com (2021) *Creating tomorrow today: seven simple rules for leaders. Blog two: Define our shared purpose by Helen Bevan and Göran Henriks – The official blog of BMJ Leader.* blogs.bmj.com/bmjleader/2021/02/16/creating-tomorrow-today-seven-simple-rules-for-leaders-blog-two-define-our-shared-purpose-by-helen-bevan-and-goran-henriks/ (archived at https://perma.cc/NUV6-ZW5C)

Bloomberg.com (2020) *Bloomberg – Are you a robot?* www.bloomberg.com/news/articles/2020-11-17/office-workers-want-to-keep-working-at-home-just-not-every-day (archived at https://perma.cc/JK6T-AQVL)

Cookson, G (2015) epichr.co.uk/2015/06/26/walkabout/ (archived at https://perma.cc/D87N-HMUQ)

Cookson, G (2016) epichr.co.uk/2016/04/14/lets-get-flexible/ (archived at https://perma.cc/2G43-8DP6)

Dale, G, and Ringo, T (2020) *Are You Ready for Long-term Flexible Working?* Kogan Page. www.koganpage.com/article/are-you-ready-for-long-term-flexible-working (archived at https://perma.cc/K7KU-NB7B)

En.wikipedia.org (2021) *Hanlon's razor – Wikipedia.* en.wikipedia.org/wiki/Hanlon%27s_razor (archived at https://perma.cc/9WQ7-PLAY)

Felstead, A and Reuschke, D (2020) *Homeworking in the UK: before and during the 2020 lockdown*, WISERD Report, Cardiff: Wales Institute of Social and Economic Research. wiserd.ac.uk/publications/homeworking-ukand-during-2020-lockdown

Goldberg, M (2021) twitter.com/mar15sa/status/1289946980676849671?s=21 (archived at https://perma.cc/WJ6C-WF9E)

Goldberg, M (2021) twitter.com/mar15sa/status/1356462768447238146?s=21 (archived at https://perma.cc/MEE3-ER5M)

HRZone (2021) *Three tips from an HR leader on the transition to hybrid working.* www.hrzone.com/lead/future/three-tips-from-an-hr-leader-on-the-transition-to-hybrid-working (archived at https://perma.cc/L2TV-3CJD)

Indeed.com (2020) *Remote Work Can Bring Benefits, but Attitudes Are Divided.* www.indeed.com/lead/remote-work-survey (archived at https://perma.cc/NL3V-SS3J)

Nadella, S (2021) *The hybrid work paradox.* www.linkedin.com/pulse/hybrid-work-paradox-satya-nadella/ (archived at https://perma.cc/92EL-ZLQL)

The Guardian. 2021) *Unilever workers will never return to desks full-time, says boss.* www.theguardian.com/business/2021/jan/13/unilever-workers-will-never-return-to-desks-full-time-says-boss (archived at https://perma.cc/RU2K-YYPX)

Weedon, M (2021) *Moving to a 'hybrid' working world.* aitchare.weebly.com/blog/moving-to-a-hybrid-working-world (archived at https://perma.cc/N5WB-ZAHM)

Chapter four

1 Microsoft.com (2021) *Work Smarter to Live Better.* www.microsoft.com/en-gb/business/work-smarter-to-live-better/ (archived at https://perma.cc/9M82-S3JV)

2 Phase 3 (2021) *Does your people technology have longevity? | Phase 3.* phase3.co.uk/connect/resources-and-templates/does-your-people-technology-have-longevity/ (archived at https://perma.cc/S9YW-J3SJ)

3, 4 CIPD (2020), www.cipd.co.uk/knowledge/strategy/hr/people-profession-2030-future-trends (archived at https://perma.cc/53LV-TZBA)

5 HRDConnect (2021), https://www.hrdconnect.com/casestudy/dropbox-building-a-virtual-first-model-to-improve-employee-experience/ (archived at https://perma.cc/FA7Y-BT8C)

6 Deloitte (2021) *The Future of Enterprise Demands a New Future of HR.* www2.deloitte.com/global/en/pages/human-capital/articles/gx-future-of-hr.html (archived at https://perma.cc/9S6B-ZHQY)

7 CIPD (2021) *Pulling the plug on digital fatigue Podcast | CIPD.* www.cipd.co.uk/podcasts/pull-plug-on-digital-fatigue (archived at https://perma.cc/VT8L-FC99)

FURTHER READING

CIPD (2019) *People and machines: from hype to reality | CIPD Report.* www.cipd.co.uk/knowledge/work/technology/people-machines-report (archived at https://perma.cc/3VW4-EEHQ)

CIPD (2020) *Workplace technology: the employee experience | CIPD Report.* www.cipd.co.uk/knowledge/work/technology/workplace-technology-employee (archived at https://perma.cc/4RQL-2842)

CIPD (2021) *Good Work Index | Survey reports | CIPD.* www.cipd.co.uk/knowledge/work/trends/goodwork (archived at https://perma.cc/2SEW-BD4T)

Cookson, G (2015) epichr.co.uk/2015/04/02/kiss/ (archived at https://perma.cc/89L9-BWKG)

Cookson, G (2015) epichr.co.uk/2015/07/13/lets-get-analytical/ (archived at https://perma.cc/7XD6-QJ4R)

Cookson, G (2015) epichr.co.uk/2015/11/04/cipd-conference-blog-4-of-many/ (archived at https://perma.cc/8P4N-V2AM)

Cookson, G (2015) epichr.co.uk/2015/11/05/cipd-conference-blog-6-of-many/ (archived at https://perma.cc/AG7E-M6AF)

Cookson, G (2017) epichr.co.uk/2017/12/11/money-for-nothing/ (archived at https://perma.cc/8PB3-M54H)

James, D (2021) *Council Post: The No. 1 Reason Corporate Learning Is Failing To Bridge The Skills Gap (And What To Do Instead).* www-forbes-com.cdn.ampproject.org/c/s/www.forbes.com/sites/forbeshumanresourcescouncil/2021/05/27/the-no-1-reason-corporate-learning-is-failing-to-bridge-the-skills-gap-and-what-to-do-instead/amp/ (archived at https://perma.cc/7NJ9-4ZPX)

Mohdzaini, H (2021) *How can HR play a lead role in digital transformation in the workplace?* peopleprofession.cipd.org/insights/articles/hr-role-digital-transformation-workplace (archived at https://perma.cc/UD8H-MD3G)

Ryan, L (2021) *Dropbox redefines employee experience in a virtual world - HRD.* www.hrdconnect.com/resources/dropbox-building-a-virtual-first-model-to-improve-employee-experience/?ru=yes (archived at https://perma.cc/53LV-TZBA)

Part two

Chapter five

1, 2 Workhuman.com. (2021) *4 Global Talent Acquisition Trends to Watch*. https://www.workhuman.com/resources/globoforce-blog/4-global-talent-acquisition-trends-to-watch (archived at https://perma.cc/6LKV-YMJN)

3 Buzzsprout (2021) *#314: How to Attract Talent During a Tsunami of Labor Movement w/ Mervyn Dinnen - HRchat Podcast - Interviews with HR, Talent and Tech Experts*. hrchat.buzzsprout.com/65006/8849551-314-how-to-attract-talent-during-a-tsunami-of-labor-movement-w-mervyn-dinnen (archived at https://perma.cc/H5W6-KPS9)

4 Baer, S (2020) *Council Post: Virtual Onboarding: How To Engage Remote Workers Early On*. www.forbes.com/sites/forbeshumanresourcescouncil/2020/10/02/virtual-onboarding-how-to-engage-remote-workers-early-on/?sh=23be03c9f0a3 (archived at https://perma.cc/MU22-P9FB)

FURTHER READING

Charles, M (2021) *The secret to remote offboarding? Kindness*. blog.learnamp.com/the-secret-to-remote-offboarding-kindness (archived at https://perma.cc/8SPE-L6PU)

Click Boarding (2021) *What is Offboarding & What is the Process? | Click Boarding*. www.clickboarding.com/what-is-digital-offboarding/ (archived at https://perma.cc/NFU3-R7QF)

Cookson, G (2016) epichr.co.uk/2016/03/25/knowing-me-knowing-you/ (archived at https://perma.cc/X6H4-WVB5)

Cookson, G (2016) epichr.co.uk/2016/03/05/the-new-boy/ (archived at https://perma.cc/ZM8U-4Z7Q)

Greenhouse (2021) *3 challenges with remote interviews (and how to solve… | Greenhouse*. www.greenhouse.io/blog/3-challenges-remote-interviews-solve (archived at https://perma.cc/9AL4-X2CR)

Hr.admin.ox.ac.uk (2021) *Challenges of virtual interviews*. hr.admin.ox.ac.uk/challenges-of-virtual-interviews (archived at https://perma.cc/WQ9H-59HJ)

HrTech Cube (2021) *Recruitment Challenges during Virtual Recruitment | HrTech Cube*. hrtechcube.com/recruitment-challenges-during-virtual-recruitment/ (archived at https://perma.cc/CC45-XS9D)

Mindtools.com (2021) *Virtual Onboarding: How to Get Your New Hire on Board – Online*. www.mindtools.com/pages/article/virtual-onboarding.htm (archived at https://perma.cc/UE3T-X35K)

Purpose HR (2021) *A Guide to Virtual Onboarding – Purpose HR*. purposehr.co.uk/a-guide-to-virtual-onboarding/ (archived at https://perma.cc/TKE8-L2EA)

Chapter six

1, 2 People Management (2021) *Can businesses cut remote workers' pay?*. www.peoplemanagement.co.uk/news/articles/can-businesses-cut-remote-workers-pay (archived at https://perma.cc/DV8N-67DA)

FURTHER READING

BDBF LLP (2021) *FAQs about the return to work and hybrid working arrangements – BDBF LLP*. www.bdbf.co.uk/faqs-about-the-return-to-work-and-hybrid-working-arrangements/ (archived at https://perma.cc/Z9W9-YHGN)

Bhattacharyya, S (2021) *How Employee Benefits May Change in a Hybrid Workplace*. www.wsj.com/articles/employee-benefits-hybrid-workplace-11628796247 (archived at https://perma.cc/CU8W-MTGU)

Cookson, G (2017) *Turkish Delight | Epic HR*. epichr.co.uk/2017/08/17/turkish-delight/ (archived at https://perma.cc/KMG9-8D4U)

Ellis Whittam Limited (2021) *The legalities of hybrid working | 6 tips for employers*. elliswhittam.com/blog/the-legalities-of-hybrid-working-6-tips-for-employers/ (archived at https://perma.cc/5LZQ-DX6F)

HR Magazine (2021) *HR Magazine – Google's pay cuts for remote workers deemed 'unfair'*. www.hrmagazine.co.uk/content/news/google-s-pay-cuts-for-remote-workers-deemed-unfair (archived at https://perma.cc/3JFE-YEFC)

Lee, S (2021) *HR in the work from home age | Torch*. torch.io/blog/hr-in-the-work-from-home-age/ (archived at https://perma.cc/9B3B-4CQ7)

Chapter seven

1, 2 Managementtoday.co.uk (2021) *Why you should call in sick more often than you think – even if working from home*. www.managementtoday.co.uk/why-call-sick-often-think-%E2%80%93-even-working-home/food-for-thought/article/1695823 (archived at https://perma.cc/3UCJ-NTPS)

3, 4 Brouard C (2021) *Remote workers and e-presenteeism: how to manage it*. www.myhrtoolkit.com/blog/remote-workers-epresenteeism-how-to-manage (archived at https://perma.cc/SH2D-S84G)

5 Mindtools.com (2021) *Mintzberg's Management Roles: Identifying the Roles Managers Play*. www.mindtools.com/pages/article/management-roles.htm (archived at https://perma.cc/D54X-GE2Q)

6 Cookson, G (2015) *Engage | Epic HR*. epichr.co.uk/2015/09/25/engage/ (archived at https://perma.cc/SPD2-9Q7S)

FURTHER READING

Acas.org.uk (2021) *Disciplinary and grievance procedures during coronavirus (COVID-19) – Acas*. www.acas.org.uk/disciplinary-grievance-procedures-during-coronavirus (archived at https://perma.cc/V9S5-DZ35)

Bean, S (2021) *Home workers take fewer sick days than office based colleagues – Workplace Insight*. workplaceinsight.net/home-workers-take-less-sick-days-than-office-based-colleagues/ (archived at https://perma.cc/3ZUH-JVMW)

Cipd.co.uk (2021) www.cipd.co.uk/Images/flexible-working-lessons-from-pandemic-line-manager-guide_tcm18-92613.pdf (archived at https://perma.cc/Q3BS-YKUE)

Collins, A, Cartwright, S and Cowlishaw, S (2017) *Sickness presenteeism and sickness absence over time: A UK employee perspective*. www.tandfonline.com/doi/full/10.1080/02678373.2017.1356396 (archived at https://perma.cc/ZJE6-PZV7)

Cookson, G (2016) *Gimme some credit | Epic HR*. epichr.co.uk/2016/05/06/gimme-some-credit/ (archived at https://perma.cc/WZ58-FF5C)

HRD (2021) *Personalised employee experience: the key takeaway from recent crises - HRD*. www.hrdconnect.com/2021/06/01/personalised-employee-experience-the-key-takeaway-from-a-year-defined-by-crises/ (archived at https://perma.cc/N8Q6-8VJ5)

HR Magazine (2021) *HR Magazine – Lessons in managing disciplinary and grievance procedures remotely*. www.hrmagazine.co.uk/content/features/lessons-in-managing-disciplinary-and-grievance-procedures-remotely (archived at https://perma.cc/EB9G-BKKT)

Lexology (2021) *Pandemic-proof performance and disciplinary management*. www.lexology.com/library/detail.aspx?g=5b306c0e-770e-47b6-aece-b5e5271078ff (archived at https://perma.cc/Q9LF-HUPW)

People Management (2021) *Handling disciplinaries and grievances in the age of coronavirus*. www.peoplemanagement.co.uk/experts/legal/handling-disciplinaries-grievances-age-coronavirus (archived at https://perma.cc/99P5-6BLZ)

Chapter eight

1 CIPD (2021a) *Managing the well-being of remote workers | Podcast | CIPD*. www.cipd.co.uk/podcasts/well-being-remote-workers (archived at https://perma.cc/ZQJ2-V7EK)

2 Hellobenefex.com (2021) www.hellobenefex.com/media/3742/the-new-reward-director-2021.pdf (archived at https://perma.cc/SQX7-W88B)

3 Ibbotson, L (2021) *How we improved wellbeing on a budget.* www.peoplemanagement.co.uk/voices/comment/how-improved-wellbeing-budget (archived at https://perma.cc/J395-MNAE)

4 Harrison, J (2021c) *Wellbeing Wednesday 22 – A focus on mental health and wellbeing during the pandemic — Peak Potential.* peakpotentialltd.co.uk/blog/2021/6/3/wellbeing-wednesday-22-a-focus-on-mental-health-and-wellbeing-during-the-pandemic (archived at https://perma.cc/6X2K-BA3Z)

FURTHER READING

Cipd.co.uk (2021) www.cipd.co.uk/Images/flexible-working-lessons-from-pandemic-line-manager-guide_tcm18-92613.pdf (archived at https://perma.cc/Q3BS-YKUE)

CIPD (2021b) *Planning for hybrid working | CIPD.* www.cipd.co.uk/knowledge/fundamentals/relations/flexible-working/planning-hybrid-working (archived at https://perma.cc/3NHQ-5NLG)

Cookson, G (2015) epichr.co.uk/2015/08/03/incommunicado/ (archived at https://perma.cc/M998-BLZC)

Cookson, G (2019) *Don't you worry 'bout a thing | Epic HR.* epichr.co.uk/2019/08/14/dont-you-worry-bout-a-thing/ (archived at https://perma.cc/38DS-GBLB).

Cookson, G (2021) *If a tree falls in a forest | Epic HR.* https://epichr.co.uk/2021/03/26/if-a-tree-falls-in-a-forest/ (archived at https://perma.cc/H82W-6ML4)

Harrison, J (2021a) *Wellbeing at Work – Part 13b Wellbeing and Homeworking — Peak Potential.* peakpotentialltd.co.uk/blog/2021/3/18/wellbeing-at-work-part-13b-wellbeing-and-homeworking (archived at https://perma.cc/WNA5-2KWD)

Harrison, J (2021b) *Wellbeing Wednesday 18 – The Pursuit of Happiness Part II — Peak Potential.* peakpotentialltd.co.uk/blog/2021/5/4/wellbeing-wednesday-18-the-pursuit-of-happiness-part-ii (archived at https://perma.cc/TYR8-N32B)

Harrison, J (2021d) *Wellbeing Wednesday 24 – Leadership Lessons — Peak Potential.* peakpotentialltd.co.uk/blog/2021/6/22/wellbeing-wednesday-24-leadership-lessons (archived at https://perma.cc/944F-EPBE)

Lancaster.ac.uk (2021) *Mitigating wellbeing pressures in remote and hybrid working models.* www.lancaster.ac.uk/work-foundation/news/blog/mitigating-wellbeing-pressures-in-remote-and-hybrid-working-models (archived at https://perma.cc/4PL9-DZW2)

Snape, J (2021) *Are mental health days the wrong answer to the right questions?* www.peoplemanagement.co.uk/voices/comment/are-mental-health-days-the-wrong-answer-right-questions (archived at https://perma.cc/5KTB-RLBS)

Tomlinson, L (2021) *HR's Next Challenge – Wellbeing, Engagement and Inclusion During Times of Crisis.* www.linkedin.com/pulse/hrs-next-challenge-wellbeing-engagement-inclusion-tomlinson-mcipd (archived at https://perma.cc/7WQT-6N6F)

Chapter nine

1 Feng, Z, Savani, K *Covid-19 created a gender gap in perceived work productivity and job satisfaction: implications for dual-career working parents working from home* asset-pdf.scinapse.io/prod/3084116308/3084116308.pdf (archived at https://perma.cc/G2L9-S6L8)

2 Snape, J (2021) *Belonging – the new catalyst for remote teams.* www.linkedin.com/pulse/belonging-new-catalyst-remote-teams-jeremy-snape/ (archived at https://perma.cc/UZE3-YK4Z)

3 Harvard Business Review (2021) *What Psychological Safety Looks Like in a Hybrid Workplace.* hbr-org.cdn.ampproject.org/c/s/hbr.org/amp/2021/04/what-psychological-safety-looks-like-in-a-hybrid-workplace (archived at https://perma.cc/JHR8-CXYY)

FURTHER READING

Cipd.co.uk (2021) www.cipd.co.uk/Images/flexible-working-lessons-from-pandemic-line-manager-guide_tcm18-92613.pdf (archived at https://perma.cc/Q3BS-YKUE)

CIPD (2021b) *Planning for hybrid working | CIPD.* www.cipd.co.uk/knowledge/fundamentals/relations/flexible-working/planning-hybrid-working (archived at https://perma.cc/3NHQ-5NLG)

Cookson, G (2016) *Carpool Karaoke | Epic HR.* epichr.co.uk/2016/10/07/carpool-karaoke/ (archived at https://perma.cc/LSR5-T5RH)

Cookson, G (2016) *Don't count people – make people count | Epic HR.* epichr.co.uk/2016/10/17/dont-count-people-make-people-count/ (archived at https://perma.cc/7TYR-LLYY)

Forbes (2021) *SAP BrandVoice: How Hybrid Remote Work Improves Diversity And Inclusion.* www.forbes.com/sites/sap/2021/05/12/how-hybrid-remote-work-improves-diversity-and-inclusion/ (archived at https://perma.cc/ZP25-AQ4U)

Inclusive Solutions (2021) *This is How Hybrid Remote Work Improves Diversity and Inclusion.* inclusive-solutions.com/blog/this-is-how-hybrid-remote-work-improves-diversity-and-inclusion/ (archived at https://perma.cc/ZY59-6WMP)

Thepeoplespace.com (2021) *Which remote or hybrid work model is best for diversity, equity and inclusion? | The People Space.* www.thepeoplespace.com/brand/articles/which-remote-or-hybrid-work-model-best-diversity-equity-and-inclusion (archived at https://perma.cc/V5A3-5M85)

Chapter ten

1 Fosway.com (2020) www.fosway.com/wp-content/uploads/2020/06/Fosway-COVID-19-LD-Impact-2020_Final.pdf (archived at https://perma.cc/H8N5-S9TQ)

2, 5 Huggett, C (2020) www.cindyhuggett.com/wp-content/uploads/2020/10/2020-State-of-Virtual-Training-Infographic-from-Cindy-Huggett.pdf (archived at https://perma.cc/2XBL-HHD4)

3 CIPD (2021) *Impact of COVID-19 on the L&D profession | CIPD.* www.cipd.co.uk/knowledge/strategy/development/impact-covid-ld-profession (archived at https://perma.cc/CX7X-HPKG)

4, 6 CIPD (2021) *Digital learning in a post-COVID-19 economy | CIPD.* www.cipd.co.uk/knowledge/strategy/development/digital-learning-post-covid (archived at https://perma.cc/ARU2-9869)

7 The LPI (2021) *L&D Dashboard.* www.thelpi.org/resources/ld-dashboard/ (archived at https://perma.cc/2KCY-TU39)

8 Cipd.co.uk (2021) www.cipd.co.uk/Images/flexible-working-lessons-from-pandemic-line-manager-guide_tcm18-92613.pdf (archived at https://perma.cc/Q3BS-YKUE)

9 NHSEmployers.org (2021) www.nhsemployers.org/-/media/Employers/Publications/Do-OD/2021-resources/Digital-tools-for-doing-OD---Final.pdf

10 Parry-Slater, M (2021) *The Learning and Development Handbook: A Learning Practitioner's Toolkit.* Kogan Page.

FURTHER READING

Cipd.co.uk (2021) www.cipd.co.uk/Images/learning-skills-work-report-2021-1_tcm18-95433.pdf (archived at https://perma.cc/72E7-6GNV)

Cook, J (2021) www.youtube.com/watch?v=BEZ3e-gaCd0 (archived at https://perma.cc/68QK-2YL9)

Cookson, G (2017) epichr.co.uk/2017/11/30/from-the-touchline/ (archived at https://perma.cc/YLA6-H3PW)

Cookson, G (2018) *#HRD18 blog 2 – Putting OD at the heart of HR, and A New Approach to Digital Learning | Epic HR.* epichr.co.uk/2018/02/06/hrd18-blog-2-putting-od-at-the-heart-of-hr-and-a-new-approach-to-digital-learning/ (archived at https://perma.cc/5YHF-4H7N)

Cookson, G (2018) *A Modern Learning Professional | Epic HR.* epichr.co.uk/2018/05/09/a-modern-learning-professional/ (archived at https://perma.cc/WA8M-5E28)

Cookson, G (2021) *What's stopping L&D's transition to performance consulting?* www.trainingzone.co.uk/develop/business/whats-stopping-lds-transition-to-performance-consulting (archived at https://perma.cc/SS8Q-9XL6)

Farmer, E (2021) *10 tips for learning and development in a hybrid working world.* www.trainingzone.co.uk/deliver/training/10-tips-for-learning-and-development-in-a-hybrid-working-world (archived at https://perma.cc/UC47-ETDV)

Gadd, K (2021) *How to make blended learning more impactful in the new era of work.* www.trainingzone.co.uk/deliver/training/how-to-make-blended-learning-more-impactful-in-the-new-era-of-work (archived at https://perma.cc/QY59-BNY3)

Hart, J (2021) *Top Tools for Learning 2021 – Results of the 15th Annual Survey published 1 September 2021.* www.toptools4learning.com/ (archived at https://perma.cc/E8TW-XJWF)

Jacobs, A (2021) *Andrew Jacobs on LinkedIn: #hybrid #learning #hybridlearning | 10 comments.* www.linkedin.com/posts/andrewjacobslnd_hybrid-learning-hybridlearning-activity-6849231868466892800-5Dgp (archived at https://perma.cc/V34X-PSES)

Labrooy, L (2021) *How to Deliver Live Learning Events in a Hybrid Working World.* www.thelpi.org/how-to-deliver-live-learning-events-in-a-hybrid-working-world/ (archived at https://perma.cc/WZV9-8VQW)

Part three

Chapter eleven

1, 5 Dale, G (2021) *We need to talk about presence.* hrgemblog.com/2021/04/21/we-need-to-talk-about-presence/ (archived at https://perma.cc/6UGX-NJA7)

2 CIPD (2021) *Planning for post-COVID working at the CIPD – The People Profession: now and for the future – CIPD Blogs – CIPD Community.* www.cipd.co.uk/Community/blogs/b/the_people_profession_now_and_for_the_future/posts/planning-for-post-covid-working-at-the-cipd (archived at https://perma.cc/28KA-GPX5)

3 CIPD (2021) *From surviving to thriving: key changes facing people practice in 2021 | Podcast | CIPD.* www.cipd.co.uk/podcasts/surviving-to-thriving-2021 (archived at https://perma.cc/48EF-A62X)

4 People Management (2021) *Returning to the office: what are other HR professionals doing?* www.peoplemanagement.co.uk/news/articles/returning-to-the-office-what-are-other-hr-professionals-doing (archived at https://perma.cc/AU4E-AXXH)

6 Goldberg, M (2021) twitter.com/mar15sa/status/1356462768447238146?s=21 (archived at https://perma.cc/MEE3-ER5M)

FURTHER READING

CIPD (2021) *Building back better post-pandemic | Podcast | CIPD*. www.cipd.co.uk/podcasts/building-back-better-post-pandemic (archived at https://perma.cc/D2WD-XL5B)

CIPD (2021) *Planning for hybrid working | CIPD*. www.cipd.co.uk/knowledge/fundamentals/relations/flexible-working/planning-hybrid-working (archived at https://perma.cc/3NHQ-5NLG)

Dale, G (2021) *Where hybrid goes wrong (and how to stop it)*. hrgemblog.com/2021/03/17/where-hybrid-goes-wrong-and-how-to-stop-it/amp/ (archived at https://perma.cc/2VF3-UDQ3)

Gratton, L (2021) *How to Do Hybrid Right*. hbr.org/2021/05/how-to-do-hybrid-right (archived at https://perma.cc/WUU8-YB7W)

People Management (2021) *Who's scooped the Oscars of HR?* www.peoplemanagement.co.uk/long-reads/articles/whos-scooped-oscars-hr-2021 (archived at https://perma.cc/WK9F-ECEE)

Chapter twelve

1, 4 CIPD (2021) *People Profession 2030 future trends | CIPD*. www.cipd.co.uk/knowledge/strategy/hr/people-profession-2030-future-trends (archived at https://perma.cc/E7TQ-WD7X)

2 CIPD (2021) *The People Profession survey | CIPD*. www.cipd.co.uk/knowledge/strategy/hr/people-profession-survey (archived at https://perma.cc/S4EP-3KW3)

3 Barozzi, G, Redevising HR to overcome new conditions, 2021 www.hrdconnect.com/2021/06/02/cisco-on-redevising-hr-for-to-overcome-new-conditions/ (archived at https://perma.cc/6VZY-7J23)

5 Go1learning.libsyn.com (2021) *Learning with Go1: Ep4 – The Future of L&D with Edmund Monk, CEO LPI*. go1learning.libsyn.com/ep4-the-future-of-ld-with-edmund-monk-ceo-lpi (archived at https://perma.cc/WB3Q-RKC8)

6 CIPD (2021) *Responsible business through crisis: senior leaders on building new cultures of trust | CIPD*. www.cipd.co.uk/knowledge/strategy/corporate-responsibility/responsible-business-through-crisis (archived at https://perma.cc/435S-PE7S)

FURTHER READING

CIPD People Profession (2021) *People Profession 2030: how people managers will play a central role in the future world of work*. peopleprofession.cipd.org/insights/articles/people-managers-central-role-future-world-work (archived at https://perma.cc/VQ73-XDUF)

Cookson, G (2016) epichr.co.uk/2016/10/29/bazuka-that-vuca-part-1-of-2/ (archived at https://perma.cc/7C7P-6L3A)

Cookson, G (2016) *Bazuka that VUCA...part 2 of 2 | Epic HR.* epichr.co.uk/2016/11/02/bazuka-that-vuca-part-2-of-2/ (archived at https://perma.cc/MD9W-N4ZS)

Cookson, G (2017) *Jack of all trades | Epic HR.* epichr.co.uk/2017/03/25/jack-of-all-trades/ (archived at https://perma.cc/WP9H-RAH4)

The LPI (2021) *The Future of L&D.* www.thelpi.org/the-future-of-ld/ (archived at https://perma.cc/5Q5U-7PZB)

INDEX

Note: Page numbers in *italics* refer to figures or tables